The Powers of the False

 FLASHPOINTS

The FlashPoints series is devoted to books that consider literature beyond strictly national and disciplinary frameworks, and that are distinguished both by their historical grounding and by their theoretical and conceptual strength. Our books engage theory without losing touch with history and work historically without falling into uncritical positivism. FlashPoints aims for a broad audience within the humanities and the social sciences concerned with moments of cultural emergence and transformation. In a Benjaminian mode, FlashPoints is interested in how literature contributes to forming new constellations of culture and history and in how such formations function critically and politically in the present. Series titles are available online at http://escholarship.org/uc/flashpoints.

SERIES EDITORS:
Ali Behdad (Comparative Literature and English, UCLA), Founding Editor; Judith Butler (Rhetoric and Comparative Literature, UC Berkeley), Founding Editor; Michelle Clayton (Hispanic Studies and Comparative Literature, Brown University); Edward Dimendberg (Film and Media Studies, Visual Studies, and European Languages and Studies, UC Irvine), Coordinator; Catherine Gallagher (English, UC Berkeley), Founding Editor; Nouri Gana (Comparative Literature and Near Eastern Languages and Cultures, UCLA); Susan Gillman (Literature, UC Santa Cruz); Jody Greene (Literature, UC Santa Cruz); Richard Terdiman (Literature, UC Santa Cruz)

A complete list of titles begins on page 265.

The Powers of the False

Reading, Writing, Thinking
Beyond Truth and Fiction

Doro Wiese

NORTHWESTERN UNIVERSITY PRESS | EVANSTON, ILLINOIS

THIS BOOK IS MADE POSSIBLE BY A COLLABORATIVE GRANT
FROM THE ANDREW W. MELLON FOUNDATION.

Northwestern University Press
www.nupress.northwestern.edu

Cover photo © Petra Gerschner

Library of Congress Cataloging-in-Publication Data

Wiese, Doro, author.
  The powers of the false : reading, writing, thinking beyond truth and fiction / Doro Wiese.
    pages cm. — (Flashpoints)
  ISBN 978-0-8101-3004-3 (pbk. : alk. paper)
    1. Foer, Jonathan Safran, 1977– Everything is illuminated. 2. Flanagan, Richard, 1961–
Gould's book of fish. 3. Powers, Richard, 1957– Time of our singing. 4. Foer, Jonathan
Safran, 1977– —Criticism and interpretation. 5. Flanagan, Richard, 1961– —Criticism
and interpretation. 6. Powers, Richard, 1957– —Criticism and interpretation. 7. American
fiction—21st century—History and criticism. 8. English fiction—21st century—History
and criticism. 9. History in literature. 10. Truthfulness and falsehood in literature.
I. Title. II. Series: FlashPoints (Evanston, Ill.)
PS374.H5W55 2014
813.609358—dc23
                                                                    2014004908

Contents

Acknowledgments

Some people go to priests; others to poetry; I to my friends, I to my own heart,
I to seek among phrases and fragments something unbroken.
—Virginia Woolf, "The Waves"

Like any book, this one could not have been written without the inspiration and help of many people. On the academic side, my first thanks go out to Prof. Dr. Rosemarie Buikema and Prof. Dr. Rosi Braidotti. When I was situated at Utrecht University, both always made room in their busy schedules for even the smallest of matters, discussing matter-of-factly or passionately the issues at stake. I am very grateful for the trust and patience they have shown me during the writing process. Prof. Dr. Michaela Hampf and Dr. Gudrun Löhrer of the John F. Kennedy Institute in Berlin, where I went to research Afro-American musicians and the civil rights movement, as well as Prof. Dr. Norbert Finzsch of the University of Cologne and Prof. Dr. Moira Gatens of the University of Sydney have also been incredibly helpful. Their wise advice and good company made this stay very agreeable indeed. The highly efficient and good-humored library personnel at the JFK Institute were a glimmer of light at the end of a tunnel of books I burrowed myself into there. Warm thanks are also due to my sister Christine, who gave me a home in Berlin during this stay.

I want to express my gratitude to PD Dr. Heiko Stoff and Prof. Dr. Maren Möhring, who read large parts of this book and gave me highly useful comments and great encouragement. Likewise, Dr. Regina Mühlhäuser, Dr. Gudrun Löhrer, Therese Roth, Dr. Chiara Bonfiglioli, and Dr. Domitilla Olivieri commented on chapters helpfully and efficiently in times of pressing questions. Dr. Alana Gillespie has been of invaluable help in correcting and improving my English. I find it still incredible how much thought and work can go into a thorough reading. Thanks also go out to all my colleagues in Utrecht who supported my work and believed in me. I want to mention especially Dr. Marianne van den Boomen, Dr. Kathrin Thiele, Dr. Birgit Kaiser, Dr. Susanne Knittel, Dr. Sandra Ponzanesi, Dr. Jamie Weinstein, Dr. Babs Boter, and Prof. Dr. Ann Rigney. Dr. José van Aelst was an incredible help, especially when I needed to keep track of administrative tasks. Trude Oorschot, the kind soul and secret brain behind the Gender Studies Department at Utrecht University, has been of invaluable assistance in all kinds of questions, from health insurance in the Netherlands to administrative and personal advice. I appreciate greatly that my research was facilitated by a Marie Curie fellowship (EU) as well as by grants of the OGC (Utrecht University) and the JFK Institute (Freie Universität Berlin).

I am grateful to the editors at Northwestern University Press, in particular to Henry Lowell Carrigan and series editor Prof. Edward Dimendberg, who never lost patience with or faith in me. Thanks also to the anonymous reviewers of the manuscript, whose insights into Deleuze's philosophy are unsurpassable. I was moved to tears by the incredibly kind and poetic response of Richard Powers that I found in my letter box barely two weeks after I had sent him this book unsolicited. Prof. Dr. Hayden White has supported me throughout the publishing process of this manuscript by offering his invaluable advice, selfless help, and unswerving belief in my work. Thanks also to *CLC Web: Comparative Literature and Culture* for publishing a previous draft of chapter 2 in issue 14 (4), 2012. I would like to let all of you know that your kind responses to my work taught me that intellectual generosity and helpfulness truly exist. Thank you for letting me catch a glimpse of this best of all possible academic worlds in which a community of scholars exchange ideas, offer critique, and enrich one's thought.

This book is a hymn of praise about friendship. Without my friends, it would not exist. Wherever they live—Amsterdam, Barcelona, Berlin, Hamburg, Marseille, Montreal, Munich, Toronto, Utrecht, Valencia—my friends have given me inspiration, comfort, kindness, and happiness. They have offered me hot meals and places to stay; they have laughed with me and wept with me. In a period in which I truly changed "countries more often than shoes" (Brecht), they have kept the doors to their homes wide open for me to enter and stay. As such, they have allowed me to square the circle and live in several cities and countries, languages, and communities. I want to thank Heiko, Silke, Susanna, Anita, Bettina, Lorena, Gudrun, Sophie, Finzsch, Michaela, and Muriel for sharing their hospitality and friendship with me. The Dutch group of Ojala has persuaded me to believe in international solidarity. The feminist self-defense meetings in Spain have been an inexhaustible source of inspiration, good humor, passionate discussions, and very funny outbursts of performance art. My Shinson Hapkido and Shotokan Karate trainers and partners have given me Ki and Do and taught me again and again that only the sky is the limit. I want to thank Begum and Jule for convincing me that Istanbul and Barcelona have suitable cafés in which to write a book. I have been very moved by the generosity and helpfulness of my Amsterdam landlord and landlady, Letteke and Gerard. Moira, Marianne, Kriss, Marjolein, Susan, Lisa, Maren, Didi, Judith, Lena, Christina, Claude, Regina, Therese, Nina, Jenneke, Ipi, Isa, Titch, Evi, Ulf, Marten, Ilona, Johanna, Joana, Jo, Alexia, Bettina, Andreas, Eberhard, Cilja, Laura, Domitilla, Sabrina, Risk, Chiara, Annabel, Sibylle, Ruth, Michael, and Petra are just some of the people that I need to thank for all the good times we shared (and the bad times we endured together, like horses turning our backs on it).

Special thanks go out to my family: Werner, Christine, Anke, and Robin Wiese. While I was writing this book, my mother passed away and we stood firm together. I am deeply grateful to have enjoyed their solidarity and helpfulness, patience and thoughtfulness in this difficult time. To my mother, Marlies, who loved life and faced death fearlessly, who was a truly selfless, giving, sagacious person with great forethought, I dedicate this work.

Abbreviations

The following abbreviations are used throughout the text and notes for commonly cited references.

B   Deleuze, Gilles. 1991. *Bergsonism*. Translated by Hugh Tomlinson and Barbara Habberjam. New York: Zone Books.

CC   Deleuze, Gilles. 1997. *Essays Critical and Clinical*. Translated by Daniel W. Smith and Michael A. Greco. Minneapolis: University of Minnesota Press.

D2   Deleuze, Gilles, and Claire Parnet. 2006. *Dialogues II*. Translated by Eliot Ross Albert. London: Continuum.

DR   Deleuze, Gilles. 2004. *Difference and Repetition*. Translated by Paul Patton. London: Continuum.

F   Deleuze, Gilles. 1999. *Foucault*. Edited and translated by Séan Hand. London: Continuum.

K   Deleuze, Gilles, and Félix Guattari. 1986. *Kafka: Toward a Minor Literature*. Translated by Dana Polan. Minneapolis: University of Minnesota Press.

MI   Deleuze, Gilles. 1986. *Cinema 1: The Movement Image*. Translated by Hugh Tomlinson and Barbara Habberjam. Minneapolis: University of Minnesota Press.

N   Deleuze, Gilles. 1995. *Negotiations, 1972–1990*. Translated by Martin Joughin. New York: Columbia University Press.

P   Deleuze, Gilles. 2000. *Proust and Signs*. Translated by Richard Howard. Minneapolis: University of Minnesota Press.

SP   Deleuze, Gilles. 1988. *Spinoza: Practical Philosophy*. Translated by Robert Hurley. San Francisco: City Lights Books.

TI   Deleuze, Gilles. 2005. *Cinema 2: The Time-Image*. Translated by Hugh Tomlinson and Robert Galeta. London: Continuum.

TP1   Deleuze, Gilles, and Félix Guattari. 2004. *A Thousand Plateaus*. Translated by Brian Massumi. London: Continuum.

TP2   Deleuze, Gilles and Félix Guattari. 1987. *A Thousand Plateaus*. Translated by Brian Massumi. Minneapolis: University of Minnesota Press.

WP   Deleuze, Gilles and Félix Guattari. 1994. *What Is Philosophy?* Translated by Paul Patton. New York: Columbia University Press.

The Powers of the False

Introduction

Altogether, I think we ought to read only books that bite and sting us. If the book does not shake us awake like a blow to the skull, why bother reading it in the first place? So that it can make us happy, as you put it? Good God, we'd be just as happy if we had no books at all; books that make us happy we could, in a pinch, also write ourselves. What we need are books that hit us like a most painful misfortune, like the death of someone we loved more than ourselves, that make us feel as though we had been banished to the woods, far from any human presence, like a suicide. A book must be the ax for the frozen sea within us. That is what I believe.

—Franz Kafka, letter to Oskar Pollak, January 27, 1904

When a history is too painful to relate to, when there is no possible account for the lives that have been lost, when there is no one who will listen to the witnesses, when the testimonies are repressed by the dominant forms of historical representation—then literature might configure a space in which unvoiced, silent, or silenced difference might emerge. This is made possible through the gaps, the fissures, the silences, the mysteries of a text, the effects it describes, the language it uses, the concepts of time and space it employs, and its self-reflexive turn toward its own limitations. Taking up Gilles Deleuze's vague and sketchy configuration of *the powers of the false*, I argue that literature is able to deal constructively with the inability to represent events from the past.

Jonathan Safran Foer's *Everything Is Illuminated* (2002), Richard Flanagan's *Gould's Book of Fish* (2003), and Richard Powers's *The Time of Our Singing* (2003) are three novels that deal creatively with histories that cannot be passed on. I do a close reading of these novels, showing how each of them allows its readers to relate to historical events that are commonly considered to pose problems to historical transmission. Foer's (2002) novel situates its main characters, the Jewish American Jonathan and the Ukrainian Alex, against the background of the Shoah. Both are confronted with their family's entanglement in the Nazis' annihilation of the Jewish shtetl Trachimbrod. They are asked to accept the legacy of the past, while confronted with the task of making responsible choices for the future. The novel thereby performs the need for a postmemorial ethical standpoint that is characterized as being indebted to the memories of the Shoah without being able to claim them; it displays a conscious awareness of the unspeakability of the trauma it relates, but still engages with it (see Hirsch 1997, 1999). Flanagan's literary work invents the narrative voice of a character called Gould who is modeled on a historical persona, the convict-painter William Buelow Gould, who was imprisoned in the 1820s on Sarah Island, Tasmania, when the island was still a penal colony. By taking up the perspective of Gould, the novel forges an account of the Tasmanian convict system that was left out of historical recordings compiled exclusively by the ruling powers during those early years of Tasmania's colonization. Powers's piece of literature tells the fictional story of the mixed-race family Daley-Strom. The novel brings "the problem of the color line" (Du Bois 2002) to the fore by dramatizing how its characters are exposed to racial thinking with devastating effects. It exhibits how modernity's notion of "race" is intricately linked to a concept of time that is seen as progressing in a linear fashion: constant and unchanging. Powers presents an alternative view on time and temporality that is informed by the insights of relativity theory and an ontological understanding of Bergson's *durée*. This vision assists in a fruitful deconstruction of essentialistic notions of race. To read, write, and think about these three novels, I take Deleuze's philosopheme of *the powers of the false* as a point of departure.

The powers of the false are an assemblage of political yearnings and literary possibilities that Deleuze evokes in *Cinema 2: The Time-Image* ([1985] 2005, hereafter cited as TI). Toward the end of the eighth chapter (207–15), Deleuze diagnoses a rupture in the conception of politically informed art, caused by events pertaining to fascism, Stalinism, and colonialism.[1] The political filmmaker and the writer of "minor literature," he argues, have to face a situation in which it has become impossible for them to dedicate their art to a people who are deemed potentially revolutionary (see TI 208). It is the people who are missing, Deleuze claims, referring in his statement to Franz Kafka and Paul Klee, the first artists who are described as having taken notice of the absence of a people to whom art could address itself (see TI 209). For Deleuze, fascism, Stalinism, and colonialism have subjected the masses to the devastating biopolitical ends that are epitomized by the Gulags and death camps, and by colonial exploitation and genocide. This biopolitical subjection of people destroys any hope of the masses acting as a revolutionary subject (see TI 208). However, the acknowledgment that the people are what is missing does not prevent the political filmmaker and the literary writer from creating films or literature. On the contrary, this acknowledgment becomes their driving creative force (see TI 209). Political filmmakers and writers of minor literature are compelled to invent a people through a form of storytelling that affirms "fiction as a power and not as a model" (TI 147). This "story-telling of the people to come" (215) is, according to Deleuze, related to the artistic possibility of envisioning a future that is not a prolongation of the past but a possibility called into being by the arts' specific forces, which he calls their *powers of the false*.

In Deleuze's account, the powers of the false are constellated with the need to invent a people who are missing as the addressee for a politically informed art. Literature has capabilities of transference that undermine political oppression by making something perceptible. However, in this formulation, the intuited thesis of this work dedicated to the powers of the false (and even more so to "the people who are missing") would remain very vague. Nonetheless Deleuze's philosopheme of *the powers of the false* can indeed be made a usable term for reflecting on literature's relationship to reality and its potential to incite readers to go beyond their frames of reference. To make this term fruitful for literary analysis, I posit that it must be made more precise so that the generality of the philosophical term can be surpassed. I argue that only singular readings can determine how novels undermine a clear-cut division between reality and fictionality. Like Barthes, who defines the essence of photography as existing only in a particular, contingent, absolute, and sovereign photograph (see Barthes 1993: 4), the powers of the false, pointing as they do toward a form of knowledge that is not yet here, can be described only by listening attentively to the singular propositions of literary works.

How do the selected novels—Foer's *Everything Is Illuminated*, Flanagan's *Gould's Book of Fish*, and Powers's *The Time of Our Singing*—perform the powers of the false? In other words, how do these novels add something to historiography, an addition that is not opposed to historical accounts but adds perspectives, questions, and riddles to readers' knowledge? How do these novels account for the people who are missing, inventing them in a way that readers can relate to their stories, although these accounts might be shameful or painful? To answer these questions, the specificity of literature must be taken into account. It is the literariness of fictional texts that allows for specific interactions with their readers. Throughout this work I define this literariness as fiction's use of vocabulary, syntax, semantics, characters, narration, and plot—the whole configuration of the fictional text's chronotopical world, as it were (see Bakhtin 1981: 84–258).

Chapter 1, "The Truth of Narration and the Powers of the False," therefore presents important concepts that Deleuze and his collaborators Claire Parnet and Félix Guattari have developed and used in writing about literature. I find it particularly important to show that Deleuze|Guattari and Deleuze|Parnet see writing as a technique and literature as a tool (or rather a "machine") that brings two different but related events into existence.[2] On the one hand, writing is considered to bring about a confrontation through which a writer is confronted with a sensation not yet heard of or seen (see Deleuze and Guattari 2004, hereafter cited as TP1). This happening provokes the writer to abandon the safe haven of subjectivity and go beyond the division between observer and observed world. The writer becomes a perceiver who lets some of her or his forces connect to other forces. She or he will give this intermingling and interaction of different forces a new form and expression in literature. What is expressed in literature is inspired by the world, but it undergoes such a complex transformation that it expresses neither a correspondence nor an analogy: between literature and the lived "there is ultimately roughly the same relationship as between the barking animal-dog and the celestial constellation-Dog" (Deleuze and Guattari 1994 [hereafter cited as WP]: 172). Because literature foregoes correspondence or analogy with the world, it is able to call the second event into existence, namely the event of learning. Readers can undergo an "apprenticeship to signs" (Deleuze 2000 [hereafter cited as P]: 4), an apprenticeship that entails searching for a truth, a search that is mobilized by involuntary or unconscious levels of existence (see P xi). I consider literature's singular proposition for learning in greater depth in the conclusion of this book.

Readers can become involved in the construction of a narrative through their interaction with a text, established through the turns and twists of a given narrative, through a fictional text's development of characters, and through the schemes and tropes of the language employed by that text. Their involvement can be triggered by rhetorical or narrative devices such as metalepsis, ekphrasis, palimpsest, temporalization and duration, focalization, and character or plot development. In my reading of the selected novels, I explain these narrative and rhetorical devices in greater detail and delve into discussions of the possible effects that narratologists such as Mieke Bal, Gérard Genette, Wolfgang Iser, or Michael Riffaterre have attributed to them. Feminist literary criticism as well as poststructuralist and postmodern approaches to literature will allow me to embed the narratological insights into a larger discussion in which Deleuze's philosopheme of the powers of the false always remains central. I see it as indispensable to complement Deleuze's (and, in their collective works, Deleuze|Guattari's) understanding of literature with the insight of literary critics. As Ronald Bogue (2007: 91–107) has shown, Deleuze's (and Deleuze|Guattari's) access to literature is affected by their focus on antinarrativity, as well as through their use of literature to illustrate philosophical concepts (see Bogue 2007: 102–5). This limited focus does not do justice to the complexity of literary works, which is why I deem it necessary to pay attention to all of those stylistic, narrative, and rhetorical devices that play a role in constituting the literary work's specific powers of the false.

In chapter 2, my reading of *Everything Is Illuminated* (Foer 2002) will show how the novel induces its readers to confront and experience the ineffability of the Shoah. As an epistolary novel, it is mainly composed of letters written by Alex and Jonathan. However, Jonathan's personal letters are missing from the book, thereby constituting a blank that the readers have to fill in (see Iser 1978: 226). Readers thereby become the co-addressees of the entire correspondence, drawn in to witness the unfolding of the novel's story. Through Alex's peculiar language use, they are furthermore encouraged to retranslate his idiom into one that makes sense to them. In my analysis I ask what it means for a novel to demand that its readers participate in the making of its story. I show how readers become translators of Alex's idiosyncratic language and how they are permanently confronted with editorial decisions centered around questions of "faithfulness" (see section 2.8). This confrontation with editorial decisions comes into being because parts of the novel discuss details of a book that Alex and Jonathan are writing together. This book, by way of metalepsis, turns out to be *Everything Is Illuminated*. While Alex often suggests that their collaboratively written book should be composed in a way that portrays the characters' choices and actions as acceptable, even "more premium than life" (179), it is obvious that Jonathan does not comply with Alex's suggestions. He does not alter text passages that Alex wants him to change, and he inevitably never depicts any of the characters as better than they are. In a twisted way Jonathan's refusal makes him an extradiegetic writer who is trustworthy and faithful. This is all the more surprising considering that those parts of the story line that are attributed to him are told in the most fantastic way, which establishes his as a magical-realist narrative.

In their coauthored book, Jonathan depicts the story of the Trachimbroders. In a fantastic-realist fashion, he tells how their shtetl, Trachimbrod, was founded before going on to describe life in the shtetl up to the day that the Nazis march into the village and murder its Jewish inhabitants. Alex takes up the story of the Trachimbroders by narrating events that he, his grandfather, and Jonathan experience on their quest for Augustine, presumably the only survivor of the entire Jewish shtetl's population who is still alive. In an intricate way, the novel displays how neither Jonathan's nor Alex's narrative is able to depict the actual event of the population's annihilation. Rather the task of accounting for the murder of a people constitutes a crisis in the narrative. The novel thus highlights the inadequacy of language and other signifying systems when it comes to representing death and destruction. The signifiers of language are by definition iterable in other times and places, their sense is mobile, and their capacity for expression exceeds an individual self or event. This iterability, mobility, and expressiveness of language stands in stark contrast to the singularity of death. The novel's narrative dramatizes this contrast by showing how a mobile and expressive linguistic signifier, "Brod," represents and acquires multiple meanings. Brod is not only a character's name but also the name of a a a river running through the shtetl. The morpheme goes on to extend its applicability to even more meanings, but despite its mobile expressiveness, it is necessarily unable to render the singular event of death and destruction in all its totality. This means that the novel confronts its readers with the failure to account for the murder of a people, a failure that readers witness in the process of reading.

It is precisely this seemingly paradoxical reading position—one that consists in using literature to testify to its own failure of representation—that I connect with literature's powers of the false. I argue that to witness literature's failure means to "[listen], not without fear, for something beyond words" (Celan 2005: 168). Paul Celan has seen this as being intricately connected with the lingering impossible hope that gives language its direction. Listening to something "beyond words" entails making room for an experience of incomprehensibility, as well as experiencing the desire to include what cannot be integrated into one's perception. Precisely because literature makes both perceptible— the fact that there is something "beyond words" and the readers' wish to include the ineffable in their sensation—is it able to unleash its powers of the false. In my analysis I consider it particularly important that the novel's employment of narrative devices assures that it cannot pass itself off as anything resembling testimony.

Its creation of a reading position that requires readers to become the novel's translators and editors is equally important. On the one hand, the constant highlighting of the novel's fictionality assures that its literary world is "a galaxy removed on planet Auschwitz" (Sicher 2000: 66), which respects its unrepresentability. On the other hand, readers have to testify to the effects of the Shoah's ineffability. I consider this creation of a postmemorial reading position to be one of the novel's most important contributions to a post-Auschwitz generation.

In my analysis of *Gould's Book of Fish* (Flanagan 2003), I explore the question of how the novel uses the powers of the false to create a different account of Tasmanian events in the early years of its colonization.[3] The novel "concur[s] with the known facts only long enough to enter with them into an argument" (16). These "known facts" refer to the steadfast opinion of an eminent historian who is a character in the novel. This remark poignantly describes the novel's specificity. Although it constantly alludes to historical events and even bases its main character on a historical figure, its story is rendered in such a fantastic way that it hardly "concur[s] with the known facts." The novel's narrative employs metafictional and self-reflexive devices and uses parodic and fantastic interventions. Most important, its main characters and narrators, William Buelow Gould and Sid Hammet, are convicted forgers and confessed liars; they are therefore highly unreliable. It can safely be stated, then, that the novel does not comply with positivistic historiographical conventions. Does this mean that *Gould's Book of Fish* does not add an important perspective to historical accounts of Tasmania's convict system? I argue that the novel's narrative strategies are important insofar as they raise the question of which narrative devices can be used to depict at least some aspects of the inhuman cruelty in the penal colony of Sarah Island, Tasmania. Called "the worst spot in the English speaking world" (Hughes 1987: 372) during its existence (1822–33), this convict station was known for its brutal conditions. In my analysis I provide detailed historiographical background information to show how the novel engages with Sarah Island's history in general and the fate of the historical figure William Buelow Gould in particular.

Ultimately this novel's most effective addition to historiography might lie in Flanagan's configuration of the ineffability of life and death. This topic is staged explicitly and implicitly in the text, most forcefully through the inability of one of the implied authors, the convict Gould, to create truthful replicas of the fish he has been ordered to draw so that the surgeon Lempriere can send the drawings to the natural historian Mr. Wheeler in London for cataloguing and categorization. Repeatedly Gould notices in horror or astonishment the transformations and metamorphoses the fish undergo, which prevent him from getting a lasting hold on them. Despite, or perhaps because of, the mesmerizing and slippery quality of his subject, he soon finds himself so involved in this task that it becomes his life. "I could not then have known how such madness, this job of painting fish . . . would come to overwhelm my life to such an extent," he confesses, only to continue describing the many uses to which he puts the fish, so that, in his words, "I would, as I am now, be seeking to tell a story of fish using fish to tell it in every way" (Flanagan 2003: 127). Is this assertion true? It can certainly be stated that a certain Gould—the historical Gould—really did paint fish and that his *Book of Fish* can be admired in the Allport Library and Museum of Fine Arts in Tasmania. Replicas of this Gould's pictures are shown on the cover and in the pages of a *Gould's Book of Fish*, preempting all possibility of grasping the concept of originals and displaying a threatening technique of proliferation. However, it needs to be stressed that Gould's literary double is in no way telling a story of fish, unless the only way to tell his story is to proliferate stories that elude capture and start to live a life of their own. In short it might be quite natural for a book that seeks to tell a story of fish to become ensnared in its own description, as the fish itself—with its silent, mute nature—can only be transmuted into another medium, in an endless play of transference and deferral of corresponding to the nature of their being.

I argue that Gould's attempt and failure to grasp the "essence" of the fishes' being is an important feature of the novel, especially because it is not staged as a defeat. Rather Gould's perception of the fish he paints conveys a sense of wonder for life and a love of it. Although this description of Gould goes beyond historical accounts, it is not inconceivable that he lovingly perceived the fishes' lovability. This means that the novel adds something to historiography, an addition that has far-reaching consequences. It allows readers to comprehend that the life of a convict and forger cannot be lumped together with the conditions in which he lives, although they are harsh and harrowing. I contrast the perspective on life presented by the novel with Giorgio Agamben's (1998) theoretical account of "bare life," which has become so important in contemporary debates about biopolitics and their determination of life.

In my reading of *The Time of Our Singing* (Powers 2003), I give particular attention to forms of time and temporalizations used in the novel. It tells the fictional story of the mixed-race family Daley-Strom, whose protagonists are all either outstanding musicians or talented natural scientists. As a piece of historiographic metafiction, *The Time of Our Singing* embeds its characters in historical events that pertain to the history of "race" and racism as well as to social movements and protagonists that tried to counter the devastating effects of racializations. It brings numerous Afro-American performers of classical music back into remembrance by alluding to concerts or musical events that—despite their historical importance—are nearly forgotten. However, I suggest that the novel's most enabling intervention in naturalizing notions of race consists in its performance of an understanding of time that is neither common nor commonsensical. Reconciling Bergson's suggestion that time is essentially continuous change with Einstein's special relativity theory and ensuing notions of a block universe, the novel shows that being-in-one's-time and being-in-time can diverge from each other. It shows that datable historical events and experiences of time do not actually coincide, and dramatizes their potential conflict. In doing so the novel asks whether time loses to a history (see Powers 2003: 329) that is understood as seemingly unchanging when it comes to the notion of race. Or does the ontology of time, performed as a dynamic exchange between past, present, and future, have the capacity to change the course of a cruel, murderous, and exploitative social history of race, of which violence, disempowerment, and injustice are dependent on a naturalizing idea of it?

By analyzing a central conflict between two characters in the novel, I follow this question without losing sight of a particular semiotic model that *The Time of Our Singing* calls into being. It is my main thesis that the novel not only performs a notion of time inspired by Bergson and

Einstein, while also reconciling their theories, but also makes use of an aural semiotic model to evoke an idea of time in which its different temporal layers coexist, without canceling each other out. My discussion takes up Alia Al Saji's (2004) description of an intersubjective, overpersonal, and nonlinear mode of memorialization and temporalization, best captured by sound's ability to allow listeners to perceive different echoes, reverberations, and voices at the same time. Going beyond Al Saji's enabling postulation, I argue that not only hearing but also singing can serve as suitable metaphors for capturing those processes through which memories and times come into existence. In my analysis of the novel, I propose that race should be *heard*, not seen, so that different voices that interact with each other can be perceived without negating each other. When race is heard and not seen, a solidarity in singularity can be perceived that encompasses a "social heritage of slavery" (Du Bois 1975: 116), one that identifies contemporary racism, and attends to utopian propositions. When captured by an aural semiotic model, past, present, and future are all dimensions of time that constantly interact with each other, once we lend our ears to their echoes and reverberations while simultaneously singing their song into being. The novel enacts literature's powers of the false by providing a written score to accompany this suggestion.

I will reflect on whether the powers of the false are in fact synonymous with literature's ability to provide a fake account of history, to potentially spread blatant lies or biased propaganda about events of the past. While I am convinced that it is undeniable that literature can invent distorting and discrediting stories about the past, I maintain that the powers of the false are not the same as lying about it. Literature's powers of the false elicit "structures of historiographic desire" (Rody 1995: 97). The powers of the false evoke readers' longing to bridge the abyss between an ineffable past and a present that has been manipulated by the historical catastrophes enfolded in its silences. But at the same time, readers are confronted with the possibility of there being no remedy for the erasures of the past. Affected by the agency of literature, readers might become responsive and attentive to the omissions in historiography. They might learn to listen closely to the silences that encompass history and to embrace what cannot be seen and what cannot be heard, since it has been lost to the past.

The three novels at the center of this study do not purport to be truthful. Their employment of narrative devices constantly thematizes their fictionality. They invent what is missing from the respective historical accounts they relate to: a reading position that can confront the ineffability of the Shoah and include it in readers' perceptions; a voice of a convicted forger and confessed liar that has not been recorded in the historical archives compiled by the ruling powers of its time; and an idea of race that severs all ties to naturalizing concepts of race while eliciting a notion of time that reconciles the need to remember the social history of race with a utopian vision. The political efficacy of such literature can be enormous because it facilitates congress with collective experiences of an untold or ungraspable past, even if neither language nor any other form of representation can master them. It is exactly this acknowledgment of the failure of mastery over an ungraspable past—established through literary means—that creates a space in which unvoiced, silent, or silenced difference might emerge. Literature invites us to imagine something beyond the limits of the already known; it calls forth different times, peoples, and worlds by calling on readers' desire to know stories about an unfathomable past. Literature provides a space for this desire: it makes it perceptible; it makes it real. In other words, it unleashes the powers of the false.

CHAPTER I

The Truth of Narration and the Powers of the False

Écrire c'est être sans histoire en faveur de cette autre histoire que se cache aussi dans la langue.

—Joost de Bloois, "Bartleby, du Scribe: 'Personage conceptuel' et 'figure esthetique' dans le pensée de Gilles Deleuze"

I.I. AN INTRODUCTION TO WHAT IS UNFAMILIAR AND NEW

Deleuze's scattered remarks on the powers of the false make it difficult to grasp their meaning and possible applications. His terminology, meant to construct the possibility to think anew, to be creative, and to be inspired, is hard to understand for readers unfamiliar with his work. In this chapter I therefore constellate the powers of the false with other relevant concepts and ideas from Deleuze's work as well as the work of other contemporary thinkers and collaborators of Deleuze (such as Félix Guattari and Claire Parnet). Clarifying why Deleuze (and Guattari) posit the writer and her or his activity of writing as central to the development of a literary theory, it quickly becomes clear that these theorists transpose traditional terms. Writing becomes a technology of undoing self and subjectivity, through which the writer is able to confront, sense, and register that which is unfamiliar and new. I link this notion of writing with Deleuze|Guattari's concept of minor literature (see K), their specific linguistic understanding (see TP1 83–123), and the conception of the fold that plays a major role in Deleuze's portrayal of Foucault's philosophy (see Deleuze 1999 [hereafter cited as F]: 78–102). Furthermore I embed Deleuze|Guattari's specific understanding of writing into the literary debates of their contemporaries. These debates took shape after Foucault's and Barthes's suggestion that the idea of the author could be abandoned (see Irwin 2002) and with the ethical demand of feminist critics to read differently by keeping the multiple meanings of a text open while still responding to it (compare Buikema 2009, 2010; Felman 1975; Spivak 2003, 2005: 238–57).

Above all I engage critically with Deleuze's proposition that the powers of the false need to be applied in a political situation in which "the people are what is missing" (TI 209). Deleuze suggests that in such a situation—one that is arguably conditioned by grave violations of human rights by, for example, (neo)colonial, fascist, or Stalinist violence—the writer of minor literature can engage in a "story-telling of the people to come" (215). I argue that Deleuze's view on literature entails its ability to add contradictory, polyvocal, and manifold voices to historical accounts. The creation of these manifold voices in literature invites readers-to-come to respond to a fictional account that is not opposed to reality, that is in fact false. Literature, in other words, is not the memory of the world, nor is it intended to reproduce the sensory. Rather it works like a brain, a faculty of thought, allowing for novel perceptions and sensations, for new relations with the world. In a situation in which "the people are what is missing" (TI 209), literature might be able to stage a mourning and a yearning for the missing people to emerge from the edges of time.

1.2. THE ADVENT OF THE SUPERHUMAN WRITER

Unlike most contemporary philosophers, Deleuze|Guattari posit the writer and her or his activity, writing itself, as their starting point for developing a literary theory.[1] A whole range of author heroines and heroes seems to emerge from their reflections on the subject, including monographs on Proust (P), Sacher-Masoch (Deleuze 1989), and Kafka (K). Are Deleuze|Guattari therefore reinventing a God-like writer who, due to her or his genius and outstanding personality, has a superhuman ability to create a work of art?[2] Surely enough, the texts are interspersed with biographical data that also support several of their arguments, so that, for example, Kafka emerges as a lawyer and a bachelor in Deleuze|Guattari's text, combining desire and legal statements (see K passim), while coughing away his tuberculosis-induced ill health with a writerly "athleticism": "an athlete in bed, as Michaux put it" (Deleuze 1997b [hereafter cited as CC]: 2). This "affective athleticism" is neither muscular nor organic but "an athleticism of becoming that reveals only forces that are not its own" (WP 172). The writer, at once "seer, becomer" (171), "athlete" (172), "inventor and creator" (175) is therefore someone who is confronted with something "in life" that, according to Deleuze|Guattari, is "too great, too unbearable also, . . . so that . . . [what] he sees, accedes to a vision that . . . composes the percepts of that life, of that moment, shattering lived perceptions into a sort of cubism, a sort of simultaneism, . . . which have no other object or subject than themselves" (171). The writer is someone who co-creates forces that belong to life, only to transcend the ordinary perceptions, affections, and sensations, the opinions that hold sway over life, to compose a universe in which "the possible" is brought into existence (see WP 177).[3] Thus, in the conception of Deleuze|Guattari, the writer is someone who achieves extraordinary "visions," transcending life through an encounter with it, transposing it into a universe made of words and sentences that make "the standard language stammer, tremble, cry or sing: this is the style, the 'tone,' the language of sensations, or the foreign language within language" (176).

This conception of literature runs counter to critics who would prefer to see the author symbolically dead rather than alive and kicking. At the end of the 1960s prominent critics like Roland Barthes (2002) and Michel Foucault (2002) declared the symbolic "death of the author," seeing the writer as a stronghold of a capitalist ideology that needs to be overthrown.[4] In their view the author is first and foremost a tyrannical figure (see Barthes 2002: 4) or a principle of thrift (Foucault 2002: 21): a factor that controls the possible meanings of a text. To them, the author was born in the wake of modernism when "the prestige of the individual" (Barthes 2002: 4) was discovered. Presumably imagined by critics and the public as a prestigious, outstanding genius in whom the work of art originates, the author is an authoritative figure that determines how a text is understood.

For Foucault and Barthes, the quasi-religious approach in which texts are seen as recording, representing, annotating, or depicting their originator's most remarkable insights should be abolished in favor of a different conception. For Barthes (2002: 6), texts should instead be conceived of as a "tissue of quotations" whose multiplicity can be "distangled" by an "anti-theological" activity that refuses to assign a fixed meaning. Accordingly a text comes into existence by being inscribed into a space called "reader," and it is her or his birth that Barthes wishes to provoke while announcing the symbolic death of the author. Similarly Foucault (2002) sees the author above all as a discourse function that reduces the threats that *fiction* poses, namely, a proliferation of meaning. For him, the author-function neutralizes contradictions, transformations, and distortions in an author's work or oeuvre (the former being designated as such by being assigned and grouped under the author's name). Furthermore, in the case of "founders of discursivity" like Freud and Marx (see Foucault 2002: 18), the author-function defines discrepancies and variations in a given discourse. It imposes "the possibilities and the rules for the formation of other texts" (18). As a means to overcome the limitations established by the author, Foucault suggests analyzing the way they function in discourse: "What are the modes of existence of this discourse? Where has it been used, how can it circulate, and who can appropriate it for himself [or herself]? Where are the places in it where there is room for possible subjects? Who can assume these various subject functions?" (22). By doing so, we—the readers of discourse—could then perceive "the stirring of an indifference: What difference does it make who is speaking?" (22). In the anonymity of a murmur that is yet to come, the legitimacy of taking up a voice would thus be extended to include "anyone."

Barthes and Foucault's approach to literature has been challenged, although most critics agree that there is nothing—be it subject, history, culture, psyche—that can impose on us a once-and-for-all unified meaning (see Irwin 2002). Yet many literary theorists have argued that the abolishment of the author does not serve their case. For one, long before the 1960s literary criticism had abolished the conflation of author with meaning (Holt 2002; Walker 2002), as anti-intentionalism has shown (see Beardsley and Wimsatt 1954). In this light, in his attack on author-centered criticism, Barthes seems to be shadow-boxing. Furthermore the existence of the author does not prevent multiple interpretations of a text, as was claimed by both Barthes and Foucault. Readers are actually able to have a whole range of aesthetic experiences with, for example, a play by Shakespeare, even if they know it was written by him (see Lamarque 2002). Moreover not every possible conception of the author can be considered as good as dead, so to speak; in some cases there is good reason not to abandon the idea of the author. For example, the prevention of copyright infringement is valuable to individuals working as writers. Even perceiving a work of art as a manifestation of a creative act does not necessarily confine readers' freedom of interpretation (see Lamarque 2002).

Therefore I think it is necessary to ask what is really gained—or lost—by sacrificing the author. After all, what Barthes (2002: 6) is erecting on the grave of the author might not be the liberating monument it seems to be at a first glance, considering his claim that the "anti-theological activity" of abolishing the author as a referent for meaning is "truly revolutionary." This consideration might help us to understand what is actually gained by Deleuze|Guattari's silent and irreverent offenses of not taking into account the position of a symbolic death of the author and instead taking her or his activity as literature's starting point. It will lead us back to the particular configuration of the author-creator which their texts not only proclaim but also perform. Although their use of a nearly all-male, canon-affiliated artist|philosopher ensemble is open to criticism from any kind of nonhegemonic perspective,[5] the theoretical implications of their author configuration might, on the contrary, be reinforcing this nonhegemonic point of view.

Let us therefore turn to the feminist reception of Barthes and Foucault's suggestions. Here again we find appreciation of a reading strategy that refuses to decipher the text's meaning by aligning it to a single referent called "author" (see Greene and Kahn 1985; Moi 1985). In addition, a whole range of feminist literary critics see reading and writing strategies as two sides of the same coin. They appreciate both activities for being able to deconstruct or undermine notions of unified subject positions. For example, in French feminist theory, Luce Irigaray's (1974, 1977, 1979) mimetic writing strategies expose phallogocentrisms; Hélène Cixous's (1980, 1994) *écriture féminine* tries to invent new ways of writing and speaking in which "the other" and "otherness" are crucial to the construction of the self, which is conceived of as being open to this experience. Marginality, subversion, and difference are of decisive importance in Kristeva's (1974, 1977, 1980) theoretical writings and have the power to haunt centralized power (1977: 4). One of the aims of deconstructive feminist critics is reading the construction of differences in texts; in doing so they decompose and expose its internal (for instance, phallogocentric)[6] logic (see Vinken 1992).

In a way, feminist critics, with their particular experience in deploying what could be called "reading as a woman"—a configuration that Culler (1983: 64) posits as the construction of a critical reading position that refers to experiences as "woman," a similarly constructed position—have on the whole been suspicious of any kind of unifying reading or writing strategy. This is because a unifying strategy seeks to obviate differences—any kind of position that is not embodied by a male, white, bourgeois, heterosexual, Western subject. Similar critiques have been put forward by lesbian and gay, queer, postcolonial, and disability theorists, which have challenged monolithic reading and writing strategies that neglect the (hidden) voices from the margins of history.[7] But while Barthes (2002: 6) seems to exorcize not only the author but also any kind of "meaning" from a text, stressing that writing is "carrying out a systematic exemption" of it, feminist criticisms do not claim an absolutely liberating, "truly revolutionary" reading activity of purely "distangling" and "ranging" over a text, as Barthes proposes. Instead "reading as a woman" still entails asking, "How should we read?" (Felman 1975: 10) and thus evokes a question about an *ethics of reading* that seems to have no easy answer but solely calls for a responsible and politically informed *reading practice*.

The target of feminist criticisms is not the redemption of meaning as such but rather the deployment of reading|writing strategies that allow for the perception and construction of difference(s). In this vein Cheryl Walker's (2002: 155) feminist response to Barthes might be understood as follows: "To Barthes I would want to say, writing is not 'the destruction of every voice' but the *proliferation of possibilities of hearing*." Instead of getting rid of meaning, feminist critics engage with the text and listen to its propositions without shutting out other possible understandings. Or, in Spivak's (2003: 72) words, "One must learn to read. And to learn to read is to learn to dis-figure the undecidable figure into a responsible literality, again and again." Without reaching any finality, feminist critics pay meticulous attention to the text and transform it, knowing not only their limitations of response but the stakes involved in responding. To put it slightly differently, feminist critics, among others, leave the question(s) and the multiple meanings of a text open while still responding to it and persistently acknowledging the incomplete and preliminary nature of this response. In short, these feminist critics practice an ethics that evokes the text as an unknowable Other, a radical alterity.[8]

Thus what is at stake here is the possibility of reading meaning otherwise, of engaging differently with a text without closing it. By accepting the unsolvable, endless, radical alterity of the text, the critic engages in an investiture of the text as theorized by Silverman (1996: 86–101): she or he bestows upon it "the gift of love," paying it productive attention despite the impossibility of ever incorporating it into the self. Precisely here, in this loving embrace of a radical textual alterity, Deleuze|Guattari's construction of literature comes into play again. To them, literature, at least in its minor form, creates an encounter with something *new*, which in turn has an intimate relation with the future and in fact emerges from it: "This literature [i.e., minor] . . . is in an exemplary situation for the production of *new* statements" (K 83, my emphasis).

Visions of art come about by slitting open the protective membrane of conventions and opinions, by tearing open "the firmament itself" (WP 203). This tearing open is an act brought about through the artist's confrontation with chaos—an escape from the comfort of resemblance, contiguity, causality, and imagined mastery (201). The artist is thus someone who forgoes all forms of protection in order to confront a sensation not yet heard of or seen—an act that is connected to "struggle," "crisis," "shock," "catastrophe," and "the land of [the] dead" approached by crossing the Acheron (202–3). But while this confrontation could easily be perceived as an act of bravery, a superhuman deed, the artist is not the *subject* but the *inject*[9] of this confrontational action (212). Her or his "present" soul preserves the confrontation in contemplation: it contracts that which composes it, thus engaging in a "passive creation" or "pure passion" (212).

For Deleuze|Guattari, the creator, instead of being the originator, is someone *with whom* something happens, someone *affected*, a *perceiver*, one gripped by forces that "are not its own" (WP 172), which in turn emerge from an unthought-of "outside": an "outside, farther away than any external world, [which] is also closer than any internal world" (F 97). Literature, as an outcome of this encounter with chaos, the unthought-of, the outside, or even with a "beyond life," is thus a diagrammatical tool through which the unregistered can be perceived. As "a watch that is running fast" (Kafka, qtd. in K 59) it points to "a possible future haunting the present" (Wiese 2009: 362), precisely because in any given moment it shows an accelerated time that is incongruent with the time defined as our present. In this way literature, like the cinematic time-image (see TI), is able to bring readers into contact with the forces of time, with time as becoming. Those who let themselves be gripped by the forces they face, those whose "lived perceptions [shatter] into a sort of cubism" (WP 171), can be said to be engaging lovingly with a radical alterity.

This is to say that they allow an encounter to take place through which the outside enters them, creating a fold that could be defined as an "interiorization of the outside." In Deleuze's (F) reading of Foucault, the outside comes into play when thought *cannot* relate forces to each other, when it is confronted with its own (in)ability to think. He defines the outside as being not a fixed limit but a moving matter (80). The outside is a moving matter that creates "folds and foldings that together make up an inside: they are not something other than the outside, but precisely the inside of the outside. . . . If thought comes from the outside, and remains attached to the outside, how come the outside does not flood into the inside, as the element that thought does not and cannot think of? The unthought is therefore not external to thought but lies at its very heart, as the impossibility of thinking which doubles or hollows out the outside" (80). The fold is thus a topographical space that is neither external nor internal. It allows for the emergence of this "other in me" that cannot be appropriated, incorporated, wholly rejected, or made abject. Nothing can be as close and yet as distant as a fold that separates as much as it connects—"farther away than any external world, . . . closer than any internal world" (97). Literature creates *the spaces of the folds* and *the haunting forces of time*, a phenomenon I would like to call "chronotopia": a place where "the other in me" can emerge without merging (with me); a virtual time that is "opposed to the actual" (TI 40) but not to the real.

This conception of literature raises a number of questions, especially since Deleuze|Guattari seem to use a double strategy of naming when writing about art. Although they continually speak about "great artists" and their "outstanding creations," they nevertheless incorporate their ideas into a completely different assemblage. For the writer, as we will see, disappears as soon as the literary machine is actuated. In the same way, the reader-critic is eternally absent, deferred to a possible future, showing herself or himself only as part of a "virtual community" that nevertheless occupies a place in the written creation. Thus Deleuze|Guattari's writing inserts *disjunctions* into their conception of the literary machine. On the one hand, writers and readers exist as they form a part of the literary enunciation. On the other hand, they are never actualized but only haunt the present in their virtuality.

How can this formula be understood, and what purpose does such a conception of literature serve? Furthermore what kind of literature are they talking about? Their peculiar way of *repeating* traditional literary terms in fact transposes them and gives them completely new meanings. For example, they speak of the writer as an "outstanding genius" who produces an "extraordinary" piece of "art," which in turn is appreciated by the reader when she or he perceives its overwhelming "otherness." This method simultaneously ensures that the terms' historical function is still evoked. Thus the bourgeois understanding of literature is conjured up but is constantly haunted by its own double, namely, "minor" literature.

1.3. MINOR LITERATURE

What is "minor" literature, then, and how are writers and readers integrated into this literary machine? In *Kafka*, Deleuze|Guattari specify three different characteristics that define "minor literature": first, it has a "high coefficient of deterritorialization" (K 16); second, "everything in [it] is political" (17); and third, "everything [in it] takes on a collective value" (17). They apply their theory in their reading of Kafka's diary entry of December 25, 1911, so that Kafka's taxonomy of "Kleine Literaturen"[10] is transformed into a political program. What for Kafka may have been simply a jotted-down private reflection is here treated as a theoretical outline for "a revolutionary machine-to-come" (17), since Kafka not only writes about "small" literatures but functions as Deleuze|Guattari's primary example in describing the prerequisites for minor literature and its implied politics of writing. In this way Kafka's classificatory in(ter)vention is immediately connected to the sociolinguistic conditions of "Prague German," a language cut off from the majority of German speakers, since during Kafka's lifetime it was spoken by only 7 percent of Prague's inhabitants, mostly rich bourgeois merchants who had settled there during the Austro-Hungarian Empire (see Stölzl 1979). As such it was a language that, due to its restricted geographical and socioeconomic situation, led its own particular kind of insular life[11] and is often described as a "paper language," a highly artificial idiom that has almost no connection to other kind of sociolects that are defined by heterogeneous class-, region-, or profession-specific language usages. As a German-speaking *Jewish* Czech Austrian Hungarian, Kafka was also part of an even smaller religious minority in this already small language community—especially considering the growing anti-Semitic tendencies in the 1920s that caused Jewish people to experience social isolation (see Goldstücker 1967).

For the development of a minor literature, this specific linguistic situation is crucial for Deleuze|Guattari, because it poses a problem (which to them is the prerequisite for a possible new solution, as it is a force from the outside), namely, "the impossibility of not writing, of writing in German, of writing otherwise" (K 16). Giving up writing, writing in another tongue or in another genre or style, does not seem to have been an option for Kafka, although some of his contemporaries did choose this path, as the growing number of Yiddish artifacts in the nineteenth century and the beginning of the twentieth show.[12] But instead of opting to write in Czech or Yiddish, Kafka stuck to German

and used it in a completely new way, which Deleuze|Guattari charac-
terize as "intensive" but "sober" (K 25): "He will tear out of Prague
German all the qualities of underdevelopment that it has tried to hide;
he will make it cry with an extremely sober and rigorous cry. He will
pull from it the barking of the dog, the cough of the ape, and the bus-
tling of the beetle. He will turn syntax into a cry that will embrace
the rigid syntax of this dried-up German" (26). In other words, they
perceive Kafka's language politics as using the material of language
itself to exploit its sparseness until it vibrates from the intensive use
it is subjected to, while it deterritorializes its sense to the point that it
becomes pure sound:

> Kafka, too, is a minor music, a different one, but always made
> up of deterritorialized sounds, a language that moves head
> over heels and away. . . . An escape for language, for music, for
> writing . . . Wörterflucht. To make use of the polylingualism of
> one's own language, to make a minor or intensive use of it, to
> oppose the oppressed quality of this language to its oppressive
> quality, to find points of nonculture or underdevelopment, lin-
> guistic Third World zones by which a language can escape, an
> animal enters into things, an assemblage comes into play. (27)

Although it could be argued that the specific deterritorializations
that occur in Kafka's stories are caused less by his specific use of words
than by a complete exploration of the literariness of fictional texts—
their use of vocabulary, syntax, character, narration, plot, the whole
configuration of the fictional text's chronotopic world, as it were (see
Bakhtin 1981: 84–258), a dream-like sobriety can still be found in
Kafka's texts. Benjamin (1992: 40) describes Kafka's texts as a rendering unimpressive of the experiencing character, in which the character
is placed at the heart of a banal situation. Examples from Kafka are
Gregor Samsa's waking up as a bug in *Metamorphosis* (2005a), something that is not as much of a problem as his inability to open the door
for the chief clerk, and Josef K.'s ignorance of the crime of which he is
accused in *The Trial* (2005b).

Kafka's characters, with their inability to influence the course of
events, seem to exist in a world that has assigned them undefined
functions, while the world itself is constantly transforming itself
unpredictably. Rather than abandoning sense "in order to liberate a
living and expressive material that speaks for itself and has no need

of being put into a form" (K 21), Kafka puts senses into play that vary from situation to situation, according to hidden rules that also seem to undergo constant changes. He thus stages incredible events that form a stark contrast to the dispassionate language that describes them.

In this manner Kafka's writing seems rather connected to the method of the AND, "this and then that," which, according to Deleuze|Guattari, undermines BEING and subjectivity, as it is not the subject that enables continuity (see TI 174). Elsewhere they call the AND function—to be connected without necessarily being coherent—"stammering" or "generalized chromatism," indicating how signifying systems undergo a form of "continuous variation" (TP1 105–11), in which themes, constants, or invariables are repeated on another scale and the frame of reference undergoes change as well.[13] Rather than being reduced to words themselves, Kafka's minor literature connects to musicality in its tendency to "escape" unifying meaning through continuous variation, "replacing the centered forms of continuous development with a form that constantly dissolves and transforms itself" (TP1 105).

In its connection to music, the term *minor* now acquires a new speed and demonstrates its ability to show "the difference of a self *within* itself" (Deleuze 2004a: 27, my emphasis)—or, in other words, "pure difference" (see Deleuze 2004b [hereafter cited as DR]).[14] This ability derives from a variation constituted by the minor scale within the diatonic scale. In Western music a diatonic scale has seven notes spanning one octave. The intervals in the scale (the musical distances from one note to the next) can be divided into half steps and whole steps. For Western ears, a scale is harmonious if it consists of whole steps interrupted by two half steps between the third and fourth and between the seventh and eighth notes. Two of the scale degrees involved in these half steps (IV and VII) are dissonant with the tonic pitch (I, with which the scale starts) and therefore call for a "resolution," meaning the progression downward (IV to III) or upward (IV to V, VII to VIII) toward the following note, that is, the mediant (III), dominant (V), or tonic (VIII).

If we take the two scales without any accidentals in the key signature (C major and A minor), we see that the scales differ in two respects: in the minor mode, the piano keyboard does not offer a whole step from II to III, while it does provide one between VII and VIII. This means that the interval between the tonic (I) and the third (III, the mediant) consists of four half steps in the major key and three in the minor, while the whole step between the VII (subtonic) and VIII (tonic) in a minor scale modifies the "call for resolution," insofar as VII is no longer "gliding toward" VIII. The reason there is no natural pull toward the tonic is the flattened seventh. In major keys it is the half step between VII and VIII that creates the necessary tension and subsequent resolution when VIII (the tonic) is heard. In a minor key the gap between VII and VIII is a whole step, and the tension (and therefore the resolution) is significantly reduced. This problem can be artificially balanced by using accidentals, so that an artificial half step is introduced between VII and VIII. But it cannot solve the problem that in a minor scale the III (mediant) is not an integral multiple of the fundamental (I, tonic)[15] and thus disturbs harmonics in general, because the transposition of a theme cannot rely on an inherent "suggestion" toward tonic resolution in a variation on a theme. The III and the VII in the minor keys thus have the ability to stand on their own and are therefore in line with twelve-tone music, in which the octave is divided into twelve equally spaced tones and neither resolution nor resonance of the tonic in a transposition is called for—therefore abandoning one of the most important compositional tools in Western music.[16] The minor scale also gestures toward the chromatic scale, in which notes are used that do not belong to the prevailing scale. G-sharp, for example, is the leading (chromatic) note in A minor. In a chromatic scale one could even use notes such as D-flat or E-flat that do not occur in any natural expressions of A minor.

With these particularities of the minor scale in mind, the extent to which its workings are connected to the notion of "pure difference" as put forward by Deleuze in *Difference and Repetition* become obvious. Although single notes do not change from major to minor (both modes use exactly the same piano keys), their nature and function in the piece of music varies considerably. While major keys might smoothly adapt to well-tempered harmonics, minor keys require constant use of accidentals to maintain a sense of harmony (unless one slips into a relative major). However, in its pure, unaltered state a minor key poses a problem, as it does not call for a resolution in the main key (based on the I, tonic). Minor is therefore an "unmediated difference" par excellence, as the exact repetition of the same pitch displays a "differential" at work: a differential, as Deleuze has pointed out, that should be understood in the sense of a mathematical function (see DR xiv), which serves as a method to determine the gradient of a curve through a tangent whose osculation point is infinitely small and whose gradient triangle is infinitesimal (see Leibniz and Newton 2007). A differential is thus a mathematical operation that uses infinitely small numbers that are nevertheless determinant for a calculation. Transposing this notion into literature cautions us against the assumption that the same words will have identical functions: even if the difference between the use of words in major and minor literature might be infinitely small, even imperceptible, their function in the construction of "lines of flight" (like the infinitesimal gradient or the escaping minor chord) through which "'one' leaves the territory" (TP1 559) might differ considerably.

It is precisely this notion that Deleuze|Guattari employ in their development of a linguistic concept (TP1 83–123), which might help us to determine the function of minor literature: a function that might design and designate the powers of the false that are the proper subject of this study. For if they define major and minor exactly in these terms—"'major' and 'minor' do not qualify two different languages but rather two usages or functions of language" (TP1 115)—it is not without bringing forth a whole new conception of language that gives rise to a "chromatic linguistics" (108), that is, a linguistics that conceptualize a "continuous variation" in language use (see TP1 104).

To arrive at this suggestion, one has to pass through the understanding of "content" and "expression," which Deleuze|Guattari put forward in this context (TP1 95–101). In contrast to linguistic studies that search for the (phonological, syntactic, semantic) *constants* in language, which then *refer* to a body or a state of things, Deleuze|Guattari suggest that "things" and "signs" are two different formalizations, regardless of the fact that "signs are at work in things themselves just as things extend into or are deployed through signs" (96). Yet this intermingling has nothing to do with their separate existence; if "things" and "signs" connect, it is by "attributing" an expression to a body or state of things that then might "intervene" in this state as a *speech act* and cause a transformation. But the power to intervene does not come directly from the verbal expression itself. It derives its power through circumstances that make it performative: "Anybody can shout 'I declare a general mobilization,' but in the absence of an effectuated variable giving that person the right to make such a statement it is an act of puerility or insanity, not an act of enunciation" (91). This means that language can be considered pragmatically, given the circumstances and its outcome, only in the "incorporeal transformations" it triggers. Yet even if we consider that situations vary, as do the functions of language, according to Deleuze|Guattari there is no reason to presume that statements "remain constant in principle" (104). Assuming a pseudo-constant of expression (signs, statements) is no better than assuming a pseudo-constant of content (bodies or state of things). If we suppose that expressions, signs, or statements remain constant, we construct their "function as a center" like the "laws of resonance and attraction" in the diatonic system of music (105) that I have illustrated with the function of the fundamental, I, and the dominant, V, in the major scale. In other words, we endow it with "stability and attractive power [*pouvoir*]" (105). Only if we consider that expressions vary, only if we grant them the "power [*puissance*] of variation" (112),[17] do we make a minor use of language accessible, one in which language is an event and escapes its usual function of "giving orders."

1.4. ESCAPING ORDERS, ACCEPTING INVITATIONS

Deleuze|Guattari believe that "the elementary unit of language—the statement—is the order-word" (TP1 84).[18] This means that utterances aim for their effectuation and cause a change in the state of things or bodies (transformations that might even be "incorporeal," such that a body takes on a different function). They nevertheless maintain that an important point of departure is missed if one constructs invariants (92). Taking Labov's example of a young black person who switches constantly between Black English and Standard English, they argue that "it is not certain that the phonology is the same, nor the syntax, nor the semantics" (104). To assume constancy in these utterances, although they might differ greatly in style, is a political decision that cannot reveal the virtual otherness of the utterance, its potential to signify differently, thus allowing for a rejection and dissolution of constant forms (see 104–16). This virtual function of the statement is real without being actualized. Just as notes may be minor or major—depending on how they are used—the function of utterances depends on their position and connection with regard to other signs and things in a particular assemblage. To determine their function we therefore need to ask whether it supports stable arrangements of meaning, circulating them like slogans or giving orders. Or does the utterance construct a line of change or creation?

How do we perceive this virtual function of a statement that is realized without being actualized?[19] Insofar as it has no actuality in the present, it follows that it lacks its own representation. Rather than being present, I would like to suggest that the virtual function is *an invitation*[20] to perceive other possibilities of meaning, to pay close attention to possible unexpected changes. The *act of resisting* habitual recognition—"it is grass in general that interests the herbivore" (TI 43)—*by constituting* an attentive recognition is able to conceive the singularity of an event: grass. The virtual is therefore closely connected to perception, to an *openness* to perceive differently. The perception of a virtual statement could be seen as an act of resistance to habitual recognition. Brian Massumi relates the virtual to the imagination, or more precisely, to the intuition. He describes it as "a thinking feeling. Not feeling something. Feeling thought—as such, in its movements, as process, on arrival, as yet unthought-out and un-enacted, postinstrumental and preoperative. Suspended. Looped out. Imagination is felt thought, felt as only thought can be: insensibly unstill. Outside any given thing, outside any given sense, outside actuality. Outside coming in" (2002: 134). The intuition, read in this way, has the ability to connect immediately and immanently with an outside of thought. It can sense the arrival of something new and is able to perceive the haunting forces of a "pure power of time" (TI 46): a time that exceeds all memory of the past and all anticipation of the future. Writing, in this sense, is the creation of a passage in which this "newness" might arrive. It is a process that "raises itself to these becomings and powers" (CC 3) through which the writer becomes "exhausted" (3). This is an exhaustion provoked by "a dealing with reality that is exhaustive" as Asja Szafraniec (2007: 122) has pointed out, since in Deleuze's definition, "only an exhausted person can exhaust the possible, because he has renounced all need, preference, goal, or signification" (CC 154). Szafraniec (2007: 121) argues that this is "the systematic disconnecting of all patterns of choice and preference which makes us into beings that we are." The exhausted and exhausting writer, who has dissolved her or his identity "into an impersonal, multiple, machinelike subject" (Braidotti 1994: 116),[21] confronts an idea, but this idea does not resemble anything known to the mind. It is an image that "emerges in all its singularity, retaining nothing of the personal or the rational, and by ascending to the indefinite as if into a celestial state. A woman, a hand, a mouth, some eyes . . . some blue and some white" (CC 158). In short, it is an image that attains its power from the impersonal, not the general, while the writer affirms this vision by remaining open to "all of chance in one throw" (DR 251).

The writer, in this sense, resembles Nietzsche's superman—or, to be more gender-inclusive, superhuman—someone who frees life within herself or himself by letting the forces within the self exceed the self, by entering "into a relation with forces from the outside" (F 109). In Deleuze's reading of Foucault (F), the writer might open life to new possibilities of connection and connectivity because of the specific qualities of her or his creation, namely literature. According to Deleuze, Foucault grants literature the capability of overcoming linguistic restraints. The writer of literature might create new linguistic rules or a new structure of meaning, as she or he might show that language can be senseless. The writer might point to or go beyond actual language use, thereby making the ontological qualities of language accessible. Deleuze calls these ontological qualities a "being of language" (F passim). This "being of language" has an absolute and unhistorical a priori quality, and its totality, through its endless ability to change, can never be re-presented.

The writer's moment of inspiration—the moment of confrontation with something unthought of in thought—is the affirmation of Nietzsche's "divine game," the throwing of dice in the eternal return. It is the affirmation of a "pure difference" and a "disguised" repetition, since all possible compositions "for each item and for all times" (DR 251) are affirmed, while that which is repeated is "affirmation": "Only affirmation returns. . . . At the cost of the resemblance and identity. . . . For 'one' repeats eternally, but 'one' now refers to the world of impersonal individualities and pre-individual singularities. . . . The eternal return is the internal identity of the world and of chaos, the Chaosmos" (372). What returns here too is the force, even the violence[22] of that which must be thought, of the unthought of in thought that makes "one" think—a "one" fractured by the problem posed by the cogitanda[23] (249). The imperative to think is forced upon those who happen to perceive it. These forces "enter and leave only by that fracture in the I, which means that another always thinks in me, another who must also be thought" (250). It is not the "I" that engages in thinking, but some of its forces, namely, those that are able to connect to another outside and an outside other. This other—hinting through its effect toward the fundamental openness of living beings[24]—introduces the possibility of another world, and therefore difference, into thought (see WP 17; Deleuze 1997a: 327). But not only does it enable the perception of the other and other possible worlds; it also enables the self to be ephemeral: "'I' now designates only a past world" (WP 18), because the "I" that "must be registered"[25] is replaced by a new perception of "me." As something that is "added" to matter, this perception is purely temporal and spiritual (see TI 46); as such, it describes the "I" as a passing entity: "I" am . . . an irreducible multiplicity.

1.5. THE MISSING PEOPLE

The possibilities of literariness, that is, the use of vocabulary, syntax, character, narration, plot, the whole configuration of a chronotopic world (see Bakhtin 1981: 84–258), might link up with the formula of a "missing people" appearing a number of times in the works of Deleuze (TI 151–216; 1998: 19) and in his joint productions with Guattari (K; WP 108, 176). In *Cinema 2: The Time Image*, Deleuze names Kafka and Klee as the first artists who took note of the absence of a people and paradoxically grounded their notion of creativity on its nonpresence. While Kafka believed that minor literature ought to fulfill collective tasks if the people are missing, Klee regarded the missing people as the decisive force that "brings together all the parts of 'its great work'" (TI 209).

To understand these far from self-explanatory ideas of Kafka and Klee and to get a grip on Deleuze|Guattari's appropriation of these notions, one has to keep in mind that they all allude to very specific conceptions of art that displace conventional notions of creators, works of art, and recipients. Additionally Deleuze|Guattari employ a different understanding of time, as time becomes a force independent of a subjective sense or historical notion. Only against the background of this altered conception of art and time does it become clear how they employ the notion of a "missing people" and why art in general and literature in particular have privileged access to express previously unvoiced experiences. This expression of silent and silenced experiences is urgently called for by, for example, postcolonial critics.[26]

If one looks at Kafka's (1948: 148–51) understanding of "small literatures," the literal translation of Kafka's *kleine Literaturen*, it immediately catches the eye that Kafka's jotted-down taxonomy is a description of the role that literature could fulfill in a "small nation" (*kleine Nation*). The very first sentence of his diary entry allows us to infer which "nations" he has in mind: on the one hand, he refers to Czech literature, and on the other hand, to Yiddish literature in Warsaw as it was depicted by his friend Jizchok Löwy. What he knows about these literatures leads him to assume that their influence in society is far more direct than in "great nations": "Literature is less a concern of literary history than of the people" (149). Although he depicts several instances through which the literature of a "small nation" permeates the life of a people—lively discussions of the literature of a "small nation" will appear in newspapers and journals, and everyone knows it thoroughly (148)—there is no coherent group of people at which it is directed, "since people lack a sense of context" (150). In fact Kafka writes about a fragmented community in which the concerns of the individual do not connect to similar concerns, because "even though something is often thought through calmly, one still does not reach the boundary where it connects up with similar things" (150).

Kafka depicts politics as the only topic in literature in which the boundary between individual and collective concerns is crossed, and it is through political slogans that literature is disseminated. But although literature is spread through politics, it does not lose its artistic integrity and autonomy: "The inner independence of the literature makes the external connexion with politics harmless" (Kafka 1948: 150; see Robertson 1985: 1–38). As Robertson (1985: 24) has pointed out, in his taxonomy of "small literatures" Kafka develops "nothing less than an essay on the sociology of literature." Yet it is a literature that does not lose its autonomous status and furthermore precedes the imagined community of its readers. One could even claim that it is literature that constructs a common ground for a people whose commonality is otherwise missing, as the circumstances do not allow the individual's concerns to connect to each other.

It is exactly this constructive function of literature that is taken up by Deleuze|Guattari, because to them "the literary machine alone is determined to fill the conditions of a collective enunciation that is lacking elsewhere in this milieu" (K 18). Literature has the ability to express collective concerns, but what it expresses is not actuality, but virtuality (see K 48), a mode of expression Deleuze claims to be real, without being actualized (see DR 260). How does the literary statement express virtuality? Insofar as virtuality has no actuality in the present, it follows that it lacks its own representation. Yet, as Bergson (1919: 112–36) and Deleuze (TI 133) have pointed out, although virtuality is not represented, it can nevertheless be perceived. To them the virtual is the "memory of the present" (TI 79) that accompanies the present as a shadow accompanies the body (Bergson 1919: 130) and connects it with the "whole of the past."

To understand this formula it should be kept in mind that for Bergson, as well as for Deleuze, succession of time does not exist. Present and past coexist; there is a "general past" alongside the concrete "perception" taking place in the present. Even though past and present are radically different, they do intermingle. On the one hand, the past is pressing onto the present, coloring perception. On the other hand, the present moment is always split: it simultaneously projects itself toward the future and becomes its own past. Only when we perceive these processes do we have contact with virtuality. If for Deleuze|Guattari the expression of collective concerns in literature can only be virtual, then in my view it serves as an invitation to perceive other possibilities of meaning, encouraging the reader to pay close attention to possible, unexpected changes, an invitation for which I provided the philosophical outline in the previous section. This explanation might also link up with Deleuze|Guattari's definition of literature as "a watch that is running fast" (K 59), pointing to a possible future haunting the present. Through its expression of virtuality, literature is an assemblage capable of registering what is not yet given, of what is yet to come: "the diabolic powers of the future that for the moment are only brushing up against the door" (48). It might allow us to question legitimized versions of the past and to conceive of a possible future through its "accelerat[ion of] a whole movement that already is traversing the social field" (48).

The close relation of literature to virtuality, its construction of a perception that is neither wholly present nor can be assigned to a remembered past, might also explain why, for Deleuze|Guattari, literature "leaves no assignable place to any sort of subject" (K 84). In *Kafka: Toward a Minor Literature*, they define the function of literature as follows:

> When a statement is produced by a bachelor or an artistic singularity, it occurs necessarily as a function of a national, political, and social community, even if the objective conditions of this community are not yet given to the moment except in literary enunciation. From this arise two principles in Kafka: literature as a watch that moves forward and literature as a concern of the people. The most individual enunciation is a particular case of collective enunciation. This is even a definition: a statement is literary when it is "taken up" by a bachelor, who precedes the collective conditions of enunciation. This is not to say that this collectivity that is not yet constituted (for better or for worse) will in turn become the true subject of enunciation or even that it will become the subject that one

speaks about in the statement: In either case, that would be to fall into a sort of science fiction. No more than the bachelor, the virtual community—both of them are real—are components of a collective assemblage. (83–84)

This construction of the literary machine destroys the notion that literature expresses any kind of subjectivity: the literary act of enunciation does not "belong" to the writer, nor is she or he referred to by the utterance of speech. Rather the writer precedes the statement while the addressed community remains eternally to come. Neither effects nor products of the literary machine, writers and readers "exist only as gears and parts of the assemblage" (84). While the writer is a "function" of a collective enunciation, a release point in a societal assemblage that is able to "take up" its tendencies and to assemble and dismantle them in the literary machine, the "virtual community" of readers might be considered an important motivation for its construction.

Therefore I suggest that the virtual community partakes in the necessity of writing, the necessary search for the "line of escape" that Deleuze|Guattari encounter in Kafka's writing (see K 28–42): "a micropolitics, a politics of desire that questions all situations" (42). It is this notion of "escaping" and "questioning" micropolitics that Deleuze takes up in *Cinema 2: The Time Image* when describing the narrative function of minor literature and political cinema after World War II. To him the rise of fascism and Stalinism destroyed the hope for progressive artists ever being able to dedicate art to revolutionary masses, since under both regimes the masses were subjected to biopolitical ends and thus lost their connection to truly liberating revolutionary forces. Similarly the oppressed and exploited nations belonging to the Global South "remained in the state of perpetual minorities, in a collective identity crisis" (TI 209). But when politically informed art cannot dedicate itself to a people because they are necessarily absent as a presupposed addressee, it can nevertheless contribute to their formation (209). In an "intolerable" situation (211) the line of escape available to the political artist who knows that the people are missing is to invent a people, "not the myth of a past people, but the story-telling of the people to come" (215).

For Deleuze, this mode of storytelling is a form of free indirect discourse, elsewhere defined as a "constellation of voices . . . from which I draw my voice. . . . Speaking in tongues" (TP1 93). "The story-telling of the people to come" is thus a mode of narration that is impersonal, whose narrator cannot be tracked down to a single, unified voice. By showing language in its most impersonal state, as a multiplicity of tongues, the narration folds back onto itself to show "the pure and simple story-telling function" (TI 145), what Deleuze calls *the powers of the false*: powers that break down the dichotomy between truth and fiction to become not truthful narration but the truth of narration, its creative, fabulating, and polyvocal function whose manifold and perhaps contradictory voices make what has happened appear indeterminate and therefore question the legitimized and homogenized versions of events. It thus "affirms fiction as a power and not as a model" (147); it shows what the narration is capable of, its "power to affect and be affected" (135). It is here that Deleuze (and Guattari) fully connect to an understanding of literature as a preconfiguration of the people who are missing and to an understanding of literature as a practice of re-, pre-, or postmemory.[27] Acknowledging that the people are missing, yet creating prefigurations for the people to come, literature can stand in for lost memories and stories that are yet to be told, while similarly questioning the divide between fiction and history. Grasping the power of the false, literature forms an assemblage "which brings real parties together, in order to make them produce collective utterances . . . (and, as Klee says, 'we can do no more')" (215).

1.6. THE TRUTH OF NARRATION

To get a better grip on the full dimensions of literature's ability to stand in for lost memories and stories yet to be told, it is useful to follow a Deleuze already infected by Foucault's understanding of truth and its relation to power. A configuration of truth and power that is seen as being inspired by Foucault might explain why Deleuze|Guattari have such high esteem for fiction and its ability to prefigure a "people to come." As Deleuze (1995 [hereafter cited as N]: 86) explains in an interview with Robert Maggiori, he attempts to find in his monograph *Foucault* the latter's "double," so that not only their "intellectual understanding and agreement" can come to the fore, but also the "intensity, resonance [and] musical harmony" that characterize their mutual influence.

In *Foucault*, Deleuze not only follows Foucault's theoretical development in chronological order, thereby giving his readers a sense of the latter's most important contributions to the history of thought. He also sets up an assemblage in which he transposes Foucault's conceptions of knowledge formation, power, and subjectivation into his own terminology, in such a way that it becomes indistinguishable whose ideas are displayed: a posthumous, reciprocal "pick-up" or "double theft" that Deleuze explains elsewhere as an "a-parallel evolution" that happens not between persons but between ideas, "each one being deterritorialized in the other, following a line or lines in which are neither in one nor the other, and which carry off a 'bloc'" (Deleuze and Parnet 2006 [hereafter cited as D2]: 14). In other words, this mutual deterritorialization into a bloc allows for a "strengthening of desire instead of cramping it, displacing it in time, deterritorializing it, proliferating its connections, linking it to other intensities" (K 4), so that a transfer and transposition is given that may allow for a new understanding of given terms. In the case of "the missing people" and their evocation by way of the powers of the false, we then have to pass through a bloc in which the possibility of "thinking otherwise" is explored—a possibility that Deleuze stresses in his reading of Foucault, since to Deleuze there is a difference between thought as an archive and thought as a strategy, the latter being an emergent, powerful force (see N 95). To Deleuze this thought as a strategy is a force that Foucault explored in his own work, thereby making it possible to grasp what Deleuze calls "actuality" (see N 95).

To arrive at this conclusion Deleuze sees two readings of Foucault as decisive (see F 72): his article on Nietzsche (Foucault 1977: 139–64) and the one on Blanchot (Foucault 1987: 7–61). In "Nietzsche, Genealogy, History" (Foucault 1977), through a rereading of Nietzsche, Foucault develops a critique of history that he replaces with a new form of historical research. Genealogy, as it is called, is dedicated to challenging traditional understandings of history as the discovery of "origins": the origin of knowledge in truth, the origin of the present in a continuously developing past that animates it, and the origin of the subject in their synthesis. In Foucault's view all three notions disguise the fact that things "have no essence or that their essence was fabricated in a piecemeal fashion from alien forms" (142). Rather there are no essences that are not "hardened into an unalterable form in the long baking process of history" (144), through forces whose interpretations have become victorious in a struggle for meaning. The unity of history, its ideal continuity, is a form of narration that disguises a more fundamental dispersion of phenomena, entangled or lost events, leaving us "without a landmark or point of reference" (155).

Genealogy, in contrast, becomes effective by recording the history of interpretations, while being attentive to a microhistory of singular events, whose different scenes and roles should be recorded, including their unrealized and absent states (see Foucault 1977: 140). In "Maurice Blanchot: The Thought from Outside," Foucault (1987: 55) displaces a traditional notion of language, in which it acts as "the future bond of the promise and as memory and narrative." Counteracting this definition, Foucault displays how the proposition "I speak" will undermine its generality as soon as the speaker falls silent, thus showing a being of language that precedes subjectivity. In Foucault's eyes, Blanchot refrains from containing this experience in the safeguard of a reflecting interiority in which the "outside" is repatriated as "the experience of the body, space, the limits of the will, and the ineffaceable presence of the other" (21). Rather Blanchot undoes the binding of language to "common" sense, until their images "burst and scatter in the lightness of the unimaginable" (23), while showing to what extent "the invisibility of the visible is invisible" (24).

Language becomes "language about" (Foucault 1987: 56) its own outside and its invisible side. It circulates the void around words, while remaining eternally outside of the outside, forever reaching out. Such a form of language undoes its own certainties and betrays its referentiality because it contains nothing and holds nothing. It is a void that carries neither subject, time, nor truth; therefore it puts us into contact with death itself, "the threatening promise of its own disappearance" (58). The essays on Nietzsche and Blanchot thus both display the contingency of truth: this is a truth that one might undo by following the intricate path of its becoming "hardened into an unalterable form" (Foucault 1977: 144)—a history intricately bound to a dynamics of power or even domination.

In Deleuze's understanding, History is the name for this hardening of meaning through time; it is that which determines what can be seen and what can be said in a given age, "beyond any behaviour, mentality, or set of ideas" (F 42). "What is visible" and "what is sayable" are, in turn, Deleuze's translations of Foucault's definition of "statements" and "evidences" as developed in *The Order of Things* (1992) and *Archaeology of Knowledge* (1972). For Deleuze|Foucault, the sayable and the visible are neither linguistic utterances nor things. Instead they come into existence through complex procedures that establish them as truths. The sayable, or what Foucault calls "statement," and the visible—the "evidence" or "visibility"—form the "base" or "condition" of what can be seen and said at a given moment in time. To extract "statements" and "visibilities," one has to "break open" words and things and determine under which modalities they come into existence.

Although statements and visibilities determine what can be seen and what can be said at a particular time, their historical variations point to other possibilities of seeing and saying. These other possibilities of seeing and saying are enabled by the ontological qualities of language and sight, ontological qualities that are a priori, unconditional, and transhistorical. In Deleuze's terminology language's ontology is called "there is language" or "the being of language," and sight's ontology is called "there is light" or "light being." Statements and visibilities come into existence only because there is language and there is light. Language and light are absolute yet historical, as they need to fall into a "formation" or "corpus." Still they are separate forces with different qualities, and even if the sayable and the visible are contained in an "audio-visual archive," the latter is disjunctive and consists of heterogeneous forms, a condition (discursive) and a conditioned element (nondiscursive) "that force one another to do something or capture one another, and on every occasion constitute 'truth'" (F 56–57). Yet their disjunction allows them to break apart and thus remain open to new conceivabilities, while language remains spontaneous and light remains receptive. In this way, not only does the audiovisual archive come into being by procedures of truth, but so do "relatively free or unbound points, points of creativity, change and resistance" (37) that "testify to the twisting line of the outside" (38).

To grasp the conception of the outside, it is crucial to note that "knowledge" is not only defined as the linkage between the visible and the sayable. It is also power that causes both divergent forms to combine and integrate, to cause and limit our seeing and speaking. Therefore "truth" is neither transcendent nor transhistorical, since it is realized in shifting power relations that are the "set of conditions" (N 106) for the visible and the sayable. But if power determines and limits what we can see and what we can say, this does not mean that everything remains within its reach. Rather, in Deleuze|Foucault's conception, there is still an "outside" to power in which the he-autonomy of the sayable and the visible is realized in a nonrelation. Similarly if power is defined as a relation between forces, nothing precludes the possibility that these forces too remain nonrelated. If the power of forces is defined as their ability to affect and be affected, forces realize themselves in an "irreducible encounter" (F 60), but this encounter entails that forces in themselves are necessarily disparate and distant from each other. Therefore it is possible to find not only existing truths but also an outside from which forces emerge unrelated and unformed. For Deleuze, it is this emergence of forces *"which doubles history, or rather envelops it"* (71), so that preceding realities and significations are unmade by creative and unexpected conjunctions. To paraphrase Deleuze, these conjunctions do not belong to history but go beyond it: they are the actuality of the event, unknown to the existing modes of knowledge. As such, they are determined by history but do not belong to it: they emerge as something new with which we can experiment and experience, yet in a rather philosophical manner (see N 106).

Giving Foucault a further twist, Deleuze configures Foucault's latest work on "subjectivation" as going beyond his early understanding of the outside as linked to death and a fundamental void. In an interview with Didier Eribon he states, "What Foucault felt more and more, after the first volume of *The History of Sexuality*, was that he was getting locked in power relations. And it was all very well to invoke points of resistance or 'counterparts' of foci of power, but where was such resistance to come from? Foucault wonders how he can cross the line, go beyond the play of forces in its turn" (N 98). To Deleuze the line of escape drawn by Foucault takes shape in the figure of the fold, through which he is able to rethink subjectivity. Instead of placing intentionality at the heart of the subject, as phenomenology would have done, Deleuze's Foucault posits the "fold of Being, Being as fold" (F 91): a complicated move, since this fold creates interiority by folding the outside in on itself, so that there is not only an interiority one could reach through reflection but also "an inside deeper than any interior" (91), where one is other to oneself.

To be able to think a subjectivity without intentionality, but still capable of resisting and of willing, Foucault arrives at an experiment to *double* the play of forces by "folding forces" (F 93) in such a way that *"optional rules"* (N 98) are created, making it possible to invent "new ways of existing" (98). Yet this invention is not done by a subject; rather it is another "dimension" of being—"a specific or collective individuation relating to an event (a time of day, a river, a wind, a life . . .). It's a mode of intensity, not a personal subject" (99). Through this haecceity ("thisness"), as Deleuze (and Guattari) have called this occurrence elsewhere (see TP1 253, 260–65), in which the forces of the singular person connect with other forces, we can be "beyond knowledge or resist power" (N 99), while in a throw of the dice, accept living a *"life within the folds"* (F 101).

1.7. THE POWERS OF THE FALSE

If we take into consideration Deleuze's shifting and very specific notions of truth, power, and subjectivity, we can, by way of conclusion, approach his understanding of the powers of the false. This notion seems directly linked to the production of a different kind of knowledge, a knowledge that, as the term *false* suggests, refrains from the will to truth. Its forces necessarily cannot belong to the hardened meanings that came down to us by history but rather must come from an outside where they are unrelated and unformed. These forces confront us per definition with a nonrelation between the visible and the sayable, so that a new perception might be created while they fold into our actuality, affecting it with hitherto unthought-of possibilities. Deleuze explains in an interview, "We always get the truths we deserve, depending on the procedures of knowledge (linguistic procedures in particular), the proceedings of power, and the processes of subjectivation or individuation available to us" (N 117). This enables us to catch a glimpse of specificities of relationality created by literature. For if we take Deleuze|Guattari's conception of literature seriously, we can inhabit a space-time that does not belong to us. As we have already seen, literature assembles only virtual existences—the preceding writer and the yet-to-come community of readers—whose untimely becomings point to an indeterminate past and an unforeseeable and unthought-of future, while asking us simultaneously to engage in a becoming of "us," to oppose the ignominies of existence, and to resume a responsibility "before," not "for" the victims (see WP 108).

The virtual, as I suggested earlier in this chapter, is connected to an openness to perceiving differently, to the creation of a passage through which newness might arrive. To conclude, the untimely becomings of and through literature add another dimension: they allow us to be "othered," to inhabit the fold by accepting being positioned at the limit where "it is a self that lives me as the double of the other" (F 81). This position, in which one is lived by me, is exactly the kind of self-relation brought about by the "folding of forces." And this folding is not done by a subject but by an intermediate or intervening substance (see Chun 2006: 3), that is, by a medium containing its own forces. Deleuze|Guattari have called this a "literary machine": a machine that might be capable of holding those forces coming from an outside and that countereffectuate the historical occurrence—"a becoming in itself which constantly both awaits us and precedes us, like a third person of the infinitive, a fourth person singular" (D2 48). And if, to stay with this picture, a verb in the infinitive is impersonal and awaits and precedes the kind of conjugations we might subject it to, a fourth-person singular has yet to be invented.

In such a way literature adds something to History, an addition that literature is capable of making, which, in Deleuze|Guattari's conception, is "the event": that which evades history while being born of it, that which becomes "aternally" when it finds its proper milieu (see WP 110). That is, literature's constructive function, as diagnosed by Kafka (1948) and taken up by Deleuze|Guattari (K), allows for the establishment of a geophilosophical zone of contact that crisscrosses through time only to find the untimely and the time out of joint,[28] rejoined on a new plane so that we might experiment with what it suggests.

Literature, in other words, is not the memory of the world, nor is it intended to reproduce the sensory. Rather it works like a brain, a faculty of thought, allowing for novel perceptions and sensations, for new relations with the world. Undoing preconceived versions of experience and personal and historical time, it gives readers a time and a space to reconnect their shattered pieces in different ways. Engaging its readers in its ongoing construction, it allows them to make it credible. It thereby establishes itself as a force through which new perceptions, sensations, and ways of relating to the world are created. As such it shows that the false is opposed not to the real but to fiction. To arrive at this conclusion it is crucial to consider that literature does not necessarily need to represent "reality." Fictional accounts create a "world" that depends on the possibilities of literary expression. When readers engage with a literary work, they can surrender to its forces that create new ways of sensing and perceiving. Under these conditions readers might be able to suspend preconceived opinions and judgments and to undo preestablished knowledge, perceptions, and beliefs. When reading a fictional work, readers are able to discover and explore what remains unaccounted for, that which is new and unknown to them. Relieved from their referential function, none of the components of literature—such as its use of figurative, narrative, or linguistic devices, its rhetoric, its creation of characters—needs to mirror what could be conceived as a "truthful" account. However, as we will see in the following chapters, literature can involve its readers in the construction of the story who ascribe credibility to it when they engage with the "fictional" account. In such a way fiction can add something to history, since it is precisely its literariness—or, in Deleuze's terms, its "power to affect and be affected" (TI 135)—that allows its readers to engage with stories that would otherwise be too painful or too shameful to relate to.

CHAPTER 2

Accepting Complicated Legacies by Being Once Removed from the World

Everything Is Illuminated *(Foer 2002)*

The bounds of politics are extended precisely because this tradition of expression refuses to accept that the political is a readily separable domain. Its basic desire is to conjure up and enact the new modes of friendship, happiness, and solidarity that are the consequence of the overcoming of the racial oppression on which modernity and its antinomy of rational, western progress as excessive barbarity relied.

—Paul Gilroy, *The Black Atlantic*

L'ambiguïte du pronom je—ou du nom propre commun, si j'ose dire, au narrateur et au protagoniste d'une autobiographie—forme donc assez clairement ce qu'on peut appeler un opérateur de métalepse. . . . Cette forme de métalepse est sans doute moins manifestement fantastique que les autre, mais elle est, plus sournoisement, au coeur de tout ce que nous croyons pouvoir dire ou penser de nous mêmes, s'il est vrai—puisqu'il est vrai—que je est toujour aussi un autre.

—Gérard Genette, *Métalepse*

How can some other irreplaceable and singular date, how can the date of the other be deciphered, transcribed, or appropriated by me? Or rather, how can I transcribe myself into it and how can the memory of such a date still dispose of a future?

—Jacques Derrida, *Shibboleth*

2.1. FOR THE LOVE OF THE WORLD

If there is one clearly identifiable topic in the highly acclaimed novel *Everything Is Illuminated* by Jonathan Safran Foer, it is love.[1] Just as the more than seven hundred novels written between 1850 and 1853 by the Trachimbroders are, regardless of their genre, "all about love"

(Foer 2002: 202), Foer's novel does not differ in this regard from his invented community. The Trachimbroders he describes, inhabitants of a Yiddish shtetl straddling the border between Ukraine and Poland, are human beings falling in love, not falling in love, "searching for something deserving the volumes of love" (80), and loving their loving more than the object(s) of their love. They love their lovers and they love their wives; they love their fathers and mothers, cigarettes, books, and heated debates. In fact the energy created by their lovemaking can even be perceived by the first man on the moon. "I see something," he says, gazing down at the shtetl, seeing the coital radiance collectively produced by the Trachimbroders during their annual festival, Trachimday. "There is definitely something out there" (99). In fact the obviousness of the topic, illuminated by numerous descriptions of the Trachimbroders' thoughts on love and loving acts, somehow seems to elude the fact that *Everything Is Illuminated* deals, in much less outspoken and secretive ways, with this perennial hot subject of human concern on a more abstract level as well. The twists and turns of the narrative, the development of characters, and the tropes and schemes of the novel's language all reflect (on) the possibility of love—a form of love that should not necessarily be understood as erotic but that signifies a turn toward the world that is driven by a "desire" to accept and affirm what lies beyond one's reach, which one can only address.

2.2. CONSTRUCTING COMPLICATED LEGACIES

This "love of the world" constitutes the quest to understand—and this quest is carried far in this novel. Its two main characters and principal narrators, Alex and Jonathan, have vastly different geopolitical, religious, and historical backgrounds. The story line eventually discloses that their family history directly opposes them: Jonathan is the Jewish American grandson of an Ukrainian survivor of the Shoah, Alex the secular Ukrainian grandson of someone who betrayed his best friend to the Nazis when the latter threatened his and his family's life. In some ways the novel thus reflects on the possibility of love against a background of dark times,[2] epitomized by Auschwitz, and of which the influence has extended to later generations because they point to a "subterranean stream of Western history" (Arendt 1968b: 96–101) that has come to light through the atrocities committed in the name of Western superiority, be it in the guise of colonialism or fascism. The two main characters

and principal narrators in *Everything Is Illuminated*02) thus have to face
the horrors of Nazism and the (familial) closeness of it, while at the same
time negotiating their own legacy. Yet this legacy is not conditioned by
causality; rather, confronted with a grim past, they have to construct
their own "complicated 'legacy'" (Bar On 2002: 44), to find out for
themselves how they could, despite or because of their ethicopolitical
and historical positioning, relate to the past and build a future influenced
by their responsible choices (themselves of questionable status).

Everything Is Illuminated can thus be seen as an experimental setting
in which the ethical possibilities of choosing right conduct for a good
life are explored against the background of Auschwitz. A challenging
topic, to say the least, since the atrocities of Nazism have created a "rupture or paradigmatic shift in moral understanding" (Lang 2007: 278),
because the countless crimes of the Nazis that culminated in the death
camps bring to light "the scandal of evil for evil's sake" (Fackenheim
1987: 163). This evil in extremis remains inexplicable, meaningless, and
purposeless, so that (moral) reasoning is no longer an adequate response
(see Adorno and Horkheimer 2002; Arendt 1945, 1948, 1968a, 1968b,
1994; Fackenheim 1968, 1987; Lang 2007; Morgan 2007). Facing the
reality of Auschwitz, the Western philosophical tradition must realize
the breakdown of its concepts and categories. The promise of reason
and progress, the conditions of which were so exhaustively studied by
Enlightenment thinkers such as Kant (1964, 1967, 1974, 1998) and Hegel
(1977, 1978, 1984, 1993), verges on becoming obscene when confronted
with industrial mass murder and systematic ethnic or racial killings.
Western thought must therefore ask itself how its own categories and
methods were involved in bringing about these historical catastrophes.
As Adorno|Horkheimer argue in *Dialectics of Enlightenment* (2002),
the Enlightenment conception of reason has transformed itself into a
disenchanted tool for domination. The dialectical movement between
reason and myth does not lead to humanity's progress in a dialectical
"solution." Rather reason becomes a murderous rationality that aims to
subdue and extinguish otherness. In a similar vein and much indebted to
Adorno|Horkheimer's thought, the postcolonial critic Paul Gilroy (1993:
39) claims that plantation slavery and colonial regimes have proven to
be connected to rationality and the practices of racial terror. Therefore,
he concludes, "the meaning of rationality, autonomy, reflection, subjectivity, and power" (56) must be reconsidered through the conditions of
slaves—or, as I would like to argue, against the background of dark
times. All in all, if the purpose of ethical thinking is to find grounds for

rightful action, it has failed miserably throughout Western history and has been unable to prevent and oppose the various genocides committed in the name of Western reason and rationality.

Still, as the Jewish philosopher Emil Fackenheim (1987: 165) has stated, there remains a difference between "seeking a purpose" and "seeking a response," thereby pointing to the necessity of a 614th commandment, whereby it is forbidden "to grant posthumous victories to Hitler." If we accept this commandment, we have to recognize simultaneously the rupture in the tradition of Western thought in the wake of Auschwitz, while seeking post hoc ways to oppose the crimes committed in the name of Western rationality. In the course of this chapter I will elaborate on how *Everything Is Illuminated* proposes ethical standpoints that respond to this (philosophical) legacy, while pointing to likeminded thinkers. As we will see, the practices of action developed in the novel do not stand alone. In fact they can be conjoined to philosophical propositions developed by philosophers who take the rupture in Western thinking as their starting point and which resonate in the novel. I will also establish points of contact with Deleuze|Guattari, whose philosopheme *the powers of the false* informs the entire framework of this research. Although Deleuze|Guattari reflected directly on the Shoah only occasionally, they were, as I want to show, implicitly guided by its legacy.

2.3. LITERATURE AS AN ETHICAL APPARATUS

This section aims to embed the ethical "suggestions" made by the novel in a broader discussion about the possibility of ethics after the Shoah, thereby simultaneously trying to overcome the fundamental separation between ethics and aesthetics in Western thought (see Gilroy 1993). If we take for granted my previously elaborated understanding of Deleuze|Guattari's literary machine, literature is able to realize a conceptual apparatus, a way of looking at and speaking about topics that is inventive and responds to problems posed, while simultaneously addressing and engaging the reader in its ongoing construction. Literature is a tool for placing us within the folds—a mechanism I described at length in chapter 1—a place where forces that come from the outside, unregistered in the audiovisual archive, create an inside that is deeper than any interiority commonly used to describe subjectivity. Located within the folds, we might experience readerly becoming-other.[3]

For it is literature's ability to involve readers in a teleopoeisis,[4] to encourage an exercise of the imagination that invokes a literary world that is singular and unverifiable, virtual and therefore, in Deleuze's understanding, real. This is a future perfect world that will have been after "us" (the implied readers who do not exist but need to become "ourselves" by assuming the position offered to actual readers in the literary machine), after we will have imagined it. The intricate time lines of this becoming are worth noting here, since the literary "world" will not have existed before the readerly practice of imagination. The readers called for by the literary machine are simultaneously never present, since we are asked to become ourselves in a way that is made possible only by answering literature's call to become other to ourselves. In other wor(l)ds, literature captures the forces of an untimely time, so that the readers can "speak in tongues" (TP 93) by being gripped by voices other than their own, by being engaged in the process of becoming-other and of being overwhelmed by forces that can change them. And it is literature that makes possible this exploration of becoming-other precisely because it is an experimental construct that does not need to express and refer to an "external" world but follows its own intricate laws of creation.

Therefore I would like to suggest that literature is *in itself* an ethical apparatus, a way of suggesting new ways of thinking and inducing possible changes of perception. But literature does not propose its ethics in philosophical statements. As I have argued throughout this study, literature makes its propositions with its own literary means. To grasp the latter's potential forces, close attention must be paid to what is said and how it is said, but care must also be taken to capture the cracking up[5] of words and sentences. The point must be reached at which language can be experienced as failing to pass itself off as referring to reality, hinting at the abyss between being and language, where—as I suggested earlier—*new meaning* is assembled. As I want to show in the following section, *Everything Is Illuminated* not only points to this abyss but situates itself with all its might in the gap between being and language—so that one can safely assume that its main narrative principle consists in asserting that its text by no means represents a pregiven reality. *Everything Is Illuminated* is a narrative in which even purely intradiegetic events are distorted and told belatedly, whereby it distances itself as far as possible from realistic representation.

Yet although all literary devices are used to expose the fictional nature of the novel's account, this paradoxically does not lead to its incredibility.

As the literary theorist Gérard Genette (1972, 1983, 1997a, 1997b, 2004) has argued, the exposure of fictionality may create a different generic contract between the work of art and its recipients. To read fiction normally entails voluntarily suspending disbelief, but when fiction underscores its fictionality and exposes the mechanisms that make it a fictional account, it paradoxically does not evoke the opposite effect. Rather, as Genette (2004: especially 23–25) has argued, the reader is encouraged to playfully simulate credibility, so that she or he becomes directly engaged in the "fictional" account. The reader becomes coauthor of the text by faking belief in its story line, by giving credibility to an account that she or he knows is fictional from the start. If this complicity itself already questions the divide between fictional and realistic accounts by considering fiction to be possibly "credible," the rhetorical devices used in *Everything Is Illuminated* enhance this blurring of boundaries even further.

The narrative makes frequent use of metalepsis,[6] palimpsests,[7] and ekphrasis,[8] all of which generally indicate the breakdown of a clear-cut division between "reality" and "fiction" by always pointing toward a "real," albeit inaccessible, "original"; the palimpsest and the ekphrasis allude to a previously accessible "reality," the overwritten manuscript or the medium described, and the metalepsis alludes to the "presence" of the author and/or the reader in the story's construction.

2.4. THE BLURRING BOUNDARIES BETWEEN FICTION AND REALITY

I want to provide a detailed reading of the ways the boundaries between fiction and reality are blurred, illuminating specifically what I consider their ethical and political consequences. Yet I also want to stress that these border violations may serve as excellent examples to illustrate the workings of the powers of the false. Involving the readers in the construction of a story whereby they give it credibility already means exposing them to "the pure and simple story-telling function" (TI 145), a function that we can also understand in mathematical terms, as I pointed out in section 1.3, as the outcome of a differential calculus through which extremely small yet constant change can be perceived (see DR xiv). Literature thus enables readers to perceive otherwise, however small the difference from a previous perception might be, because it subjects the readers to a procedure that affects them and is affected by their reading, while evoking a bloc of sensation.

To understand this formula, one has to keep in mind that Deleuze|Guattari, following Spinoza, differentiate between affection and affect. Affection is first and foremost a state of the body, a state that might allow one to form an idea of the effect produced by the action of another body. Affect, however, is enveloped in an affection as the transition of one state of being to another, and this lived passage entails the experience of a differentiation taking place between those two states, thereby making it possible to determine whether one's power of action increases or decreases in the process (see Deleuze 1978–81). The "past" affection does not disappear but forms part of the transition process, while the "present" affection might reflect back on the experience of the "past" one, thereby undoing a linear understanding of time.

By involving its readers in the explication[9] of the enveloped affect, literature allows them to become, to crisscross different layers of time, and to assemble events anew, thereby establishing new connections between different temporal series and dimensions. Thus literature in no way functions as a memory, as it does not aim to reproduce the sensory. Instead it becomes brain, a faculty of thinking that is able to create new perceptions and sensations by relating in a novel way to the world, by imagining it anew. Literature's powers of the false are closely related to this creative potential to reconnect differently and to its ability to undo preconceived versions of experience and personal time or historical time, allowing for new constellations and assemblages of their shattered pieces.[10]

In this way literature allows for a different take on the grand narratives of the human, life, and history, simply because its "world" is not necessarily referential. Yet its severed ties with the material world do not make literature any less persuasive. It even has the power to open up perception, to postpone its need to "select and move according to life" (Colebrook 2006: 7), in this way allowing for complexity, difference, and potentiality to emerge. Fiction postpones the need to act according to established judgments or opinions; it allows its readers to take in a surplus of meaning and to engage in a micropolitics capable of questioning situations (see sections 1.3 and 1.5). I argue that this questioning is necessary because it enables us to think anew.

2.5. READERLY BECOMING-OTHER

This chapter considers how *Everything Is Illuminated* allows its readers to engage in a becoming-other to themselves by its multiple use of metalepsis, palimpsests, and ekphrasis. To do so, I will discuss the different story lines in which these rhetorical devices are grounded. I will also pay close attention to their possible ethicopolitical function. As I have already pointed out, metalepsis, palimpsests, and ekphrasis are narrative devices that blur the boundaries between fiction and reality, especially by using intradiegetic, metadiegetic, and extradiegetic narrative levels, since the latter two rhetorical devices by definition point to a "reality" that cannot take part in the novel's discourse, because neither a reflected medium nor an actual reader and/or writer can ever "really" be present in a written text. As narrative devices they also regulate how a story unfolds, to whom, and when it is told. In this way they allow for a complicated notion of time to emerge, in which the past will be mediated in the present, while the present is changed by the past.

This mutual dependency is further complicated by the use of narrative devices that have their own temporality. For instance, the use of a photograph as a main driving force in the narrative changes the concept of time in the novel, since, as Barthes (1977: 44) has pointed out, the photograph incorporates a specific temporality, "an illogical conjunction between the here-now and the there-then," constituting "spatial immediacy and temporal anteriority . . . giving us, by precious miracle, a reality from which we are sheltered." Even if the readers of *Everything Is Illuminated* cannot see the photograph, they know its characteristics from their own experiences with the medium[11] and can therefore consider how Barthes's formula of photography's reception is represented and/or altered in the novel.

In a similar vein the use of metalepsis and palimpsests establishes these new connections between different temporal series and dimensions that enable anew the constellation of experience, personal time, and historical time. As I have indicated, this process is closely connected to the powers of the false. *Everything Is Illuminated* creates a notion of generational distance in which the latter is not radically separated from the past. On the contrary, distance in time and space is a prerequisite for having a possible perspective on past events, although it might be a distorted or necessarily idiosyncratic one.[12] This creative interaction with the past will be analyzed later as the advent of postmemory, a term introduced by Marianne Hirsch (1997, 1999) in a discussion of generational transmission of Holocaust experiences. But before discussing postmemory, I will focus on those rhetorical devices that allow the powers of the false to emerge.

2.6. TURNING READERS INTO TRANSLATORS

As an epistolary novel, *Everything Is Illuminated* is mainly composed of letters written by the two main characters, Alex and Jonathan. Alex works as a Ukrainian translator at Heritage Tours, a travel agency for Jewish people visiting Poland and Ukraine "to unearth places where their families once existed" (Foer 2002: 3). The Jewish American Jonathan, referred to as "the hero," had engaged Heritage Tours on his visit to Ukraine, where he had hoped to find Augustine, the woman who saved his Jewish grandfather from the Nazis. Yet the letters they exchange differ greatly in style, content, and narrator. Jonathan does not appear as a character in the story he tells; instead he opts for an omniscient third-person narrative voice to tell the story of the Trachimbroders. Alex's voice, on the other hand, is expressed in multiple ways. Parts of *Everything Is Illuminated* consist of the letters he writes to Jonathan, in which he describes daily affairs and personal feelings, makes confessions, and, above all, discusses critical details of a book they are writing together.

Furthermore Alex is characterized mainly through his peculiar use of language. Although he was Jonathan's translator during their search in Ukraine, the version of English he employs seems strangely remote from any ordinary usage; it seems as if he is overly dependent on a dictionary that is dated or incorrect, leading him to constantly just miss the mark in expressing himself correctly. Cars are rotated rather than turned, trains are dilatory instead of late, and the standard formula he uses at the end of a letter is not *sincerely*, but *guilelessly*. His slightly off-key usage of language emphasizes the fact that he is translating from one language to write a narrative in another language that he is a relative stranger to.

At the same time, the readers are turned into translators themselves. To understand Alex's idiom, they have to retranslate his translation into a language that makes sense to them, a requirement that directly involves them in the creation of the story they are reading. Far from being an unimportant feature, this constant alteration of words and phrases is, I argue, another exploration of what friendship could mean, or, in other words, whether language in literature can establish a notion of friendship for readers. With this in mind, I would like to suggest that some literature is guided by loving friendship insofar as it permits meaning to fray and reveals the productive forces of an unknown outside of language. Gayatri Chakravorty Spivak (1992: 188, 196) has described this type of friendship as an intimate reading in which "I surrender to you in your writing, not you as intending subject," or "a friendly learning by taking a distance."

Alex's language involves the readers in such a way that they must invest in the text and invent possible meanings. It also urges them to allow themselves to be drawn into an idiom that is not "theirs" and of which the "original sense" is lost through the act of translation. In his reading of Benjamin's "The Task of The Translator" (1969), Paul de Man (1986: 80) points out that translation generally means to transpose an "original" text, so that "the translator can never do what the original text did. Any translation is always second in relation to the original, and the translator as such is lost from the very beginning." As Benjamin outlines it in his text, the task of the translator is always ambiguous. The original German title, "Die Aufgabe des Übersetzers" (Benjamin 1977), illustrates this well: translating *die Aufgabe* as "the task" only catches one of its meanings, since it could also mean "being defeated" or "giving up."[13] For Benjamin—and in de Man's reading—the translator not only transposes the text into another language but necessarily has to abandon the original text.

By connecting this insight to the novel's thematic engagement with the Shoah and with its postmemorial point of view, we can conclude that the process whereby the readers become translators distances them from an "original" experience that cannot be recovered. The unrenderability and inapproachability of this "original" experience is furthermore enhanced by deferring it in multiple altered mirrorings. This deferral is accomplished by the belatedness of Alex's narrative, its delivery through the medium of writing, and its complexity. Narrative metalepses cause a multiplication of worlds: the translator is translated by his readers; the readers become—through the vexing absence of Jonathan's letters[14]—the addressees of the entire correspondence; the name of the author Jonathan Safran Foer is reflected in the narrator Jonathan; Alex does (not) translate the utterances of his grandfather (the appointed "driver" during the search for Augustine) but nonetheless renders everything else meticulously, including omissions, belatedly in his letters to Jonathan; and the village Trachimbrod might be a literary disguise of the historical shtetl Trochenbrod, especially since nearly all of the events that took place in the latter are depicted in the novel.[15]

These multiplications result in a blurring of boundaries between the novel's intradiegetic world and the world of its readers. As such the narrative metalepses cause "a perturbation or an uncertainty about the boundaries between fiction and reality and how they can be identified" (Häsner 2005: 8, my translation), so that narrative levels become indistinct through mise-en-abyme.[16] The metaleptic narrative transgresses the distinction between the event of telling and the events told,[17] while both are deprived of an original version. As I argued earlier, a metaleptic narrative encourages readers to playfully suspend judgment about whether a document is truthful and to become directly engaged in the "fictional" account, thereby superseding the generic contract that entails the voluntary suspension of disbelief while reading (see Genette 2004: especially 23–25; see section 2.3). Furthermore readers are encouraged to experience "incompossible worlds"[18] that introduce "inexplicable differences to the present" (TI 127) into the plot. The metaleptic narrative enables a notion of alterity to emerge that allows for a "heteropathic identification," which expresses, as Hirsch (1999: 9) has argued, "'It could have been me; it was me, also,' and, at the same time, 'but it was not me.'"

Heteropathic identification is respectful and distant: it entails having knowledge of the alterity of the other. Furthermore it is congruent with Spivak's (1992: 181) description of translation:

> Paradoxically, it is not possible for us as ethical agents to imagine otherness or alterity maximally. We have to turn the other into something like the self in order to be ethical. To surrender in translation is more erotic than ethical. In that situation the good-willing attitude "she is just like me" is not very helpful. In so far as Michèle Barrett is not like Gayatri Spivak, their friendship is more effective as a translation. In order to earn the right of friendship or surrender of identity, of knowing that the rhetoric of the text indicates the limits of language for you as long as you are with the text, you have to be in a different relationship with language, not even only with the specific text.

For Spivak, making a translation requires a very special form of reading, writing, and relating: it is a "surrender of identity." Furthermore translation has the privilege of escaping the logic of self-identity, insofar as the translator "earns permission to transgress from the trace of the other— before memory—in the closest places of the self" (178). This highly complex statement hints at a form of relationality in which self-perception is brought about by the other and not the self. In other words, in translation one's "closest places" are experienced by approaching the self through this trace of the other—if permission has been granted to do so.

To complicate matters even further, the self-approach through translation does not point to a unified subject, but the experience of the "other" in language might refer to its "random contingency, beside language, around language" (Spivak 1992: 178). Such dissemination "cannot be under control" (178). As language use is fundamentally split between logic and rhetoric,[19] it can disrupt knowledge by pointing to "the silence between and around words" (179). The translator, who surrenders to the text by becoming its intimate reader, needs to show how it points to the "limits of language," the "silence," and "the absolute fraying of language the text wards off" (181). Through its figuration and its rhetorical nature, the loose ends of a text come into being and point to the salvage of language and logic, but only if the translator surrenders to an experience "where the self loses its boundaries" (178). When a translator lovingly facilitates the transfer of the fraying of language to the reader, then she or he has fulfilled what Spivak considers the translator's task (see 178), giving de Man's intervention another twist. Logic and rhetoric are split up through the agency of the translators, an effect of translation warded off by the original text (see 181) that comes into being when the translator surrenders to the experience of the "other" in language.

Taking up the position of a translator can show us how "a world is made for the agent" (Spivak 1992: 179), since the splitting up of language makes accessible a threefold notion of language as rhetoric, logic, and silence. Conceiving of this notion in this way means that we take up an ethical position that Spivak sees as a facilitation of "love between the original and its shadow" (178), a love that not only shows a yearning to close the abyss between being and language that presents itself exactly in the fraying of language split up by logic and rhetoric but that also allows the exchange between "the original and its shadow." Yet this exchange is possible only on the condition that the fundamental difference between the two positions is accepted, while it is simultaneously infected by the structure of its staging. In other words, the literariness of the text allows a "heteropathic identification," which becomes the vehicle for a heteropathic memory that spans different times and through which we are othered to ourselves. The literariness of *Everything Is Illuminated* provides us with an ethical position that lovingly embraces alterity and accepts a fundamental difference while engaging with it.

If we depart from this theoretical approach to embark on a reading of *Everything Is Illuminated*, we begin to look for those features that allow "acts of friendship" in which a fundamental surrender of "self-identity" takes places in favor of a different relationship in which precisely this identity is questioned by virtue of something "other." If we take for granted Spivak's propositions, in literature this "otherness" might be the configuration of language itself. This configuration points to its outside, which is precisely that which cannot be said in a given time and therefore must remain silent or cannot make sense. At the same time, though, it can initiate other forms of signification in which the fraying and breakdown of language and its silence are fundamental. Here I would like to suggest viewing the figure of the translator as a "guide"—or rather a *non*guide,[20] someone who guides us to lose ourselves, to give ourselves up[21]—in more than one sense. Not only does a translator named Alex guide us through the narrative—as a character in the story and as a storyteller with a peculiar use of language—in such a way that we might not be sure what to think afterward. As a guide he instructs us, the readers, not to become translators ourselves, translators who need to know the source language and the target language in order to realize a translation. It is precisely here, through the choice *not to translate an "inappropriate" language*, that the "being of language" reveals itself, in its absolute and unhistorical a priori quality, in its ability to point to its own outside through its creative and unregistered use—in other words, if we as the reader-translators decide to *leave the language as it is*, to let it acquire a new meaning that is as precise as it can be although, or maybe because, the words and phrases used differ from their common uses. In this way we reader-translators let a familiar language—in this case English—become estranged, de-familiarized, and perhaps even *unheimlich* in a Freudian sense as the *unheimlich* points to the fraying of language and the limits of sense. If we let language happen—a strange, de-familiarized language—without integrating it into our horizons, then we come closer to the condition of thought proposed by Deleuze|Guattari in *What Is Philosophy*, because it is the friend, the possibility of another perception of the world itself that makes thinking possible and which also makes another world possible, a perceptible field in which a fundamental newness can happen. Any form of guidance necessarily fails in this fundamental newness, because no guide has ever drawn a map of this unexpected new terrain.

Through this second possibility of reading, through the choice not to translate a deferred and strange language—allowing it to take effect and to unfold its forces—signifiers might acquire new meanings. The "task of the translator"—her or his choice to let language "be"—permits the exploration of the ahistorical and a priori "being of language" (F), its ability to advance new meanings (see section 1.6). At the same time, a deferred and strange language points to its own unregistered outside, thereby revealing "the visible" and "the sayable" (F) as unique properties of a certain time that are therefore changeable. Differing expressions allow such language to grasp speechlessness, silence, and the breakdown of significance as unregistered regions of a "being of language." If we allow language to happen—a strange, uncanny language that cannot be integrated into the horizons of understanding—if we permit this language to enter our thought, we near an "image of thought" as described by Deleuze|Guattari (WP). Confronted with the other's discourse and another discourse, thought can be opened up to a new and alien "world."

That an encounter with and in language "*on behalf of the other, who knows, perhaps of an altogether other*" (Celan 2005: 163), has remained possible was and is the hope of many survivors (of the Shoah and other genocides) who speak up to bear witness. In the words of Paul Celan,

> Perhaps an encounter is conceivable between this 'altogether other'—I am using a familiar auxiliary—and a not so very distant, a quite close 'other'—conceivable perhaps, again and again. The poem takes such thoughts for its home and hope—a word for living creatures. (163)[22]

That this "hope that has gone wrong" needs to be "mindful of its dates" (163)[23] might be the paradox of writing after the Shoah, a paradox to which *Everything Is Illuminated* has remained true and has respected by refusing to provide an "original" account. Nevertheless its narrative metalepsis allows its commemoration in the presence of the readers.

2.7. AN EXPERIENCE OF INCOMPOSSIBLE WORLDS

Everything Is Illuminated creates incompossible worlds: a past world that is only partly accessible through distorted and deferred mirrorings—for example, through Alex's belated report—and a world of readers who partake in the play of signifiers. This might be one explanation for Alex's remark that in Jonathan's stories "everything is one world in distance from the real world. Does this manufacture sense? If I am sounding like a thinker, this is an homage to your writing" (Foer 2002: 103). Nevertheless *Everything Is Illuminated* offers a perspective with which the inaccessible world of the Shoah can be seen. The man on the moon referred to earlier might provide a narrative instruction about how things can be perceived regardless of how removed, distant, and distorted they may be: "And neither of them hears the

astronaut whisper, *I see something*, while gazing over the lunar horizon at the tiny village of Trachimbrod. *There is definitely something
out there*" (99). This distance between worlds that allows for the transfer of translation—"a friendly learning by taking a distance" (Spivak
1992: 196)—makes a different construction of the world perceptible. If
readers are open to experiencing it, they might be able to get a glimpse
of new horizons.

If readers' attitude can allow them to experience an unknown world,
what is the consequence of this transfer? To answer this question, I will
analyze the transferring metalepsis of *everything is illuminated*, which
is mirrored in the title of the novel and in the title of one of the chapters.
This might point toward the possibility of the reader's involvement in
the novel's topic of the Holocaust. The origin of the illumination in the
chapter of this name (Foer 2002: 243–52) is the sparks of a match used
to set fire to the shtetl Kolki's synagogue, in which the shtetl's Jewish
inhabitants have been locked up: "It illuminated those who were not
in the synagogue those who were not going to die" (251). It is this
spark that can trigger readers to think about their own relation to the
Shoah, to be likewise immersed in the light of the Shoah—a triggering
that is facilitated by Alex's translation of his grandfather's language.
The "illumination"—caused in the only chapter running under the
title "Illumination"—recounts the story of a friendship in which Alex's
grandfather does not choose for his Jewish friend Herschel, exercis-
ing a choice not between love or not-love but between life and death,
between evil and a "smaller evil" (246). The Germans enter Kolki, a
small Ukrainian town, and order the inhabitants to stand in rows and
point out those who are Jews. Alex's grandfather—then called Eli—
stands between his wife, Anna, who holds their baby in her arms, and
his friend Herschel. When nearly all the Jews have been gathered in the
synagogue to be burned to death, the German general starts to shoot
those who tell him that there are no Jews left to denounce. When it is
Eli's turn, he points at his best friend and says that he is a Jew.

While this story in itself displays an impossible choice—how can
someone denounce his best friend, and how can he not denounce his
friend if it means losing his own life or that of his family?–for once
it is not the choice of words that translates the terror of choosing for
or against someone, but the breakdown of word borders and syntax.
In this way we read that the rabbi says "No no nonono" (Foer 2002:
249) when his wife is seized by the Germans, and we read Herschel
saying, "Iamsoafraidofdying Iamsoafraidofdying" (250). There are no

full stops to halt the account, so it continues recounting: recounting the murder, recounting survival, recounting "the cryingofthebabies and the cryingoftheadults" (251) and the way the burning synagogue "illuminated those who were not in the synagogue those who were not going to die" (251). This breakdown of spelling and punctuation conventions results in a form of writing that is more like speaking: it makes the written speak out, cry out, tremble in pain and fear, while borderless sentences continue to give an account that is rendered limitless and timeless. This creates a *continuous present* of murdering, witnessing, and surviving, illuminating those who stand there, in the dark of the night, and watch their best friends die.

This illumination is a merciless, blinding brightness that might help us understand why the grandfather, Eli, is called "a blind driver" throughout the novel. He is someone who has seen too much of the truth, someone who is blinded by his knowledge of the world, so that he cannot be our guide, despite the reported fact that he "know[s] a beefy amount from all his years at Heritage Touring" (Foer 2002: 6) and the fact that his son even calls him an expert. Expert or not, there is no way the grandfather can act as a guiding friend to us, the readers, when he is also the one who illustrates the breakdown of this category in the story and the way it is told, because although we are protected, there is no guide in this continuous presence of terror:

> If you want to know who would be the guide, the answer is there would be no guide. Father said that a guide was not an indispensable thing, because Grandfather [participating in the journey as a driver] know a beefy amount from all his years at Heritage Touring. Father dubbed him an expert. (At the time when he said this, it seemed like a very reasonable thing to say. But how does it make you feel, Jonathan, in the luminance of everything that occurred? (6)

So, at the very end of the book, it will be the grandfather who walks in darkness: "I will walk without noise, and I will open the door in darkness, and I will" (276). These last words of the book give an account of Eli's thoughts in a letter to Jonathan written before he commits suicide. The letter is translated by his grandson Alex. "All is for Sasha and Iggy," the grandfather writes, thereby dedicating everything to his grandchildren. "Do you understand? I would give everything for them to live without violence. Peace. That is all that I would ever want them. Not money and not even love. It is still possible" (275). And it is this possibility of a hope that might go wrong that the novel conveys to the readers. Like Alex, who in his last letter to Jonathan writes that he wants to be "the kind of person who chooses for more than chooses against" (241); like Alex, who signs this letter *Love*—we who live in the present might have more choices than just life or death. Alex and Jonathan represent the third generation after the Shoah. Like them, we—the future generations—might go forth to meet a future in which we have to choose between love and not-love and in which lives count for something. *Everything Is Illuminated* is dedicated to this wish; it is committed to a past that is ultimately inapproachable and is accessible only through the deferred and altered mirrorings of a metaleptic narrative. Through the twists and turns of its language and tropes, we are positioned in the presence of a transferring translation whose task it might be to allow the reader-translators to surrender to a story and to experience it with an unbridgeable distance as a possible history that might be illuminated in the future: "It is still possible" (275).

2.8. ONCE-REMOVED FROM THE WORLD

Wondrous things happen in the story line Jonathan writes and sends to Alex in installments. It stars his great-great-great-great-great-grandmother Brod, who was born during an accident in which her parents did or did not die, and who gives a nameless shtetl the name of Trachimbrod. Brod is a woman who is loved—or envied—by everyone, who has read innumerable books and charted many different forms of sadness. She is a woman who is in love with love yet does not know much about her foster father Yankel because they are both constantly pretending. Jonathan's narrative also stars Brod's husband, the Kolker, who abuses her verbally and physically after having an accident in the local mill when a saw blade becomes stuck in his head. The Kolker becomes a symbol of luck after his death, as his body is turned into a bronze statue that stands in the shtetl's central marketplace. The narrative also stars his grandfather Safran, who has sex with countless women because they are particularly attracted to his dead arm, but falls in love with the right woman, the one he marries. Jonathan's narrative also includes a multitude of stories about life in the shtetl, which is shaped by different religious alignments, such as the Uprighters, the Slouchers, and the Wisps of Ardisht (a clan of artisan smokers);

countless discussions, love affairs, sexual dreams, philosophical treatments; and recurrent festivities and festivals during which the founding of the shtetl following Brod's birth is reenacted and retold.

As several critics (Behlman 2004; Collado-Rodriguez 2008) have pointed out, this story line uses magical realism, particularly in its myth orientation and its fantastic elements and cyclical temporal structure. Of specific interest for the present discussion of literature's powers of the false is magical realism's tendency to ground its reality firmly on signifying practices. In the words of Frederic Jameson (1986: 311), the reality created in magical realism is "in and of itself magical or fantastic," so that plausibility is called into existence not by a comparison between a describing and a described world—a world seen as an external referent—but solely by the plausibility and coherence of the fictional world itself. Magical realism tries to overcome the fundamental divide between being and language by moving beyond the divide into a realm in which language creates its own "being" in a fictional world openly and self-referentially (Jackson 1981; Reeds 2006; Simpkins 1988).

As I suggested earlier, this failure to refer back to a "real world" should not be regarded as a weakness of the literary text. On the contrary, it involves readers in the text in which they simulate its credibility. In addition it unleashes the powers of the false, which are the proper subject of this work. By situating the reader in a nonreferential narrative space, literature is able to show itself not as a model but as a creative power, one that creates the possibility of undoing preconceived opinions and perceptions and of assembling events anew, crisscrossing time's different layers and dimensions. In *Everything Is Illuminated*, this power of literature, and specifically the use of magical realism's qualities to carry readers away from earthly realities, is reflected in the metaphor of being "once-removed from this world." This self-reflexive image, which surfaces at different points in the novel, allows for reflection on its message and form, since self-reflexivity per definition serves this end (see Gearhart and de Man 1983; Kao 1997). It thereby stresses literature's mediality (Gearhart and de Man 1983) and the fundamental gap between "verbal expression and the referent" (Kao 1997: 59).

Furthermore, in *Everything Is Illuminated* this self-reflexive image "of being once-removed from the world" is split up between two forms of narrative articulation, since Alex comments upon it, being first vexed and later angry about its use in the story line, while Jonathan embeds this metaphor into the narrative and ascribes it to the intradiegetic characters. When it first surfaces, it is attributed to Brod, who distances herself from the world she lives in with her self-affecting imagination, while later it becomes Alex's judgmental description of Jonathan's storytelling:

> You are a coward, Jonathan, and you have disappointed me. I would never command you to write a story that is as it occurred in the actual, but I would command you to make your story faithful. You are a coward for the same explanation that Brod is a coward, and Yankel is a coward, and Safran is a coward—all of your relatives are cowards! You are cowards because you live in a world that is "once-removed," if I may excerpt you. I do not have any homage for anyone in your family, with exception of your grandmother, because you are all in the proximity of love, and all disavow love. I have disclosed the currency that you most recently posted. (Foer 2002: 240)

Through the recurrent surfacing of being once-removed from the world, *Everything Is Illuminated* engages in a metalepsis through which the different worlds become mirrors for each other, since it is not only the intratextual character Brod who is once-removed from the intradiegetic reality. To reconcile herself with the world, she lives a "once-removed life, in a world once-removed from the one in which everyone else seemed to exist" (80). The metadiegetic narrator Jonathan is also accused of telling the story in such a way that makes him once-removed from the world, which, in Alex's view, makes Jonathan's story unfaithful. However, since Jonathan has not accepted Alex's editorial suggestions about changes,[24] the readers have no other choice than to read about thrice-removed realities. We are presented with a narrative written by a narrator who is already once-removed from the world, in which we read about a distant world from which the characters are estranged. In terms of editorial choices, the readers are therefore in the same position as Alex and have to decide whether or not they believe the story to be faithful—a decisively different category from "realistic," that is, "as it occurred in the actual" (240).

2.9. "THE KIND OF PERSON WHO CHOOSES FOR MORE THAN CHOOSES AGAINST"

Interestingly enough, the only example of Alex's use of the term *faithful story* occurs in one of his letters near the end of the novel, when as a narrator he refrains from creating a written version of himself that is larger than life, a man whom women adore and are "carnal with" every night, a man who is always on top of things. Instead he discloses this version as a lie that he acquired by habit to appease his father and tells a story about his grandfather and him, in which his grandfather asks Alex to give him the money he has earned from the literary exchange with Jonathan. Alex stresses several times in this letter that he has to make a choice concerning his grandfather's request, because to give his grandfather the "currency" means that he and his little brother, Igor, will not be able to go to America, as his grandfather will not be able to pay him back. "Our dreams cannot exist at the same time" (Foer 2002: 218), he states, referring to his wish to leave Ukraine and to his grandfather's desire to use the money to find Augustine.

In Alex's next and last letter, he tells of his decision regarding his grandfather's request: he did not give him the money, although his reasons have changed. He decided against giving it to him because he did not believe in the Augustine his grandfather was searching for—a figuration standing in for people that his grandfather loves and misses but who have died, an aspect of Augustine that I will explore in more detail in the next section. Alex thinks that finding the real Augustine would have killed his grandfather, a strange interpretation considering that he tells Jonathan about his grandfather's suicide in the next paragraph, which underscores the fact that keeping his grandfather from searching for Augustine could not have saved his life (241–42). Nevertheless it can be argued that deciding not to give the money to his grandfather saved Little Igor, Alex, and their mother from their violent father and husband—a choice that the grandfather accepts and cherishes, as he tells Alex, "You are a good person, doing the good and right thing. It makes me content" (241).

Several questions arise from this. First of all, it needs to be stressed that Alex's reflection on his possible choices point toward a larger discussion of the possibility of ethics after Auschwitz. As part of Alex's coming-of-age story, the narrative comes to a close here—even if it is a contradictory and possibly unsatisfactory close,[25] since several questions and problems posed by the narrative are addressed and solved. The quest for Augustine is halted by Alex's decision to withhold the money; the grandfather commits suicide, although his last words have not been spoken yet; the letter and money exchange between Alex and Jonathan is broken off; Alex decides to rebel against his father, to send him away, and to take care of his family himself.

In addition his character development fulfills the requirements of the typical coming-of-age story (see Boes 2008; Esty 2007; Karafilis 1998). He not only accepts his (worldly) obligations but also comes to terms with a less than perfect world by learning to take responsibility within it. This character development is expressed through his decision to speak his mind (Foer 2002: 242) and his wish to "be the kind of person who chooses for more than chooses against" (241), a decision he puts into practice by choosing to keep the money for the survival of his family. He thereby repeats his grandfather's act of choosing his immediate family in exchange for the life of another person. This development is sealed by Alex's decision to sign his last letter to Jonathan with *love* (242); the uniqueness and context of this decision suggest that word choice is not coincidental here but might be directly linked to the vision of love the novel displays and enacts—a questionable, even uncanny kind of love that nevertheless shows a secret understanding between Alex and his grandfather.

2.10. NOMADS WITH THE TRUTH

For the current discussion that deals with the generic qualities of Jonathan's narrative, it is most remarkable that Alex seems to differentiate between "faithful" and "actual" forms of storytelling and that these different forms evoke contradictory reactions. Strikingly, as an editor he never has any problems encouraging Jonathan to modify the narrative or the characters. "With writing, we have second chances" (Foer 2002: 144), he states when reflecting upon the writing process, only to ask Jonathan to modify the grandfather's story line. "I beseech you to forgive us, and to make us better than we are. Make us good" (145), he writes, since he does not see his grandfather reflected in the murderous deeds told in the narrative Jonathan writes for him. At other times he asks himself why they are not making up a story in which they appear larger than life instead of writing in a way that makes them seem like fools. He even suggests that his grandfather could be Augustine, or "August, perhaps. Or just Alex, if that is satisfactory to you" (180).

As these reflections are embedded in a larger discussion of the truth of nomadism undertaken in the story line, its general frame might be helpful to understand the general structure of the novel and to reason about the story line narrated by Jonathan. Alex asks if it is "acceptable" (Foer 2002: 179) to write about things that have happened and thereby points to an extradiegetic reality that has found its way into the story, only to reason, "If your answer is no, then why do you write about Trachimbrod and your grandfather in the manner that you do, and why do you command me to be untruthful? If your answer is yes, then this creates another question, which is if we are to be such nomads with the truth, why do we not make the story more premium than life?" (179). From the start Alex's reasoning indicates that it is questionable to write the way both of them do and that the assessment criterion is acceptability in the face of "things that occurred." However, further arguments in this line become obscure, since we as readers do not know of any command of Jonathan's to be untruthful, nor do we know how Jonathan positions himself when writing about things that happened. The absence of Jonathan's letters in the novel removes a space in which his opinions and feelings might be displayed, highlighting once more his decision to be absent as a self-reflecting voice—an editorial decision that leaves it again to the reader to puzzle out the connections between the narrative levels of narrator(s), (implied) author(s), and (implied) editor(s). Yet we know that Alex is constantly making suggestions about how Jonathan could alter the story, to indeed make it more "acceptable" by eliding painful events in which characters are compromised through their—often anti-Semitic—actions or their admitted cowardice in failing to tell the truth.

Since Jonathan as the final editor has not omitted these painful and compromising parts in which the characters appear in a bad light, which Alex wanted him to alter, in a twisted way he seems to be more "truthful" than Alex. In case Jonathan believes it is acceptable to tell "of things that occurred," Alex voices bewilderment that radiates from the strange and disconnected world of Trachimbrod that nevertheless has *not* been depicted as being "more premium than life." While the passage is meant to accuse Jonathan of being a nomad "with the truth," it establishes the contrary and affirms that Jonathan has refrained from making his characters larger than life and that there is indeed a connection with "things that occurred"—although it is impossible to know the exact nature of this connection, whether its conjunction is causal, disjunctive, concessive, final, instrumental, conditional, consecutive, proportional, or temporal. Yet one could infer that being "nomads with the truth" means to constantly displace the truth rather than to abandon it. This interpretation is sustained by Alex's statement that he and Jonathan "have always communicated in a misplaced time" (Foer 2002: 218), a proposition that suggests that their letter exchange is inaccurate because its temporal dimensions cannot be transferred.

2.11. WATERSHED MOMENTS IN TIME

The most important reason for Alex's and Jonathan's different narrative styles might be the watershed moment in the story in which the Jewish inhabitants of the shtetl Trachimbrod receive no help from their gentile neighbors and are murdered by the Nazis. When a woman who survives is asked if she could forgive the gentiles, she answers, "It is not a thing that you can imagine. It only is. After that, there can be no imagining" (Foer 2002: 188), which points to the eternal present of a moment in time that always "is" and also to the impossibility of "imagin[ing]"—forgiveness—in the face of death and destruction. This is the point in time at which the story lines of Alex and Jonathan respectively depart and arrive, and neither of them will go beyond it, making it a point of origin and termination, respectively. Taken as a directive rather than a description, the woman's utterance means that "forgiveness" and "imagining" may be part of a story until a point in time in which the Judeocide takes place, while neither "forgiveness" nor "imagining" are possible afterward. At least this is the case for her—and maybe also for Jonathan, since Alex's request, "I beseech you to forgive us, and to make us better than we are. Make us good" (145), is not complied with in the manner that Alex wishes.

Interestingly enough, the survivor's directive does not prevent Alex's and Jonathan's story lines to intertwine, and although the general setup of the novel is such that Alex's "realistic" story and Jonathan's "magical-realist" story are chronologically separated from each other, Alex still reflects on Jonathan's story line, while several phrases in Jonathan's narrative surface recurrently in another narrative context. Most strikingly, the beginning and end of Jonathan's story line mirror each other in an inversion. Jonathan's narrative begins with Brod being born in a river in which her parents did (or did not) drown, amid surfacing debris, an event repeatedly enacted in the course of the narrative, for example, during the annual Trachimday festival, and in numerous books and plays that are quoted and staged in the novel.

In this way it will be another Trachimday when the Germans bomb the shtetl—yet it is not directly narrated how the inhabitants die. Instead Brod dreams of their death, and this dream has been recorded in yet another book, a book of dreams. The page dealing with this dream has been torn out, and instead of being destroyed in the Nazi raid, it lands on the face of a child that has—unlike the page—been burned to death. It is on this page, which tells of an account of a dream appearing in a book of dreams, itself recounted in *Everything Is Illuminated*, that the readers learn of how the inhabitants of Trachimbrod jump into the river to save themselves from the bombing, only to drown in the water. Safran's grandfather's child is born during the turmoil but drowns with her mother because the umbilical cord cannot be cut. This scene inverts Brod's birth in a perfect symmetry, since Brod is born without an umbilical cord, an occurrence that makes her unprecedented, so that even the Well-Regarded Rabbi cannot find any textual precedent for her situation and decides that her birth "is about life" (Foer 2002: 21).

Yet the tales of Brod's birth amount to more than a simple juxtaposition with the death of Grandfather Safran's nameless child. Narrative fragments of her "original" story surface in the novel like the debris that surrounds her during her birth in the river. For example, the prehistoric ant "in Yankel's ring, which had lain motionless in the honey-coloured amber since long before Noah hammered the first plank, hid its head between its many legs, in shame" (Foer 2002: 13) not only once at Brod's birth, but twice, repeating its action while the shtetl is exterminated. The ant thus connects the beginning and the end, a connection also suggested by the titles of the chapters that mirror each other: "THE BEGINNING OF THE WORLD OFTEN COMES" is the title of the chapter about Brod's birth, while the chapter dealing with the death of the shtetl's inhabitants is called "THE BEGINNING OF THE WORLD OFTEN COMES, 1942–1791," differing only in its inclusion of the dates. The resurrection of the ant that lived before Noah could indicate that God's covenant with Noah and his sons, indeed with "every living creature of all flesh," is made void, in the sense that "the waters shall no more become a flood to destroy all flesh" (Genesis 9:15, King James Version). The beginning of *this* world, in which a whole shtetl can be exterminated, signifies the end of a world in which God remembers the "everlasting covenant between [Himself] and every living creature of all flesh that is upon the earth" (9:16). It is the beginning of a world in which "a flood . . . destroy[s] all flesh," a world that predates Genesis—the Judeo-Christian biblical story of how the world was created by God, when the waters and the earth and night and day were parted from each other, and plants, animals, and humans were created.

As the title of the chapter "THE BEGINNING OF THE WORLD OFTEN COMES, 1942–1791" suggests, after the extermination of the shtetl time runs backward, from 1942 to 1791, possibly returning to a time in which the world did not exist yet, or was "without form, and void; and darkness was upon the face of the deep" (Genesis 1:1), so that the horse whose death is recounted in the story of Brod's birth at the bottom of the river, "shrouded by the sunken night sky, closed its heavy eyes" (Foer 2002: 13). After the destruction of the shtetl, after the near-complete Judeocide committed by the Nazis and their henchmen, it is, as the reversal of time suggests, impossible to believe in God's protecting hand. The relationship between God and His people must be understood in a different manner, an understanding that needs to go back to a point in time in which God has not yet promised to protect creatures of all flesh, a revision that is necessary when His people drown in the waters, "the desperate mass of babies children teenagers adults elderly" (273). The mercilessness of this event is so extraordinary that time itself is reversed, that it can even cause the smallest of small creatures, the "prehistoric ant" (13) that dates from a time when time was not measured, to awake from the dead and to hide its face in shame for an event that should not have happened, a shame that even the smallest of small creatures feels in its long-dead heart.

2.12. CREATING ANEW FROM FRAGMENTS

The ashamed ant is not the only textual fragment that resurfaces in the novel. Resolutions and explanations that have been recorded come up again and again, throughout time, changing contexts, sometimes explaining a story line, sometimes linking characters, sometimes spilling over from one story line to another. These recorded phrases emphasize the mobility of sense and the enduring characteristic of writing, its ability to enclose and disclose knowledge to readers and characters alike. It thereby establishes an understanding of language that precedes subjectivity and shows itself in its pure being, a being-of-language that reveals itself as a force that *creates* meaning rather than expressing it, a force that does not belong to the hardened meaning of established truths, continuously progressing linear time, and a clear-cut self (see chapter 1, especially section 1.6), thereby making the readers responsible (and reliable) for their involvement in the story.

It is the reader's responsibility to link the different phrases, fragments, and hints to each other, to make sense out of the surfacing bits and pieces, to unravel the strands that have been caught up in each other. This activity undoes any notion of a temporal continuum, since the "things" surfacing again and again are mostly quotations that remain unchanged throughout the course of the narrative. They are blasted out of the story's continuum, only to form constellations with each other, commenting and communicating with their contexts but also with each other; if the reader establishes this connection with readerly activity, crisscrossing time's different layers, then she or he can establish unknown connections.[26] As such, a note that Yankel's wife wrote to him when she left him for another man becomes the inspirational source and material for Brod's love sonnets to her lover, the Kolker. The note acquires in this way a completely new meaning that Yankel could not have seen in the note, even though he wanted to. "And as for the note, he couldn't bear to keep it, but he couldn't bear to destroy it either. So he tried to lose it. . . . But like his life, he couldn't for the life of him lose the note. It kept returning to him. It stayed with him, like a part of him, like a birthmark, like a limb, it was on him, in him, him, his hymn: *I had to do it for myself*" (Foer 2002: 45). In a similar way the exclamation "I see something" is not only used by the astronaut who perceives the shtetl's collective coital radiance (99) but is also uttered by one of the girls who first saw Trachim's wagon sink when Brod floats to the surface without an umbilical cord from the depths of the river (12). Furthermore Brod, who travels through time, even sees the note on the back of the photo of Augustine that has caused Jonathan to visit Ukraine, and she thinks to herself that the handwriting looks like hers (88).

Through the displacement of these fragments, it becomes apparent that their sense is determined through context, which makes it clear that these utterances are "impersonal" in the sense of the term as used by Deleuze|Guattari, namely, as the affirmation of "pure difference" (see section 1.4). Narrative fragments can be displaced, can become quotations and metonymically hint at one another, which illustrates the fact that utterances can travel through time and space. It thereby affirms the force of repetition, defined as the repetition of the same in another place and/or time, a repetition that points toward a universal condition of each and every one. No one owns language; language is expressive beyond an individual self, although who utters and the conditions under which an utterance is made remain singular and unrepeatable. Even "I speak" is an utterance that can be taken up by anyone; even "this is me"—the words written on the back of Augustine's photograph—might belong to someone else, so that it is affirmed, once again, that "I" is first and foremost an other—different from "me." This understanding of subjectivity is among the crucial concepts of this work, and is one that usually pertains to poststructuralist understandings of subjectivity, as I have pointed out throughout this work, especially in my discussion of the impersonal in the work of Deleuze (section 1.4), Foucault's reading of Blanchot (section 1.6), my discussion of Genette (sections 2.3 and 2.14), and in cross-references to psychoanalysis.

2.13. THE "BECOMING-UNREPEATABLE" OF TRADITION

Nevertheless *Everything Is Illuminated* departs from this vision of "difference and repetition" in an important way. The novel suggests that an event of genocidal proportions questions whether "pure difference" can eternally return through repetition. However, I would suggest that in *Everything Is Illuminated* the force of repetition, which secures the possible emergence of "pure difference," is broken when such a traumatic event occurs.[27] This is indicated by the breakdown of traditions that occurs after the murder of the inhabitants of Trachimbrod. Prior to the extermination of the shtetl, the population had ensured that experience was passed down like the links of a chain of tradition. This passing on of experiences is evoked in the chapter "The Dial 1941—1804—1941." As already suggested by the chain of dates in the title, two stories that stem from different times are linked here to each other but are separated by nearly 150 years. The chapter tells the story of Brod and her husband, the Kolker, and is framed by a narrative in which their great-great-great-grandson Safran places himself in a tradition that arose after the death of his great-great-great-grandfather the Kolker.

As mentioned earlier, the Kolker became a symbol of luck after his body was transformed into a bronze statue, which was then placed in the market square. People visit the statue to make wishes. Traditionally every groom kneels down before the statue and vows fidelity. Safran also performs this act, thereby establishing "a perfectly unique link in a perfectly uniform chain—almost one hundred fifty years after his great-great-great-grandmother Brod saw the Kolker illuminated at her window" (Foer 2002: 140). This "perfectly uniform chain" that forms Trachimbrod's tradition is established by storytelling, by the passing on of stories through which Jonathan's grandfather Safran knows, like everyone else, "the story of the Dial, the tragic circumstances of its creation and the magnitude of its power. Each knew" (121). This knowledge is performed in *Everything Is Illuminated* as well, which takes "each knew" as its password to jump directly into Brod and the Kolker's story, a story that will be taken up again and again in the chapters that follow.

Yet Grandfather Safran is not the only one placed into a chain of tradition. The shtetl's inhabitants' need to construct a chain even leads to chain-smoking: when the Wisps of Ardisht run out of matches, they make a schedule, because "there is always someone smoking. Each cigarette can be lit from the previous one. As long as there is a lit cigarette, there is the promise of another. The glowing ash is the seed of continuity!" (Foer 2002: 136–37). In addition the people of the shtetl keep reading and writing to each other and for themselves, sometimes with the sole aim of not forgetting the lies they have made up for a loved one, like Yankel, who glues notes onto the walls of his room so as not to forget the stories he has told his foundling daughter, Brod. Love stories, novels, philosophical treaties, religious interpretations, and personal notes are passed on, mostly voluntarily but sometimes involuntarily, and several volumes of the Book of Dreams and the Book of Antecedents are collectively written to keep the record. "And when there was nothing to report, the full-time committee would report its reporting, just to keep the book moving, expanding, becoming more like life: We are writing . . . We are writing . . . We are writing" (196). This writing practice is displayed on one and a half pages of the novel that are covered with these material traces devoid of meaning, in which a lifetime has been converted into dedicated recordings of writing: "We are writing . . . We are writing . . . We are writing . . . We are writing . . . We are writing . . . We are writing . . . We are writing . . . We are writing . . . We are writing . . . We are writing . . . We are writing . . . We are writing . . . We are writing . . . We are writing . . . We are writing . . . We are writing . . . " et cetera (212–13). This practice should have ensured that something would be passed on, anything at all, were it not for the moment when the collective subject and its present continuous action were effaced in the story line and in the graphic design. After the extermination of the shtetl, "We are writing" is erased from this recording, so that all that remains are the ellipses that previously linked one declaration with another. Transformation becomes extermination through ellipses, making marks that indicate an omission of words function as veritable bombs and bullets:

"...
....
....
....
....
....
....
....
....
...."

et cetera (270–71)

This erasure and effacement of a collective subject and its writing practice results in the narrator Jonathan not being able to put himself in a line of tradition. The story line tracing Brod, her predecessors, her contemporaries, and her successors is broken off; after Brod's dream that narrates how the inhabitants of the shtetl drown in the river, their story will not continue. Where the page that has been torn out of the Book of Dreams ends—depicted on page 272–73 of *Everything Is Illuminated*—the narrative comes to a dead stop. If Jonathan wants to align himself with a narrative tradition, he has to accept that there is no original to refer to. Only fragments have survived, fragments that have been torn out of a book that is continuously "moving, expanding, becoming more like life" (196). If he wants to get close to this narrative, he has to invent it—and since the content has changed as well, this narrative has to represent not only life but, above all, the taking of life. This means that he cannot repeat the story as it is; it cannot be quoted in its entirety because only fragments remain of it, and the context has to be reestablished, again and again.

2.14. THE NECESSITY OF A PALIMPSEST IN REVERSE

Everything Is Illuminated is therefore like a palimpsest[28]—a text that is overwritten by another text—in which the original has been so distorted that it is impossible to reconstruct it entirely. On the one hand, Jonathan's text relies on previous writings. It might even be "unable to exist" without the earlier texts (Genette 1997a: 5). In fact the author Jonathan would not even be alive without his (writing) predecessors. On the other hand, *Everything Is Illuminated* reverses the temporal order of the textual relation between the hypotext—the text onto which another text is grafted—and the hypertext, which overwrites a previous text. In this novel it is not a past text that is transformed or imitated; hypertexts generally transform or imitate a text, either by saying things differently (transformation) or by saying another thing in a similar way (imitation). Instead the remains of the past are used to rebuild the past in the present, like the debris that surfaces from the watery depths during Brod's birth. This means that past and present, rather than succeeding each other, are co-present and co-constitutive. There is a past that needs to be reconstituted in a present that is deeply influenced by a past.[29]

In a way, the writing by Jonathan makes up the vellum on which the hypotext may appear, giving it a textual ground or surface (a text/ure) on which it may become readable. The story line written by Jonathan constantly stresses its own movements in constructing this ground. Brod's dream of the extermination of the shtetl can even be said to serve as an image for this textual strategy, as during her dream she transforms into a veritable riverbed: "my safran picked up his wife and carried her like a newlywed into the water which seemed amid the falling trees and hackling crackling explosions the safest place hundreds of bodies poured into the brod that river with my name I embraced them with open arms come to me come I wanted to save them all everybody from everybody the bombs rained from the sky" (Foer 2002: 272). Through the displacement of "brod that river with my name" with an "I," Brod becomes the river and thereby a ground or bed that serves as a contrast to the floating corpses, which are not adequately perceived, instead seeming like butterflies dotting the water in pretty arrangements: "the bodies began to rise one at a time until I couldn't be seen through all of the bodies blue sky open white eyes I was invisible under them I was the carcass they were the butterflies with eyes blue skin" (273). Even if Brod knows that the people are dead or dying, it is impossible for her to perceive it without being reminded of something alive. Death is the last thing that defies being meaningful. And because of the arrival of this unrepresentability, this event that occurs just once, repetition is not possible any more. The relation between hypotext and hypertext needs to be reversed in the same way as the order of time, since the interruption and interference caused by this death, by this slaughter of a people, makes it impossible to perceive a foundational or grounding (writing) tradition, one that came to an end with the erupting silence of a collective subject and its practices of inscription.

The ground, Brod, becomes invisible and concealed through "all of the bodies blue skin open white eyes," while it remains impossible to ensure that words will not signify something else, that "the blue skin white eyes" will not become butterflies or a blue sky with white clouds peacefully stretching over the earth. Because of this concealment and extinction and because of this mobility of sense that does not come to a halt when confronted with its own inadequacy to represent the unrepresentable and the singular, the relation between hypotext and hypertext needs to be reversed. Through the murder of a people and the interruption and interference caused by countless deaths, a (writing) tradition comes to its end, making repetition impossible.

2.15. CATASTROPHIC DIFFERENCE AND THE GROUNDLESS GROUND

At this point it is important to note that this inability of repetition to bring forth "pure difference" and the attendant impossibility of a difference emerging that cannot be repeated has been taken into account in Deleuze's *Difference and Repetition*. It was Deleuze's (and Guattari's) concern to free both terms from their bond with identity, analogy, opposition, and resemblance (DR 37), so that difference and repetition may turn into something new that forces one to think beyond the already thought. To unleash both terms from their conventional associations, it must be considered how they establish singularities, and it is here that Deleuze expresses his most original thoughts. To him, something escapes in repetition that cannot be subsumed under a unifying concept: "Reflections, echoes, doubles and souls do not belong to the domain of resemblance or equivalence; and it is no more possible to exchange one's soul than it is to substitute real twins for one another" (1). This means that in repetition, it is not the same that returns but difference in itself, since nothing exists that will not become different when repeated—although it might be a difference "without a concept," a difference that cannot be grasped in general but only in its singular occurrence. Therefore repetition does not bring about a generality of the particular but a universality of the singular (see DR 2); even words that can be repeated again and again are given a here-and-now existence when articulated in speech and writing (see DR 15). Difference, though, does not distinguish itself from something else, but distinguishes itself, like lightning from a black sky (see DR 36). It is a "unilateral distinction" that takes place when difference is created. One element makes a difference and distinguishes itself, while the other or other elements do not make a difference, although they or it acquire(s) an autonomous existence when differentiation takes place (see DR 37). In the history of Western philosophy, difference has always been tied to something else, reducing a difference in itself to a difference from (for a feminist use of this insight, see Braidotti 1994).

Western philosophy has therefore failed to think pure difference. Only difference as catastrophe has been an exception from this general tendency. Catastrophic difference acquires its own concept and its own reality, whereby it cannot be placed within a continuity of resemblances or within structures of analogy (see DR 44). Nevertheless if we stay within Deleuze's conception of difference as a process of "unilateral distinction" in which one element remains—albeit in a changed relationship—it is now possible to ask whether one has to deal solely with an incommensurable catastrophic difference. Deleuze strives for an understanding of the irreducible ground from which difference as catastrophe differentiates itself like lightning from a black sky (see DR 44)—a question that asks for a consideration not only of a difference in itself but also of that which nevertheless continues.

Reconsidering the complex and floating significations of Brod's dream and of Brod in her dream, we might at this point align the notions transferred by this passage with Deleuze's suggestion of an incommensurable catastrophic difference and forms of continuation. The passage conjures up different narrative times, being coincidentally a narrative written by Brod about her dream and a narrative written by Jonathan recounting the telling of her dream and the destruction of the shtetl. Similarly, in her dream Brod is writer, character, and floating signifier; she simultaneously represents a narrative voice, a riverbed, and a carcass. We do not know to whom the carcass belongs. The nameless carcass could belong to Brod, her parents, or the horse that pulled the wagon when Brod's parents drowned—or did not drown—in the river. The narrative thus evokes an event in which different narrative times and voices coincide, as if it indeed wants to conjure them up into *one image* through which something that otherwise threatens to disappear and be irretrievably lost can be "appropriated." Although my description was inspired by Benjamin's understanding of the dialectical image—an understanding that found its way into the fifth thesis of his famous essay "On the Concept of History"[30] (2005b: 389–401)—I see the conjuration of these different times and narrators as an instance of a form of free indirect discourse that evokes the powers of the false, as explained at length in chapter 1.

As Susan Buck-Morss (1991: 8, 76) has so brilliantly shown, Benjamin's "dialectical image" attempts to reconstruct a philosophy from *the material* of history: a philosophy that asks the viewers or readers to constellate the different (temporal) fragments anew, thereby blowing up history's continuum. This bears some resemblance to Deleuze's understanding of literature's ability to affect the readers who will then traverse different layers of time. Nevertheless whereas Benjamin engages with materiality as part of his project to contribute to historical materialism, I would characterize Deleuze|Guattari's project as an attempt to create concepts that work like a brain, a faculty of thinking, through which new perceptions, sensations, and ways of relating to the world are created. Such concepts are able to capture incorporeal events (see sections 1.4 and 2.4; Möhring, Sabisch, and Wiese 2001). Benjamin's (2005b: 391) historical materialism indeed aims at "appropriating a memory as it flashes up in a moment of danger," thereby catching "the true image of the past [when it] flits by." Deleuze's project (and, before his death, Guattari's) seeks to find those modes of storytelling that surpass the real-fictional alternative. Such modes of storytelling break away from "organic description"—"a regime of localizable relations, actual linkages, legal, causal and logical relations" (TI)—to become "crystalline," thus showing that it is not the real that is opposed to fiction, but the false.

To understand this formulation it should be kept in mind that for Deleuze, as explained in chapter 1, the present moment is always split. The present needs to pass so that a new present may arrive. It is therefore still present and already past, becoming its own past while simultaneously propelling itself into the future. Deleuze, following Bergson, therefore divides the present into the virtual and the actual. While the actual is the present that propels itself into the future, the virtual is the memory or the recollection that the present moment makes of itself—its double, its mirror image, its contemporaneous past (see TI 66–95).

A narrative thus becomes "crystalline" when the splitting of time itself is observed, when the point in time is reached where actual and virtual become indiscernible, so that we witness "the birth of memory" (TI 50) that is constituted in the present for a future to come, for a future in which this present will be past (see TI 50).[31] Yet this is not the only outcome of the crystalline narrative, since, as I would like to suggest, one might equally testify to the *impossibility* of forming a memory for the future, to the *failure* of memory-making. This impossibility and failure might be closely related to historical trauma, which is defined as the outcome of an event that exceeds immediate under-standing and defies psychic integration (Freud 1961: 1–64). The crys-talline narrative is related to the powers of the false and their ability to oppose fiction (rather than reality), precisely because of its testifying function to (the failure of) recounting. Rather than narrating an event, *Everything Is Illuminated* shows the impossibility of accounting for the murder of a people and the breakdown of a narrative tradition. It brings the problem of a historical rupture to the fore and traces its impacts and repercussions.

In the case of *Everything Is Illuminated*, I would therefore like to conclude that the floating signifier Brod serves as a time-crystal (see TI, 66–95)—a crystallized and condensed materialization through which the birth of memory can be observed—which makes the event acces-sible in which *no* memory is made for the future. Although "Brod" conjures up manifold meanings in one crystalline image, this image shows precisely how inadequate any and each possible meaning is for rendering the death or murder of a people. Yet even after the rupture caused by death, words remain repeatable; they continue to create and make sense. Their significance and signification therefore can be seen as standing in for the "groundless ground" from which difference as catastrophe differentiates itself: it is a form of continuity in the face of meaningless death and unfathomable mass murder. *Everything Is Illuminated* shows that this continuation of sense-making is inad-equate and thereby goes beyond the "groundless ground," which is, in the picture Deleuze has drawn, like a dark sky from which lightning distinguishes itself. Catastrophic difference—in this simile, the light-ning—therefore illuminates its background, changing its status as a backdrop that stays unchanged. The passing on of experience through language and other semiotic systems is no longer possible in the face of meaningless death and unfathomable mass murder, which affects the background so that it cannot stay dark. "Everything is illuminated" in the merciless light of this catastrophe.

Precisely because the novel shows its inability to make sense out of the senseless, it applies the powers of the false. The configuration of its liter-ary world allows its readers to grasp how and why it is impossible to pass on meaning and tradition in the face of death. It shows how incapable one might be when it comes to the formation of a memory of a cata-strophic past. Its ethical commitment consists in establishing a narrative context in which this inability is conveyed, so that "we" might strive to listen to this event of words falling into a silent, encompassing, and dissolving ground, which shows signs of becoming erased. Nevertheless it is impossible to continue without making sense, and here the novel allows its characters to struggle for meaning, although not "before" those who, like Alex's grandfather, have seen the merciless light that has accompanied the death of a village, and not "before" the victims, as we will see in the next section. It is possible to make meaning out of one's life and to make responsible choices, but not in continuation with historical and traumatic catastrophe, only in spite of it. In this light Alex's choice to withhold his money from his grandfather marks the moment in which he accepts that there is no way to make a catastrophe unhappen and no way to change the course of history by believing in finding Augustine. Yet, as we will see in the next chapter, even if Augustine is not "possible," she might still "have been there" as an ontic reality.

2.16. PHOTOGRAPHY AND THE TRANSMISSION OF INTERMEDIAL KNOWLEDGE

On visiting www.whoisaugustine.com, the exploratory website for *Everything Is Illuminated*, one immediately stumbles across a photograph: a yellowed, hardly discernible image of a smiling young woman, whose relaxed, uninspired pose suggests that she was caught off guard when the picture was taken. In the background a couple of pine trees can be discerned, while on the left-hand side another woman sits in a sun lounger with her head bowed, probably reading. It is impossible to be sure what the latter is doing, though, because her hands—as well as the feet of the woman in the foreground—are left out of the frame. The edge of the photograph therefore marks the border of any possible knowledge we might have about the two women, were it not for the strikingly visible name and date inscribed on the right-hand side of the picture: "Augustine 1939."

The first object encountered upon typing the URL "whoisaugustine" therefore immediately announces a dichotomy between a fading image of the past and a highly visible date that has marked world history; 1939 is commonly known as the year in which Hitler invaded Poland and started World War II. The conjunction of date, name, and fading image arguably suggests that any quest into who Augustine might be has to pass through a constellation in which the date persists, while the ravages of time consume the opportunities to know a person. We only get a short glimpse of a moment in time in which Augustine wore short sleeves and had bare legs when someone took her by surprise and made a photograph of her smiling into the camera. To add a few unknown persons to this description, there is the photographer who caught Augustine looking happy with her guard down, and the same— or another—person who jotted down a name and a date, only to guarantee that more than just an image would be handed down to someone who might, at a future point in time, come and see.

But do we really have to confine our knowledge about Augustine to the space of a photograph? Is there not more to know? Here I would like to argue that we could know more—on condition that we adjust our image of knowledge. In analogy to Deleuze|Guattari's "image of thought," defined as "the image thought gives itself of what it means to think, to make use of thought, to find one's bearings in thought" (WP 37), the photograph of Augustine might allow us to think about the precondition of knowledge. If Augustine is caught between a fading past and a history marked by dates, something else emerges as their relation: a relation defined by a gap between an unknown personal fate and a history told and passed on. If we accept that this gap is "something" that can be perceived, or, in other words, if we let ourselves be affected by an irreconcilable divide between an irrecoverable past and a recorded history, we can get closer to the creation of an "alternative epistemological and ethical space" (Grewal 1998: 10), the invocation of which is one of the aims of this study. What I am suggesting, accordingly, is to include the acknowledgment of the gap between knowing and not-knowing into our conception of knowledge itself: a gap that evokes, above all, a creative situation, since it allows the renewed assembly of meaning and the undoing of preconceived opinions, for instance, about the state of affairs.

But I am going too fast. Augustine is still confined to a photograph, although we might already have become fixated on the question of who she is. The reason I sought out the website www.whoisaugustine.com was based on having read the novel *Everything Is Illuminated*, in which another photograph of her plays a decisive role. In some ways Augustine's image—or, to put it into a literary framework, her "figure"—is the driving force, the motivation for the story told in this epistolary novel. After all, it is the photograph of Augustine that drives the Jewish American Jonathan to visit Ukraine, where he hopes to find her, the woman "who would be the only one still alive" (Foer 2002: 59) of the family who saved his grandfather from the Nazis. It is noteworthy that this photograph also has a "signature" on the back: "This is me with

Augustine, February 21, 1943" (60). As the intradiegetic characters do not fail to notice, the relation between Jonathan's grandfather—"me"—and Augustine is highlighted by this inscription, since they are not the only people in this picture. Thus Jonathan and his Ukrainian translator, Alex, begin to speculate about whether Jonathan's grandfather had fallen in love with Augustine: "It is queer that he remarks only her. Do you think he loved her?" (60), Alex asks, making a structure of attention, of singling someone out, function as a token of love right from the start, albeit speculatively so. Augustine, in other words, is the force through which the possibility of love appears on the horizon—a "there is love" or a "being of love"[32] for the intradiegetic characters, but maybe also for us, the readers.

2.17. SHE WHO HAS BEEN THERE

In a slightly different vein, Augustine's figuration makes it possible to perceive the relation of historical time to a personal life story in a different manner. Here it is crucial to note that her photograph is staged as an ekphrasis in a work of (literary) fiction, making it necessary to take two media and their intermediality into account (see section 2.5). If we consider, as a first step, what is specific about photography, we can, following Barthes's (1993: 76–77) reflections in *Camera Lucida*, rely on the following definition: "In Photography, I can never deny that the thing has been there. There is a superimposition here: of reality and of the past. And since this constraint exists only for Photography, we must consider it, by reduction, as the very essence, the noeme of Photography." What is specific about photographs is, in other words, their ability to show, immediately and doubtlessly, the former reality of a past object. Barthes translates this former reality into Latin as *interfuit*, playing with the specific notion inferred by this composite, that hints at a being at a certain time in a certain place, "s/he who has been there,"[33] concluding, "What I see has been here, in this place which extends between infinity and the subject (*operator* or *spectator*); it has been here, and yet immediately separated; it has been absolutely, irrefutably present, and yet already deferred. It is all this which the verb *intersum* means" (77). It is here that Barthes gives himself away, on purpose or unconsciously, transferring by a slip of the mind another notion he persistently clings to in his work on photography, namely, that it is a certain type of attention on the part of the observer, called for by a punctum emanating from the photograph, that will give rise to its effect. For *intersum* is not the infinitive of *interfui* but denotes the presence of a first-person singular—"I am there"—that constitutes its meaning, while the unmentioned infinitive establishes yet another signification that might be indispensable for photography: *inter-esse*, that is, "being there, existing, being," but also "being interested." Thus the presence of an observer is indispensable if the photograph is to have meaning, while its unmentioned foundation—its never-ending possibility[34]—is the exchange to and fro,[35] the mutual interest taking place. And in fact Barthes confers both limitations—the need for a specific photograph and for a singular observer—stating that his work on photography must necessarily combine two "voices": "The voice of banality (what everyone sees and knows) and the voice of singularity (to replenish such banality with all the élan of an emotion which belonged only to myself). It was as if I were seeking the nature of a verb which had not infinitive, only tense and mode" (76). Barthes considers photography as being essentially like a conjugated verb since, to him, the essence of photography exists only in the absolute, particular, sovereign, contingent photograph itself—"this photograph, not Photography" (1993: 4)—as he states right at the beginning of his work on the "illuminated chamber."[36] To him the photograph cannot be separated from the referent itself, which makes it impossible to talk about Photography in general. Yet as he also delves into those layers of knowledge that cannot be easily named and in fact might defy meaning, he also makes himself "the measure of photographic 'knowledge'" (9). Only then, so his argument goes, can he explore photography "not as a question (a theme) but as a wound: I see, I feel, hence I notice, I observe, and I think" (21). Thus any writing about photography must be limited to a specific object, which has a mode and a tense, while Barthes prefers to access its reality—maybe even its "truth"—by experiencing and giving a singular and personal voice to its effects. Yet the precondition of this experience is first and foremost the "wound": that which can be explored when one takes in a photograph through the sensory and the thinking apparatus.

2.18. THE IMPOSSIBLE SCIENCE OF THE UNIQUE BEING

At this point I would like to linger slightly longer on the notion of the wound as presented in Barthes's text. Its presence is so unimposing that it might escape notice that it actually forms the center of attraction in the text, not only as an object of inquiry but also as its very starting point. At first sight the wound relates to a semiotic experience Barthes has called—once more using Latin—"the punctum," a "sting, speck, cut, little hole" that might prick, bruise or be poignant (1993: 26–27), and that is established in an interaction with the observer. Rightly or not, we could claim that Barthes's wound is caused by the activity of the punctum, since to prick or to bruise might inflict a wound. Yet in another way the punctum—or, to use the more familiar Greek translation of "wound," the trauma—might also be seen as the starting point for the interest, the "intersum" of a singular observer, its invisible source. For it is the specific photograph that rouses Barthes from the indifference caused by the "daily flood of photographs" (77). The photo in question is of his mother as a child, one he stumbles upon shortly after her death, when he "consults" images of her, looking in vain for a souvenir that might help him to "recall her features (summon them up as a totality)" (63). Barthes is roused from a state of disinterest by his realization of an impossibility, namely, the impossibility of total recall or the the impossibility of establishing such a vivid image of someone's corporeality that her or his death seems canceled out. And although this situation arouses despair, since it shows the irrevocability of death and the irretrievability of the dead person, however much one might have loved her or him, Barthes finds a photograph that consoles him. The photograph has captured for once not his mother's identity but her essence, and in doing so it performs a science that Barthes has been looking for all along: *"the impossible science of the unique being"* (71). In other words, what photography makes us see belongs to a kind of visibility in which it is not self-sameness in time[37] that can be detected but the "being" of a person in her or his "basic element."[38] This basic element is not constituted in the visible but is recognized through the visible, a process that establishes a "science."[39] The photograph paradoxically transfers an impossible knowledge of singularity, a singularity that can be distinguished from other beings in a "clear-cut" way; this knowledge is derived from a whole chain of activities—"I see, I feel, hence I notice, I observe, and I think" (21)—caused by the wound that the photograph is essentially. Confronted by the photograph of his mother, Barthes performatively answers the research question he has announced at the beginning of his work: "Why mightn't there be, somehow, a new science for each object? A mathesis singularis[40] (and no longer universalis)?" (8). It is important to note that this performance relies completely on another medium—writing—since the photograph of his mother in the winter garden is the only one in the book that is not reproduced.[41] We might already conclude here that the trauma of photography, its punctum, cannot be captured at its origin but needs to be transformed into a written form and thus repeated in another guise.

Yet why is the photograph able to establish a mathesis singularis? And why is this science—this knowledge—inseparable from a wound, a punctum, a trauma? Here we have to keep in mind that Barthes has a very particular understanding of the nature of photography. For him, the photograph is "an emanation of the referent" (1984: 80); this is not a metaphor, but must be taken literally:

> It is often said that it was the painters who invented Photography. . . . I say: no, it was the chemists. For the noeme "That has been" was possible only on the day when a scientific circumstance (the discovery that silver halogens were sensitive to light) made it possible to recover and print directly the luminous rays emitted by a variously lighted object. . . . From a real body, which was there, proceeds radiations which ultimately touch me, who am here; the duration of the transmission is insignificant; the photograph of the missing being, as Sontag says, will touch me like the delayed rays of a star. (80)

In other words, photography does not proceed through analogy but is the direct inscription of the light emitted by an object on a silver plate, an image that can be transported through time and place. Because this image instantly belongs to another order of time, being split from from its natural referent by remaining in "the stasis of an arrest" (91), photography has an intimate relation to death. The "absolute past of the pose" (96), its irrecoverability, is transmitted through the photograph too, so it also tells about "the death in the future" (96); it will therefore also transmit an affect— when realizing that a catastrophe "has already occurred. Whether or not the subject is already dead, every photograph is this catastrophe" (96).[42]

2.19. THE RETURN OF THE LIVING TO THE DEAD

It is impossible not to note that the definition of photography's relation to catastrophe—"the death in the future" that has already occurred[43]— is precisely the same as the definition of trauma, since the latter also reverses the order of time. In trauma, as I explained earlier, the initial event exceeds understanding and psychic integration and will therefore be enacted through a repetition, one that accompanies the notion of déjà-vu. Trauma urges one to repeat (in the future) what has already taken place, what one has already seen. In Barthes (1993: 49) words, we are presented with a "trick of vocabulary: we say 'to develop a photograph'; but what the chemical action develops is the undevelopable, an essence (of a wound), what cannot be transformed but only repeated under the instances of insistence (the insistent gaze)."

Photography, like trauma, evokes repetition; it repeats those who are willing to see and insist on seeing. There is no development, no transformation, but maybe there is love. Ultimately Barthes insists that he feels "pangs of love" for certain photographs, but in a "broader current" that he wants to call pity. For this is what photography calls forth when it displays the "undevelopable, an essence" (Barthes 1993: 49): "I entered crazily into the spectacle, into the image, taking into my arms what is dead, what is going to die, as Nietzsche did when, as Podach tells us, on January 3, 1889, he threw himself in tears on the neck of a beaten horse: gone mad for Pity's sake" (117). Photography, then, might incite pity in the spectator, through which she or he will be able to bridge the gap between past and present by entering into the spectacle, while the notion of death clings to the picture. As Anselm Haverkamp (1993: 267) has pointed out, what is performed in Barthes's *Camera Lucida* is therefore not a return of the dead—a haunting—but "a return of the living *to* the dead" (emphasis mine). This return (caused by a broader current of love) calls up feelings for the dead by means of its invisible point—its punctum— a point that will remain invisible until it is transferred into language (275). It is this necessary transference that causes Haverkamp to insist that photography neither mimics nor replaces the work of memory but rather works as a quotation "cited from the text of history and quoting the texture of history" (275). This texture can be "developed" only when we insist on repeating the original image as a quotation. This is a form of repetition that will necessarily take place in another context (since a quotation is by definition a transferral of an original piece of text) but will also transform object, subject, and the interaction between them, as it takes place in an entirely different medium, namely, writing. What Barthes finds when seeking the nature of the photograph is not solely the essence of an object but also the necessary transference that this essence needs if it is to be voiced. Photography works like a verb to conjugate its observer to a past point in time, yet this transfer is made possible only through the transference of an observer who contributes her or his feelings to get close to—to embrace—the object displayed. Nevertheless this is only a felt closeness, since a photograph can be viewed only by those excluded from the image, and what one sees is always an object that is being-given-to-death, whose death-in-the-future is inscribed in the medium. In this way a photograph always confronts one with the evidence of a body that has been "real" in the past and has been able to inscribe its light onto a silver plate at an irretrievable moment in time. In photography the texture of history is therefore always one that is shaped by loss, by the irrecoverability of a past moment in the life of a "real" object, while its *effect* is necessarily transposed into another medium that performs, with all its might, the mourning of the irrecoverability of the life lost, caused by the trauma that death and its realization evokes.

2.20. A NOTION OF HOPE AND SURVIVAL IN THE FACE OF DEATH

In order to apply these insights to a reading of Augustine's figuration in *Everything Is Illuminated* we must, first of all, notice that in our readerly encounter, she—or her photograph—is enveloped[44] in a literary articulation. As such, her "reality" is distinct and hidden from view in the transfer through the medium of writing—even if it is a writing that, assuming my reading of Barthes's self-exposure to photography is correct, is able to "repeat" the experience of a photograph's punctum. Intradiegetically, however, the photograph first and foremost signifies a certain relation to her reality and to time. In other words, Augustine has been real, and this is the quintessential expression of photography. Her photograph is indeed a quotation "cited from the text of history and quoting the texture of history" (Haverkamp 1993: 275) from a given moment in time. Following Barthes's (1993) reading of photography, this means that history is mediated in photographs as something that—however close we might feel to the objects and people exposed in it—is always already past; their "real body" cannot be brought back to life but is irretrievably lost to time. Their "text" can therefore only be quoted, while the "texture" from which is it taken is so dense and infinitival that it cannot be restored. It is no wonder, then, that Barthes alludes to Benjamin's notion of the catastrophe of history (see section 2.18). The latter's vision, best expressed in his reading of Klee's *Angelus Novus*, resembles Barthes's closely, especially in its understanding of the irrecoverability of the past. For

Benjamin's Angel of History has been blown into the future by the winds of progress and can only watch how the past is assembled into one single catastrophe, a catastrophe that, for Barthes, is the being-given-to-death of the ones we love.

Yet contrary to Barthes's presumption that a photograph always expresses the death-in-the-future of the object that is photographed, the characters in *Everything Is Illuminated* see it as proof that Augustine is possibly "the only one still alive" (Foer 2002: 59), although this hope might not spring from the photograph itself but rather from the date written on its back. This indicates that Augustine at least certainly survived a certain moment in time in which, intradiegetically—but also historically—the inhabitants of the Jewish shtetl Trachimbrod were murdered one by one by the Nazis. Thus the ekphrasis of Augustine's photograph in the novel changes the text and the texture of history, since she is able to transmit a notion of hope and survival in the face of past deaths. In a way the ekphrasis of Augustine's photograph forms an antithesis to the supposed effect of photographs in real life. Photographs in general—or their noeme, as Barthes calls it—show that someone was alive when the picture was taken, but that she or he is given-to-death. The photograph of Augustine, however, is the image and proof of survival in the face of death; it shows her being given-to-life and her giving-of-life. Here we should not forget that she is the one who saved Jonathan's grandfather from certain death at the hands of the Nazis. Through ekphrasis, the photograph therefore acquires a new meaning that is juxtaposed to photography's general noeme, thus stressing its outstanding and singular character. The ekphrasis performs a kind of tikkun—or, in more secular terms, a "mending of the world." The Jewish philosopher and theologian Fackenheim has explored whether such a "mending of the world" could be possible after Auschwitz. In his reflections on the necessity of a 614th Commandment that forbids an "authentic Jew" to grant "Hitler yet another, posthumous victory,"[45] he states, "We are forbidden to turn present and future life into death, as the price of remembering death at Auschwitz. And we are equally forbidden to affirm present and future life, at the price of forgetting Auschwitz" (Fackenheim 1987: 159). Claiming that God's presence cannot be found in Auschwitz, he nevertheless believes that God, like humans, can mourn the murder of His or Her children in the death camps, concentration camps, and work camps (186), thereby performing a mending of the world by being on the side of the mourners. But while no tikkun is possible for the rupture created by Auschwitz (187), a catastrophe in which God's presence has been eclipsed, it is possible and necessary *here and now* to cherish life and to mourn the lives that have been lost. This is especially the case since in "the midnight of dark despair"—the epitome of which has been Auschwitz—there has nevertheless been the "shining light" of those who were "the target of radical evil" (Morgan 2007: 262) and still resisted the Nazis. This is not to say that resistance was possible, then and there, but that it was *actual*. For Fackenheim, the victims of fascism did not have the freedom to act—which, according to his interpretation of Kant, is a prerequisite for morality—and therefore one cannot call any act of resistance from their side possible. Yet there was resistance: it was an "ontic reality" then and there, which allows us, in the here and now, "to hear and obey the commanding voice of Auschwitz" (Fackenheim 1994: 25). In other words, the ekphrasis of Augustine's photograph signifies that it is the "ontic reality" of her *resisting being* that radiates into the present and touches us, who are here. This traveling through time and place is made possible by the citation of a photograph that provides the necessary context of resistance and of survival. Augustine therefore makes it possible for us, the readers, to "hear and obey the commanding voice of Auschwitz" (25). She is "an emanation of the referent" (Barthes 1993: 80) that illuminates our presence with the possibility—and ethical necessity—to resist the devaluation of life and the forgetting of death.

2.21. CUTTING AND PASTING THROUGH TIME AND PLACE

This is by far not the only result of the ekphrasis of Augustine's photograph in the novel, since her transposition into written language transforms her into a figuration that is by definition susceptible to teleopoiesis, a process described by Spivak (2003: 43) as a "cutting and pasting" by which we project imaginings to a space far away and into a future perfect. In other words, the staging of Augustine's photograph allows an affect to infect our notion of time. Yet this cutting and pasting is not appropriation, since there is no position that allows for personal possession. Instead, if we accept my concept of the literary machine, the addressee of literature is not us but a "we" in search of an "us," who is asking us to become an "us" who is able to witness and work through the story caught in the twists and turns of its language and figuration. And we, affected by its very form and force, might answer this call without fulfilling it, and as such we might become social and responsive agents to this call. Mediating other times, peoples, and worlds, reading is precisely one of those practices that allow us *to be othered* and to be haunted by difference in and for itself. It calls forth different times, peoples, and worlds, so that these "others" can haunt our present, called for by the close attention paid to language and the surrender to it that might be triggered by reading. Nevertheless the cutting and pasting that reading implies—the transference it allows—is a process that is generalizable per se, and for this reason, the figuration of Augustine is also susceptible to it and again forms an antithesis to photography's noeme of absolute singularity as described by Barthes (see section 2.20). This process of generalization is precisely that which is staged in *Everything Is Illuminated*, since a general teleopoiesis takes hold of the "me" that has been Jonathan's grandfather, so that it acquires different layers in time, while others are taken to be, mistakenly or justifiably, Augustine's older self. As such, the photograph of Jonathan's grandfather and Augustine is put to multiple uses, a multiplication in time and place that already shows itself in its (photographic) reproduction, quite literally so. But that is not all. Over time the image also acquires a meaning beyond its purely referential value. Alex, for example, mentions in one of the first letters he sends to Jonathan, "I have thought without end of what you said about falling in love with her. I never fathomed it when you uttered it in Ukraine. But I am certain that I fathom it now. I examine her once when it is morning, and once before I manufacture Z's, and on every instance I see something new, some manner in which her hair produces shadows, or her lips summarize angles" (Foer 2002: 24). Alex not only has a quite idolatrous relation to the image of Augustine; he also imagines falling in love with her, a position that is in no way unique, since in his account both he and Jonathan have "fathomed" this feeling. At other times the image soothes him, so that he is not in his "normal solitude" (53). The photograph's capacity to soothe far exceeds that of "normal" images, and in this way it acquires mythical qualities. But this is not the only possible use—and effect—of the photograph, since Alex's grandfather, who drove Jonathan and Alex around during their search for Augustine, is, as viewer of the picture, also exchanging the figuration *in* the image itself:

> As for Grandfather, he is always becoming worse. . . . I have witnessed him crying three times this week, each very tardy at

night when I was returning from roosting at the beach. . . . The first night I witnessed him crying he was investigating an aged leather bag, brimmed with many photographs and pieces of paper, like one of Augustine's boxes. . . . The second night he was crying he had the photograph of Augustine in his hand. The weather program was on, but it was so late that they only presented a map of the planet Earth, without any weather on it. "Augustine," I could hear him say. "Augustine." The third night he was crying he had a photograph of you in his hands. It is only possible that he secured it from my desk where I keep all of the photographs that you posted me. Again he was saying "Augustine," although I do not understand why. (102)

In this passage Augustine transforms from a person with boxes of photos into a photograph and a generalizable name, one that might be used to refer to others, regardless of their gender, nationality, religion, or age. *Augustine* thus becomes the most generalizable name imaginable, while on the other hand, it is the specific feeling that she triggers that makes her so exceptional: people love her and feel soothed or cry when they look at her. And while this quality might already make her—or rather her photograph—quite exceptional, it stands in stark contrast to the experiences of love described by the main characters who have only been *close* to love: "Really close, like almost there. . . . But never, I don't think" (110). As such, Augustine's image has the ability to call up an unthought-of feeling that remains inexhaustibly "new" and "beautiful," since Alex always discovers a different aspect of her "producing" and "summarizing" corporeality—a beauty that is able to create and to encapsulate differences in and for themselves. In short, Augustine is not only singled out by a feeling of love, but she also makes others experience a loving feeling for other people, whereby she becomes the singular cause for a generalizable "love" and the general effect of a singular "love." In this way Augustine is a "concrete image" that exceeds its status of representation through its ability to affect with a feeling that goes well beyond her. What is staged in *Everything Is Illuminated* by giving a photograph a written-down "worlding" is thus the event by which a structure of address between perceiver and perceived is exceeded. This event is already double in itself, since it is *at once* belated and becoming. Being written, it is a belated event, since writing always comes after the experience or perception it records. However, being writing, its ability to affect might entice the readers to become, to dive into the folds and place themselves at the limit where it is an other that enunciates "them."

It should also be noted that *Everything Is Illuminated* doubles these forces of belatedness and becoming more than once, creating in this way an ever-shifting field of forces, as if cutting through an ocean. Thus not only the persons who might—or might not—have fallen in love with Augustine proliferate, but the act of possibly falling in love is also recounted at various times, therefore making the act itself susceptible to the cutting and pasting of anyone who dares to do so, thereby crisscrossing time and space. Not only might Jonathan's grandfather have fallen in love with Augustine, and given this possibility away by writing, belatedly, her name and a general pronoun on the back of a photograph, but Jonathan's and Alex's falling for her is also recounted in retrospect, through comments in an exchange of letters, in which the reader participates. In other words, it seems as if Augustine's photograph is captured by a pure power of time that exceeds any subjective notion of it, since her image is generally, for all time, accessible to new interpretations, while she, simultaneously, eternally returns as an image that has lost its context and becomes a quotation for which a new context needs to be developed.

2.22. DOUBLING IN ANOTHER TIME AND IN AN OTHER'S TIME

Everything Is Illuminated allows for a third option in between a passed-on history and a fading life story. The suitability of Augustine's photograph to being cut and pasted into the lives of "others" allows for her to be doubled in another time and in an other's time. While her image is in this way continually repeated as "the same," it is also permanently transferred into a "new" context, open to unforeseeable interpretations and appropriations. Its repetition is shown to have singular effects, whereby the differences in space and time are stressed in which she finds herself repeated. Augustine's photograph, generally reproducible and therefore repeatable, also indicates, when transposed into writing, the advent of her coming as the other in "me," of the eternal other hidden in the generality of a pronoun. This event can be witnessed directly while reading, when her representation is present to an other who engages teleopoietically with her figuration. Although her photographic representation is severed from any secure knowledge about her past, her displacement in a work of fiction highlights the difference between her present articulation and what we do not know about her past, thereby stressing "the ascent of the course of time in writing the event" (Muresan 2004: 152). It is this ascending time that secures a difference in kind between original event, photographic display, verbal articulation, and act of reading, since *what* is repeated is irretrievable, lost to time, while our wish to repeat remains possible, articulating itself as "the real movement for the other, from the other, by the other" (161). As such, reading witnesses to the advent of the other as other, to what cannot be accommodated in our gridworks of knowledge and reflection: "It is not an image that can be kept in memory as recollection, but rather the movement of pure memory itself that brings to the fore something forgotten; it is a stroke that founds memory as it brings to light the recessive part of things, confronted with what eludes in them any archive" (161).

Through our readerly encounter with a figuration suitable to cutting and pasting, combined with the possibility that we, the readers, could become agents of this act of transposition, the original constellation of the fading image and well-recorded history is exceeded by the notion that it could have been "me" in the image or behind the camera, it could have been me who wrote in the margins of a photograph, me who was overwhelmed by a loving feeling and who wanted to freeze a moment for an eternity to come, while she, Augustine, was wearing short sleeves and had bare legs when she was taken by surprise, smiling into the camera.

2.23. THE COMPANY WE KEEP

But is this the only story possible to tell about "me" and "Augustine"? Here I would like to unfold another fold hidden in *Everything Is Illuminated*, in which, instead of multiplying "Augustine" in time and place, the "true" referent of the picture is sought after, thereby narrowing the interpretative possibilities down to a singular point. For the characters find, after a long day of driving around and of moving in circles, with little hope left that their search will be successful, a woman who, peculiarly enough, has never witnessed anyone in the picture of "Augustine and me" but has instead been witnessed by "them":

> "Have you ever witnessed anyone in the photograph?"
> "No." She was humming again, with more volume.

"Have you ever witnessed anyone in the photograph?"

"No," she said. "No." I saw a tear descend to her white dress. It too would dry and leave a mark.

"Have you ever witnessed anyone in the photograph?" I inquired, and I felt cruel, like an awful person, but I was certain that I was performing the right thing.

"No," she said, "I have not. They all look like strangers."

I perilled everything.

"Has anyone in this photograph ever witnessed you?"

Another tear descended.

"I have been waiting for you for so long." (Foer 2002: 118)

How are we to understand this configuration of witnessing? And who is this woman, sitting on the doorstep of a small house, surrounded by laundry drying on the grass, and peeling corn? She is the one who "knows" about Trachimbrod; in fact, as the only survivor of the shtetl whose inhabitants have all been killed in cold blood, shot one by one, made to spit on the Torah, made to watch their relatives die, who performed acts of bravery and acts of cowardice in the face of death, as if this would or could matter in the face of certain death, Augustine "is" Trachimbrod. She says she is not Augustine, and only her strange walk links her to one of the stories of Trachimbrod, in which a woman is shot through her vagina and survives because she is heavily pregnant. This story might be hers, but she does not recognize it as hers. She claims it is a story of someone close to her, her sister. But then, if the story is not hers, how can she do what she does, namely, collect the remains of the village: the watches, hairpins, diaries, and dust?

She considers herself to be among "the not-lucky ones" in surviving, because "you should never have to be the one remaining" (Foer 2002: 153). There is only one scene that explains her actions; she is there "in case," just as the ring of Rivka is there "in case." Rivka hid her ring although she knew she was going to be killed, just "in case someone came searching one day," someone who existed "in case of the ring" (192): "in case" something can be passed on, anything at all. But is this woman only a function? Is she the one who sees to it that the stories are told? Is she there "in case" someone finds her and asks her about the remains? Here we have to take into account the title of the chapter in which this occurs as well as how we are *entitled* to read it: "What we saw when we saw Trachimbrod, or Falling in Love." How are we to understand this? We might link it to the kiss Alex's grandfather gives her at the end, showing his affection for her. On a more abstract level, we might link the "falling in love" to the figure of her in the story, because the way she unfolds as a character might make us "love" her for what she is and not what she does. This reading might help us to understand her last utterance as well. "I am" (193), she says, and although she will again chain herself to the past, to the—possibly dead—baby that is missing her, in spite of her return to the dead, the rendering of the story will ensure that she is more than one particular account in one story. She is, to borrow a phrase by Wayne Booth (1988), "the company we keep": a character who accompanies us through the story, who bears the story for us, making sure that we can grasp it like Rivka's ring and making sure that we get the story without ever having to experience it personally. Precisely because literature is not reality and precisely because it is fictional, it allows us to get in touch with the unbearable, while the characters can add love, care, humor, and friendship to the story, while they guide—or non-guide—us through the events.

What we see in Trachimbrod is thus a character who recurrently emphasizes her being present, while situating herself in a chain of witnessing in which she does not take an active part. Are we then to conclude that she must necessarily be a "passive witness," someone "made witness" by the circumstances, by the wishes and will of her dead predecessors? I would like to suggest, again, that we pay attention to the way she is staged in the novel, since this reflects her specific condition of being. If we take into account that literature allows us to become "like a third person of the infinitive, a fourth person singular" (D2 48), this nameless woman might be a prefiguration of a version of ourselves, one that awaits and precedes us: a prefiguration that we might step into through reading. Such stepping in allows us to be haunted by different layers of time and different people(s), since she, our third person of the infinitive, narrates the past in our readerly present, while speaking to "us," the readers to come. One cannot fail to note the messianic structure of this staging, because arguably we will never become "us," the past will never become present, while the third person of the infinitive necessarily needs to await the conjugations we subject it to. Nonetheless this aporia is possible and allows us to get a glimpse of what might become of us if we fall in love. And we have been close. Claiming this structure for a feminist collective to come, I see something rising on the horizon of our knowledge. I hope it will be her, standing in, as a woman, to signify our impossible chances. I maintain that she would come "if we worked for her" (Woolf 2005a: 633), and it is to this end that we should stretch ourselves to become Augustine, or "August, perhaps. Or just Alex, if that is satisfactory to you" (Foer 2002: 180).

2.24. A CONCLUDING "WORD FOR LIVING CREATURES"

Is it possible to hold onto an "utopian" vision—such as the one I have sketched in the last paragraphs of the previous section—"in the luminance of everything that occurred"? (Foer 2002: 6). By way of conclusion, I would like to discuss what kinds of ethical and postmemorial positions are mapped out in *Everything Is Illuminated* with regard to events pertaining to the Shoah. As I have shown, the novel confronts us with a historical rupture, a point in time that neither of the two story lines narrated by Alex and Jonathan exceeds. Through narrative and linguistic devices the novel shows that the cruelties of the past remain inaccessible to characters and readers separated by historical and generational distance. Its aesthetic renderings are in this way built up in accordance with the paradigm of the nonrepresentability of the Shoah, which is seen as a structure that defies representation (see Adorno 1981: 34; Arendt and Jaspers 1992: 54; Blanchot 1993: 135; Friedländer 1992: 3; Levi 1988: 38; Alphen 1997; Wieviorka 1998: 172–75). The paradigm of the nonrepresentability of the Shoah comes into being out of respect for the ethical demand of not debasing an unimaginable event. Nevertheless this is not the only outcome of the novel's specific use of narrative and stylistic twists and turns, since its singularity is constituted through its move to involve the readers in the construction of the story.

I have pointed out how Alex's metaleptic translation urges readers to become translators who let language happen; how its magical realism allows readers to undo preconceived opinions and perceptions, and reason about the truth of narration; how the narrative fragments ask for a readerly constitution of a palimpsest in reverse, whereby the present is established as a text/ure on which "things from the past" may appear; how the ekphrastic representation of Augustine's photograph changes the generic meaning of the photographic medium and reveals her resistant being as an ontic, testifiable reality; how the teleopoietic cutting and pasting of reading establishes Augustine as a prefiguration of readers-to-come, while simultaneously opening up perception to the conditions of her arrival. I have shown how all these stylistic and narrative devices involve readers in the production of meaning, thus transforming the reading contract from an agreement to suspend disbelief into an agreement to bestow credibility, and this involvement is crucial if the story is to be effective and have the potential to unleash the powers of the false, which are the proper subject of this work.

Still there is another dimension that must be added, one that points back to my initial question of what kind of ethical and postmemorial positions the novel allows. I argue that the specific linguistic and narrative construction of *Everything Is Illuminated* allows readers to become witnesses who might testify to the impossibility of accounting for the murder of a people and the failure to do so, specifically because the senselessness of death cannot be conveyed through the meaning-making qualities of language. In the novel this failure is dramatized through the floating signifier Brod. At this point I would like to reexamine this particular event of failure, paying specific attention to its two-sided structure.

I have already argued that the novel not only shows that the murder of a people cannot be represented. In addition, the novel discloses how language and other semiotic systems do not cease to be after genocide but continue to "make sense," however inadequate and cruel this continuation may seem. But is it possible to regard this continuation only as cruel and inadequate, or is there another affect hidden in the persistence of language? If I constellate it with the "impossible" hope that has gone wrong, has ended, has been felt too much—which is what Celan (2005: 163) expressed when he added the suffix *ver* to the verb *hoffen*[46] in his "Meridian" speech—then I cannot help but notice that hope is nevertheless "a word for living creatures." Hope serves as a home for the poem in which it can linger and stay.[47] And this means that *there is hope*—no matter how impossible it might be—that lingers in language, giving time and space to the poem in particular, and maybe also to literature in general. In Celan's speech "The Meridian," this lingering hope in language gives the poem its direction, namely, to facilitate an encounter between two radically different others: an "altogether other" and a "quite close other" (163). The "altogether other" is a stranger or a strangeness that Celan envisions as being "turned toward the poem" (163), and the "quite close other" is an "I" at a distance from itself and is oblivious and estranged (160–61). For Celan, this encounter is possible, and it is possible precisely when someone does not listen to the "talk of art," or, as Celan corrects himself, when someone is present "who hears, listens, looks . . . and then does not know what it was about. But who hears the speaker, 'sees him speaking,' who perceives language as a physical shape and also . . . breath, that is, direction and destiny" (155). This moment, for Celan, constitutes the encounter that the poem "bespeaks" (164), which becomes "conversation—often desperate conversation" (165), and which is grounded on, questionably, "something that listens, not without fear, for something beyond words" (168).

Celan never says that the poem—the poem in general—succeeds in reaching its destination, but the poem is heading for it; it directs itself toward someone or something with the ability to perceive its orientation. That there is someone or something listening and perceiving is the singular poem's—and maybe literature's—hope. The poem in particular, and maybe literature in general, is given a "temporary" home, or at least a "meridian" as one axis of its localizability, by hope. I see this hope displayed in *Everything Is Illuminated* as part and parcel of its (fictional) letter exchange, although Jonathan's letters are missing in the book, thereby suggesting that Alex and Jonathan's "conversation" has fallen silent, since one partner has withdrawn from the exchange. Nevertheless the novel makes different instances of falling silent perceptible and directs these "recordings" at its readers, an example of a sending that "bespeaks" (Celan 2005: 164) and conjures up the hope persisting in language too, namely, to be able to transmit something and to reach someone, "in case someone c[omes] searching one day" (Foer 2002: 192). What is made perceptible in *Everything Is Illuminated* is thus not only a cruel and inadequate continuation of sense-making but also a persisting hope to be able to make sense for someone or something to which it directs itself. Such persistence might be perceptible only if one— the reader to come—listens to something "beyond words" (Celan 2005: 168), and "beyond knowledge" (Derrida 1986a: 328) that has somehow been also captured in the literary machine.

What does it mean to listen to something "beyond knowledge"? To answer this question, it must be stressed that an encounter with something that is beyond knowledge does not necessarily entail that the perceiver is defeated. On the contrary, to be affected by something that is beyond knowledge might mean that one places oneself outside and "beyond formations of knowledge and dispersed visibilities" (Colebrook 2004: 2, quoting Deleuze 1988a: 84). That is to say, one places oneself beyond those visibilities and sayabilities that, as I have shown in my reading of Foucault (1977, 1987) and Deleuze (F), have "hardened into an unalterable form in the long baking process of history" (Foucault 1977: 142). In other words, when confronted with something that is "beyond knowledge," maybe even "beyond words," one might be positioned at a location where forces from the outside that have not been related to each other by the powers that be, create an "inside deeper than any interior" (F 91) that allows us to be other than ourselves, to be othered (see section 1.6). This is the event brought into being by literature, by the addition it makes to history that attests to its powers of the false, *an addition that is brought into being by those powers*. This event in which one is forced to sense, to listen, and to think, since neither knowledge, habit, nor opinion make it any easier to confront—this event is created precisely by the powers of the false that literature can call into being. This also explains why the false is not opposed to the real but to fiction, as I stated in chapter 1: for the advent of the other in me, of me as an other, lies beyond representation. Still, it is not without effect: to shake up the coordinates of knowledge, the bits of captured life in which one is kept and stilled, might be a worthwhile undertaking if one strives to have more options for living one's life in the folds. It is an opening. "It is a word against the grain, the word which cuts the 'strings,' which does not bow to the 'bystanders and old warhorses of history.' It is an act of freedom. It is a step. . . . It is homage to the majesty of the absurd which bespeaks the presence of human beings" (Celan 2005: 156–57). The powers of the false reside here and now, when the unthought in thought and the unsensed in sense—the "non-sense" that "bespeaks" the presence of human beings, for example—is facilitated. They allow for an encounter "beyond," a questionable encounter that can only be postponed to the future but of which the anticipation, the imagining beyond the coordinates of the here and now, gives language its direction. Literature's plane-making abilities evoke the powers of the false precisely by setting up a plane, by constellating anew, by making it perceptible that "language [h]as a physical shape and also . . . breath, that is, direction and destiny" (155).

How does literature engage the powers of the false, those forces that are unleashed when a piece of literature creates something that remains "beyond knowledge" or even "beyond words"? As I have suggested, in *Everything Is Illuminated* the question that thrusts itself violently on the readers is primarily how continuations ought to be dealt with, such as the continuation of time, language, or the ordinary. An example of the continuation of the ordinary can be found, for example, in Alex's and Jonathan's juvenile obsessions with sexuality, gender roles, and questions about what their roles in life will be in terms of profession, family, and friendships. By constellating these "banalities" with "everything that occurred" (Foer 2002: 6), the novel asks characters and readers alike to create a legacy that takes both into account, both the rupture of history and the broken arrow of transgenerational experience and tradition, and the continuation of sense-making that is at once cruel and gives hope. And this hope is not confined only to the hope that someone might "c[o]me searching one day" (192) for the remains of the past, but it also entails the aim to "love" in the present and to work for a position in which one can choose "for and not against."

As I have shown, the latter position is exemplified by Alex, who chooses to sign his last letter to Jonathan *Love*. Alex decides to adopt a new structure of decision making in which he affirms his choices, possibly positively. Simultaneously his last letter also shows how he chooses to use the money from the literary exchange for his family and to withhold it from his grandfather. The latter choice seems cruel given his grandfather's wish to use the money for a new search for Augustine, since Augustine embodies everyone he has loved and mostly lost. However, I argue that this choice adheres precisely to the 614th Commandment suggested by Fackenheim. To Fackenheim (1987: 159), "it is forbidden to turn present and future life into death, as the price of remembering death at Auschwitz," which also means that one has to accept the fact that life continues and that not every choice can be made in the light of Auschwitz. In the case of Alex, I would like to suggest that he decides to withhold the money because he recognizes that his responsibility in life is not the same as his grandfather's. He accepts that he has to find a way to live in the present and have high esteem for the lives of the present, but without devaluing the present in "the luminance of everything that occurred" (Foer 2002: 6) and without measuring its importance against the importance of the past, symbolized here by the grandfather's yearning.

Yet the 614th Commandment also means that one should not "affirm present and future life, at the price of forgetting Auschwitz" (Fackenheim 1987: 159), which means that Auschwitz should be in our luggage when we travel through time. In the novel, not forgetting the Shoah means constructing a complicated legacy around it, in which, nevertheless and most important, one's own time—of survivors, of their children's children, of bystanders, of victims and their children's children—*is not* a prolongation of what happened during the Shoah. This, however, does not entail that one's time is not deeply influenced by it or that one should not try to expose the subterranean connections that run from the past to the present. But when trying to find the past, one also has to accept that its fragments have undergone such a "sea-change" and that it remains impossible to know their original shape.

> And . . . thinking, fed by the present, works with the "thought fragments" it can wrest from the past and gather about itself. Like a pearl diver who descends to the bottom of the sea, not to excavate the bottom and bring it to light but to pry loose the rich and the strange, the pearls and the coral in the depths, and to carry them to the surface, this thinking delves into the depths of the past—but not in order to resuscitate it the way it was and to contribute to the renewal of extinct ages. What guides this thinking is the conviction that although the living is subject to the ruin of time, the process of decay is at the same time a process of crystallization, that in the depths of the sea, into which sinks and is dissolved what once was alive, some things "suffer a sea-change" and survive in new crystallized forms and shapes that remain immune to the elements, as though they waited only for the pearl diver who one day will come down to them and bring them up into the world of the living. (Arendt 1968b: 205–6)[48]

In a very radical way this means that the present cannot be measured against all the events that are referred to by the name of Auschwitz. And in another very radical way it means that one has to turn into a pearl diver—if one is to obey Fackenheim's imperative—and search out those elements of the past in their "crystallized forms" and give them a new ground, a palimpsest in reverse, in which they can develop a new meaning.

Everything Is Illuminated develops a postmemorial ethics precisely by asking what kind of relationship one might develop to the legacy of the past *and* by displaying impossible hopes for the future. It is indebted to the memories of the Shoah without claiming them. It recognizes the unspeakability of its trauma but still engages with it (see Wiese 2011). It displays hope for something and someone who is "turned toward" it (Celan 2005: 163), anticipating it, imagining beyond the coordinates of the here and now, something that lies in the direction of language. Here one should not forget that the last words printed in the book are "I will" (Foer 2002: 276). The grandfather, "in the luminescence of the television" (276), writes "I will" as a promise for the future, "I will" illuminated by a vision that comes from afar.[49] Through this vision I see a common ground established at last on which the characters can connect to each other. This common ground consists of hope for the future, and this promise to direct oneself *to* the future might be their bond. This hope might be situated, like the astronaut who "sees something," on a moon circling our planet, a satellite that is illuminated only by a deflection of light. To unite themselves on this "lunatic" ground is far from naïve; in fact it is informed by "everything that has happened," and it has worked it through even to the point where the grandfather, who commits suicide, resigns from this life since it seems that he failed to keep a promise—a promise of friendship and love—beforehand.

Nevertheless all three characters who went on a search for Augustine perform acts of friendship. Jonathan does so by editing the letters and sending them to a general public without commenting on and judging them; Alex does so by becoming sincere and taking care of his family; the grandfather does so by finally facing his deed of betraying his best friend and by coming to terms with it and finding peace of mind in a darkness (see Foer 2002: 276) that is not completely illuminated by the events of the past but by a vision that comes from afar. These gestures made by literary characters and put into play by literature's geophilosophical, plane-making abilities create the conditions in which differential and different positions appear that have gone diving for the pearls of the past, thereby making the past and its continuing influences appear and create a palimpsest in reverse, a not-translating translation, a teleopoietic cutting and pasting of readerly activity. The ethics displayed in *Everything Is Illuminated* consist in creating a "connection *without equivalence*" (Smith 2007: 47) between the past and the present and between the different positionalities brought into being by genocide. As such it connects optimally with Deleuze (and Guattari's) understanding of a difference in and for itself, also made "visible" through the novel. Guided by a loving friendship, and by a yearning for the possibility of love in the future, "I will" becomes "a word for living creatures."

CHAPTER 3

"He Looked for Truth in Facts and Not in Stories"

Crimes of Historiography and Forces of Fabulation in Richard Flanagan's Gould's Book of Fish *(2003)*

To be a fish!
So utterly without misgiving
To be a fish
In the waters.
Loveless, and so lively!
Born before God was love,
Or life knew loving.
Beautifully beforehand with it all.

—D. H. Lawrence, "Fish"

Each fish is a hero.

—Hermann Melville, "We Fish"

3.1. INTRODUCTION

Gould's Book of Fish (2003) by the Tasmanian author Richard Flanagan is marketed as a novel. As such, it is firmly placed within the fields of fiction, an imaginative form of narration not usually considered to provide a reliable account of history. Furthermore its narrator is introduced as a professional forger, so his rendering of events is suspiciously untrustworthy. However, if one believes that such "unreliable narration" has no relation whatsoever to any kind of truth about the past and that exclusively historical documents or accounts can claim to be truthful, one is relying on a millennium-old dichotomy between history and fiction challenged by *Gould's Book of Fish*. "He looked for truth in facts and not in stories" (Flanagan 2003: 20) is one character's slightly appalled summary of another's steadfast opinion that historical and fictional accounts can be categorically differentiated. The novel deconstructs this belief by showing that the truth is *obscured* by historical documentation. The archivist Jorgen Jorgensen describes life on the penal colony Sarah Island by "obeying the laws of cause & effect" (287); his written account creates an image of the settlement "that would persuade posterity of both the convicts' animality & the administrator's sagacity" (287). For Gould, who writes down his memories in his intradiegetically rendered book of fish, this "universal history" is a crime through which "all he had seen & known, all he had witnessed & suffered, was now as lost & meaningless as a dream that dissolves upon waking," condemning everybody "to an eternity of imprisonment" (290). To escape this fundamental injustice, he steals the island's annals and meanders—without knowing where to turn for help—across the inhospitable, deserted, and depopulated island, most of whose Aboriginal inhabitants have been murdered, their deaths neither accounted for nor mourned.

Gould's Book of Fish is an attempt to counter the intradiegetically perceived injustice of the archive's documentation, brought about by the archivist's overriding interest in showing the moral superiority of British rule during Britain's early colonization of Tasmania in the 1820s. By using the forces of the literary machine—which, according to Deleuze|Guattari, is "the relay for a revolutionary machine-to-come" (K 26)—the book exposes the cruelty of the Tasmanian prison system and the colony's racialized order as it renders their destructive forces perceptible through the distortional effects they have on the parties involved. In a personal love story between the former inmate Gould and the Aboriginal Twopenny Sal, it furthermore points toward those Aboriginal inhabitants of Tasmania whose population of a cautiously estimated three thousand to four thousand was completely wiped out in only two generations of British settlement. (In 1803 the first Europeans settled on the east coast of the river Derwent; in 1869 purportedly the last Aboriginal Tasmanian black man, William Lanney, died [see Cocker 1998; Hughes 1987; Ryan 1981].) Recent revisionist debates[1] in Australia show how difficult it is for Australian society to acknowledge its guilt for the demise of Aboriginal society, brought about by direct violence as well as the occupation of traditional hunting grounds, starvation, and disease (see Pybus 1991). A novel like *Gould's Book of Fish* intervenes in its own way in the debate, creating a space in which disparate stories of a cruel, dehumanizing prison system and a disappearing people are related to each other. It stages mourning and sadness about a wasted chance to establish respectful interpersonal contact between individuals and groups of different cultural backgrounds. The loss of lives and loves is shown to have devastating effects on the survivors, one of whom is Gould, whose fight for an adequate voice to render stories of unfathomable suffering is interlinked with his ambition to draw mute fish. Through the inventive narrative mode that makes mourning possible, the novel bypasses the exclusionary effects of an archive compiled exclusively by white colonial invaders—whose failure to account for the subaltern voices of convicts and Aborigines alike has enormously limiting effects, as the versions they created express only the point of view of the ruling class.

By opposing these limitations *Gould's Book of Fish* converges optimally with the function Deleuze|Guattari ascribe to "minor literature" that "is determined to fill the conditions of a collective enunciation that is lacking elsewhere in the milieu . . . even if this collectivity is no longer or not yet given" (K 18). By inventing that which cannot be found in the historical record, the novel creates a space for the emergence of a collectivity no longer existing or yet to come. It employs the powers of the false to evoke a "missing people." This power can convey a sense of what is eternally missing in the present, leaving only traces of their lost lives for posterity. Reading *Gould's Book of Fish*, I would like to track literature's ability to invent history and explore the virtuality of the past—a past that is often silenced by common modes of representation, including some fundamental patterns of domination and exclusion shown in Flanagan's novel.

3.2. HISTORIOGRAPHICAL ACCOUNTS OF SARAH ISLAND

Macquarie Harbor is an inlet on the west coast of Tasmania that remained hidden from Western eyes until the end of 1815. Then Captain James Kelly managed to navigate an open whaleboat through the narrow heads of its entrance and discovered a vast expanse of water with a rugged coastline on which Huon pines grew in abundance. The remoteness of this difficult-to-access environment as well as the richness of its natural resources inspired Governor Macquarie, after whom the inlet was named, to turn the harbor into a penal station. There "absconders, thieves, gorgers and other undesirables could be exiled to work cutting timber and mining coal until they had atoned for their

crimes and indiscretions" (Maxwell-Steward 2008: 5). The wild coun-
tryside seemed so impenetrable that it would be difficult for convicts
to escape; the only access to the area remained the difficult passage
by sea—through the narrow heads that became known as "Hell's
Gates"—which the authorities considered manageable with the use of
smaller ships.

In 1822 the first prison settlement was built on a small island in the
south of Macquarie Harbor; Sarah Island, as it was called, soon gained
the reputation of being one of the worst spots in the English-speaking
world (Hughes 1987: 372). In the first years of the settlement, the commandant, Lieutenant Cuthbertson, reigned with sheer brutality; an
average of 6,560 lashes were inflicted on 175 men with a particularly
heavy and double-twisted whipcord. Frequently people who attempted
to escape were punished with one hundred strokes of the cat-o'-nine-
tails (Brand 1984; Lampriere 1954). By the end of the 1820s the number
of whippings dropped, only to be replaced by solitary confinement in
cells deprived of light and in which the prisoners could hardly stand
(Brand 1984; Lampriere 1954). Especially newcomers and untrained
convicts had to work in chain gangs, mostly to cut the Huon pines, the
wood of which was used for shipbuilding. The nutrition was so poor
that scurvy became a common disease: a convict's daily ration consisted of one pound of meat, one and a quarter pounds of bread, four
ounces of oatmeal or hominy, and salt; fresh meat, let alone vegetables,
were scarcely available, and the brine-cured pork was often enough
two or three years old and had gone bad before arriving at Sarah Island
(see Hughes 1987: 375). The prisoners had to work for twelve hours a
day and sleep in dormitories so cramped that they could not rest on
their backs. In February 1829 seventy-one convicts shared two rooms
with an average of 6 feet 6 inches square available for each of them
(Maxwell-Steward 2008: 24). Each prisoner had two sets of clothing, but because prisoners often worked in rainy or wet conditions,
both sets were often wet. The brutality of this state-inflicted violence
on Sarah Island was exceptional under the British convict system (see
Smith 2008). Yet it nevertheless served an important purpose. Convicts
knew what possible treatment might await them if they were to lapse
back into crime or tried to abscond. The existence alone of a place of
terror like Macquarie Harbor Penal Station therefore helped to keep
convicts in line (see Roberts 2009: 235; Maxwell-Steward 2008: 58).

Although the responsible authorities, such as Governor Arthur and
Lieutenant Governor Sorell, claimed that only the "most incorrectible"

and "worst convicts" were sent to the Macquarie Harbor Penal Station, a third of the prisoners had to serve their sentence on Sarah Island because they had attempted to escape during their previous sentence. Maxwell-Steward (2008: 49) holds that only 19 percent of the prisoner population had been charged by a higher court, while 72 percent were guilty only of minor offences; 9 percent had been sent without any court order, probably to serve as an example. In general the vast majority of felons transported to Australia—in total 162,000 men and women (Hughes 1987: 3)—had been sent "down under" for crimes against property, including shoplifting and theft of comestibles for personal consumption (Cocker 1998: 120–21). Transportation was thus a way to deal with the immense poverty of some of the British population (see Hughes 1987). The tripling of the Welsh and English population from 6 million in 1740 to 18 million in 1851, early industrialization, and a fast-growing urban population—consisting of those unpropertied men and women who hoped to find work in the cities—were some of the reasons for this sudden rise in poverty (Hughes 1987: 19–43). Furthermore the immense societal changes brought about by early industrialization also influenced jurisdiction. There were six times as many capital statutes in 1819 as there were in 1660; people were sentenced to death for a wide range of crimes, from brutal murder to "impersonating an Egyptian," which meant "posing as a gypsy" (29). Most of these death sentences were converted into transportation sentences. Once in Australia convicts had to do forced labor until they had served their sentence, a practice that produced an infrastructure, common goods, and capital for the British colonial powers. Although the costs of transportation were considerably high—on average £26 per convict—it only cost £4 to maintain a prisoner during a seven-year imprisonment. The net profit of a transported convict could be anywhere from £26 to £158 over a lifetime, depending on the convict's sex and age at the moment of conviction (Lewis 1988: 519).[2] On Sarah Island the convict industry consisted of pining, shipbuilding, coal mining, and farming. During its period as a penal colony (1822–33), it became the largest shipbuilding yard in Australia, building 113 vessels (Brand 1984; Bannear 1994). Charles O'Hara Booth, who was "appointed commandant of the Port Arthur convict settlement, with jurisdiction over all stations on Tasman Peninsula" (Hooper 1966: 125) had a number of favorite projects, specifically a coal mine, a unique communication system consisting of semaphores on hilltops, and "the first Australian railway, powered not by steam, but by convicts" (Hughes 1987: 406). *Gould's Book of Fish* depicts the railway as well as other objects, persons, and events known from historiography. In the following section, we will see how this knowledge is used in the novel. In 1833 Macquarie Harbor Penal Station was closed, probably because it was plagued by supply problems, and the remaining convicts were relocated to Port Arthur (Maxwell-Steward 2006).

3.3. REVEALING THE IMPOSSIBILITY OF DETACHED OBJECTIVITY

Macquarie Harbor Penal Station—a merciless place in terms of its geographic and social conditions—is the setting of *Gould's Book of Fish* and is depicted in accordance with historical descriptions that have been passed down through history. In a similar way its first-person narrator, William Buelow Gould, is drafted on a real historical character, the convict-painter William Buelow Gould (1801–53) who went down in history for his exquisite naturalistic paintings of birds, flowers, and fish (Allport 1931; Clune and Stephensen 1962; Pretyman 1970). The historical character was sent to Sarah Island for forgery and was assigned to the colonial surgeon Dr. James Scott, who commissioned him to produce his naturalistic artwork. The novel *Gould's Book of Fish* is supposed to be the journal of this convict-painter. Its fish drawings are said to be replicas that Gould painted from memory, and its story purports to be his account of persons and events on Sarah Island from 1829 on.

The literary Gould's account of his journey to and first impression of Sarah Island provides an example for the novel's use of historiographical knowledge. The tale of his first escape in Tasmania is brimming with historical details: the mortal remains of dozens of murdered Aborigines he stumbles across on the beach (see Flanagan 2003: 69), the raped and tortured Aborigine woman he encounters on his journey (69), and his general description of an undeclared war between military forces, settlers, and Aborigines. The historian Benjamin Madley (2008: 106) recently proclaimed the extinction of the Tasmanian Aborigines to be genocide and cites numerous historical sources that bear witness to a high number of brutal crimes and murders.[3] The missionary George Augustus Robinson (1966: 82, qtd. in Madley 2008: 89), for example, testifies to "multiple abductions, tortures, and murders," while Captain James Hobbs (1830, qtd. in Madley 2008: 89) writes about a common practice among sealers of stealing Aboriginal women and shooting Aboriginal men and children. Cocker (1998: 127–84) describes shooting practice sessions in which Aborigines were used as targets, instances of poisoning food, brutal gang rapes, and the practice of feeding the bodily remains of Aboriginal victims to dogs.

Similar details can be found in the passage that tells of Gould's arrival on Sarah Island, in which his first sight of a human being consists of seeing the floating corpse of a convict who drowned when trying to escape (Flanagan 2003: 99). Historically the harsh condition of the penal colony did not prevent numerous convicts from trying to abscond. Already in the first few month of its existence, fourteen prisoners—10 percent of its early population—attempted to escape (Maxwell-Steward 2008: 61–62). Many of those who tried did not survive the attempt. The rendering of Gould's first impression of the island, guarded against the wind by log fences, with a stone building serving as a commissariat and an unfinished wharf on the water (Flanagan 2003: 98), are in accordance with historical findings (Maxwell-Steward 2008). Similarly his description of the smell of death and disease, the sound of tortured men, and the poverty of the convicts' sod huts and timber sheds (Flanagan 2003: 104–7) is historically credible when looking at the architectural remains on the island and the official administrative records on convict's illness, causes of death, and individual prisoners (Hughes 1987; Cocker 1998; Madley 2008; Maxwell-Steward 2008).

Nevertheless it is not its historical accuracy that makes *Gould's Book of Fish* such an outstanding example of a literary work that applies the powers of the false. If one looks at the few examples just given, it is striking how the specific employment of literary and rhetorical devices are employed in such a way as to create an irresolvable paradox: although the novel constantly alludes to historical events and characters, it is nevertheless told in such a fantastic manner that its genre seems to situate it firmly in the field of fiction. Its nonchronological narrative heavily employs self-reflexive and metafictional devices, fantastic and parodic interventions, and frequent interruptions caused by the introduction of new story lines. All these devices ensure that the novel cannot pass itself off as anything close to historiography. Rather the novel is articulated in such a way that it stands in stark contrast to a once common positivistic style in which historical accounts were rendered, particularly by violating the formerly tacit historiographical assumption that the past must be presented objectively and disinterestedly: by the facts alone.[4]

This assumption has been heavily criticized in the wake of the linguistic turn and the rise of new social actors in the 1970s. Metahistorians such as Frank Ankersmit (1983, 1989, 1994, 1995, 1996, 2005), Paul Ricoeur (1984, 2000), and Hayden White (1973, 1980, 1982a, 1982b, 1987, 1999) have shown that historiographies are just as constructed as literature, since they are subject to the same narrative principles, such as plot structure, narration, and discourse. Feminist, postcolonial, and queer critics have argued that historical narratives have been used as a means to establish a patriarchal, imperial, and heterosexist world order.[5] The teleological and centripetal master narrative of the "progress of civilization" sustains and maintains gendered, sexualized, and racialized domination by privileging particular kinds of events, while it "renders any other history uninteresting, marginal and even non-existent" (Ashcroft 2001: 84). In contrast to a positivistic understanding of history, Flanagan manages to invent a format in which content and style account for historical events, yet in a manner that is not in the least objective, disinterested, or fact-orientated: rather the perspective of its first-person narrator is highly subjective, most often unreliable, and bound to be less than truthful since the narrator Gould—doubled and dubbed by the narrator Sid Hammet, as I will explain shortly—is introduced as a professional forger.

Nevertheless I want to maintain that neither content nor style derogates the novel's specific literary powers of the false. If one accepts the definition of the powers of the false that was given in chapter 1, these powers break down the dichotomy between truth and fiction by establishing not a truthful narration but the truth of narration that offers a different point of connection to the reader. While it seems completely impossible for Gould, the principal narrator in *Gould's Book of Fish*, to account for traumatic events without rendering them in a distorted and highly idiosyncratic way, this character performs an affective and passionate cathexis aimed at revealing exactly this impossibility of a detached objectivity. He thereby performs a longing for an "alternative epistemological and ethical space" (Grewal 1998: 10) that testifies to the distortions imposed on people by the brutal and genocidal colonial system in Tasmania, as well as to the affectionate relationships they were also capable of having. Literature, in other words, may endow us with a knowledge that differs from historical truth without being its dialectical opposite. It might construct a nonreferential narrative space in which experiences unfold that are (un-)imaginable, or it might show the urge and desire to understand historical events that

are nevertheless too terrible to relate to, thereby displaying an unful-
filled longing for an inclusion of mute, silent, and silenced voices. This
desire finds its expression in *Gould's Book of Fish* in the longing of its
first-person narrator, Gould, to tell a story of fish—an animal that is,
by human standards, voiceless. I will therefore pay particular attention
to the transformation he has to undergo to capture their stories. In this
chapter I will illuminate this transformation with Deleuze|Guattari's
concept of becoming.

Regarding the peculiar violation of historiographic rules in *Gould's
Book of Fish*, its powers of the false are established particularly through
its breach of the principles of objectivity, disinterestedness, and fact-
orientedness. It suggests that one important, albeit missing, perspective
on the past is established when giving access to a subjective, unreliable,
and—to apply the developed terminology—"false" voice that nevertheless testifies to a fundamental need to invent a story. This story ought
to be able to account for the consequences of a violent colonial system
in which a whole number of people—that is, the natives, the slaves,
and the lumpenproletarian prisoners—were dispossessed of their own
bodies and forced into unpaid labor and often tortured or even killed,
sometimes in numbers amounting to genocide. By choosing its particular—subjective, fantastic, unreliable—point of view, this approach
ensures that it does not create an impasse when the historical records do
not allow it to render the "true" voices of the dispossessed and disen-
franchised.[6] As has been my argument throughout this work, literature
provides the means to express *a credible rather than a truthful story*
to its readers. It provides a story to which they might be able to relate
because it makes an affective layer of experiences accessible, because it
affects them and is affected by their reading. As I have shown at length,
a Deleuze|Guattari-inspired reading of the literary machine does not
understand this access to affectivity and affect as being provided by
the voiced experiences of an author. The writer is neither the subject
nor the object of a literary work. Rather the writer is the inject of a
confrontational action with something unseen and unheard of which is
transposed into literature to become a bloc of sensation (see WP 164)
that does not need to refer to the real world, while nevertheless being
effective in its impact. Yet its impact is established through the specific
gears and tools of the literary machine itself that follows its own rules
and does not mirror any kind of subjectivity.

Thus a literary work like *Gould's Book of Fish* does not strive to
tell the truth but to employ specific literary means to provoke a "false"

vision that is necessary to but missing from the historical transmission. I want to argue that *Gould's Book of Fish* establishes a perspective on those dispossessed of their own body—the natives, the slaves, and the lumpenproletarian prisoners—that opens up to a horizon in which compassion, sympathy, and solidarity with them is called for. It thereby creates a point of contact that might be taken up by "the people to come": those who want to adopt this literarily evoked attitude of respect and love toward these abased and dispossessed people, those who want to include these destinies in their legacy of the past, to construct an inclusive present and future. Furthermore *Gould's Book of Fish* testifies to a subjective perspective in which the lives of these dispossessed is depicted as meaningful, loving, and lovable; they are people with outstanding talents and, above all, people with the means to resist and take flight from a cruel and distorting colonial system. This is a change of perspective that not only runs against a "history in major," as I want to call it, but allows a counterpart in minor to raise its voice in dissonance to it. It thereby stresses a vision of life that is one of the most fundamental and consequential shifts the novel offers to its readers. By putting the unreliable and distorted voice of an inmate and forger into the center of its story, it disturbs the legitimate coordinates of epistemologies, only to reconnect on an affective level with its readers who might adapt, at least temporarily, to its point of view. Yet, over and above all, the novel stresses a loving and loveable desire to render stories of unspeakable horrors through a becoming-fish of its first-person narrator. This desire expresses a hyperbolic love of each and everyone, until it becomes not general but universal, thereby including the wonders of this world in its account. At the end of this chapter I will take the novel's perspective, in which life and its conditions cannot be lumped together, as a point of departure from which to criticize Agamben's transhistorical and transnational account of biopolitical determinations of life as proposed in *Homo Sacer* (1998). In contrast to the empowering depiction of convicts and natives in *Gould's Book of Fish*, Agamben fails to invest stylistically and affectively in an account of human beings in which they are *not* dehumanized.

Deleuze|Guattari owe their highly esoteric concept of becoming to two philosophers: Baruch (Benedictus) Spinoza (1632–77) and Friedrich Nietzsche (1844–1900). As Robert Hurley (1988: i) states in his preface to Deleuze's (1988b [hereafter SP]) treatise on Spinoza, between both passes "a historical line of connection" that runs through a "form" called "Man." Their ideas are "prior to" or "beyond" this "form." For

Spinoza (2000), "Man" is an assemblage of attributes or a modification of one single substance which he calls God or Nature. Nietzsche (1997: 57–125), on the other hand, delineated an "over-man" who is able to affirm life as a "meaningless" becoming rather than as a teleological development. Both have in common that they undermine the importance of consciousness, values, and what Spinoza calls sad passions (see SP 17), notions that arose during and after the European Enlightenment. While in Nietzsche's (1968, 1974, 1994, 1997, 2002) work the will, affirmation, and the power to forget play an important role, Spinoza's (2000) contribution consists in stressing that we need to construct and acquire a knowledge that is capable of capturing what mind *and* body can do (see Braidotti 2002, 2006; SP; Gatens 1996; Gatens and Lloyd 1999). The latter's understanding is based on the belief that human beings have inadequate ideas about causes and effects. If we encounter an idea or another body, we apprehend first and only what is happening to us: "only our body in its own relation, and our mind in its own relation" (Spinoza 1985: 28–29, qtd. in SP 19). Yet to acquire an adequate apprehension of the capability of our mind and our body, we need to go beyond this first grasp. Even our own mind and our own body are capable of surpassing "the consciousness that we have of it" (SP 19), and so do other bodies and minds. To get a grip on these capabilities, Spinoza sees it as helpful to use the imagination (Gatens and Lloyd 1999). It plays a cognitive role, as it allows fictions to arise that "do not themselves yield adequate knowledge; but they re-work the materials of common perception, leading the mind on to a more adequate perception. Fictions are not true; but they are expressions of a positive mental capacity—the capacity to feign" (Gatens and Lloyd 1999: 34). From surpassing consciousness, we might be able to analyze what is of most importance to Spinoza, namely, to understand whether the relations one creates enhance joy or instead lead to sadness. To develop these relations, mind and body are equally important. In fact, for Spinoza, the mind is "the idea of the body, rather than a separate intellectual substance" (Gatens and Lloyd 1999: 2). Here we also have to understand that in Spinoza's view, the body itself is composed of infinitely small parts, so that a relation does not necessarily involve the whole body. Furthermore it is not solely the encounters between human beings that might enhance their joy and power (puissance, potestas) or evoke sadness and weakness. A relation can be composed of things, animals, human beings, or some of their respective parts. In itself, it is neither good nor bad. It can be evaluated by the possibilities it allows—limiting or enhancing—to the singularities involved in its assemblage. This point of view, which one could call an ethics of relations, has the advantage that it "opens up forms of experimentation. It is a whole exploration of things, it doesn't have anything to do with essence. It is necessary to see people as small packets of power (pouvoir)" (Deleuze 1980).

In their concept of becoming, Deleuze|Guattari have taken up Spinoza's visions, most importantly his idea of looking at the composition of relations and their outcomes rather than at the essential traits of beings, the definition of which has been, for example, one of the aims of Platonism.[7] In Deleuze|Guattari's (1987 [hereafter TP2]: 238) view, "becoming lacks a subject distinct from itself"; it is composed of extensive parts (longitude) and intensities (latitude), creating affects that express neither a subject nor a subjectivity (see chapter 1). Although becoming lacks a form that can convey its meaning, it nevertheless can be traced as a play of singular, definable moments in time, intensities and affectivities, events and accidents (see TP2 253). It thereby expresses the capability of life to escape signification and to form an assemblage that might enhance its possible joys and might even evoke a "love of the whole world" (Lawlor 2008: 173).

Gould's becoming-fish, with its unrequited love, will be at the center of the following analysis, in which I want to pay close attention to the suggestions it puts forward for a vision of life itself—a life that cannot be pinned down to the cruelties it endures and the distortions it undergoes and that is continually in the process of becoming more than itself. I will show how this vision is accomplished and how it might influence the construction of a legacy with the past and a responsibility to the future for its readers, while simultaneously evoking a vision of life that takes it to be more than the circumstances in which it becomes distorted, silenced, and mute like a fish.

3.4. PROFESSIONAL FORGERS, NOTORIOUS LIARS: NARRATOR GOULD AND NARRATOR HAMMET

The primary example of the novel's vision of historiography and its inventive "false" mode of narration is its peculiar first-person narrator, Gould. From the start he introduces himself as a drunkard, professional forger, and notorious liar:

> Call me what you will: others do, & it is of no matter to me; I
> am not what I am. A man's story is of little consequence in this
> life, a pointless carapace which he carries, in which he grows,
> in which he dies. . . . What follows may or may not be a true
> story: either way it is of no great importance. . . . I simply want
> to tell the tale of my paltry paintings, before I too join them.
> (Flanagan 2003: 44)

He thereby depicts himself and his accounts as uncertifiable, indeterminable, and generally untrustworthy. In fact it is up to the readers to decide if Gould's story is "true" or not, since "it is of no great importance" to him. It is nevertheless noteworthy that he makes a distinction between a story about himself—a self that is here reduced to an outer zoological shell without further meaning—and a story about his paintings, whose importance is emphasized by his wish to account for them. His story of fish serves a task that seems more important to him than letting others know about his life. This is a cathexis that characterizes Gould as an unselfish person who does not put too much importance on himself but stresses instead the significance of a rather strange undertaking in storytelling: an enterprise in which metalepsis is what distinguishes *Gould's Book of Fish*, since the novel is said to be the reproduction of his journal—his book of fish—from page 41 on. By stressing the importance of his book of fish—*Gould's Book of Fish*—he also emphasizes that his strange and fantastic tale has a significance that exceeds his life story.[8] The metaleptic narrative also implies that the tale told in *Gould's Book of Fish* exceeds the importance of the narrator's life story as well, since it is said that the novel is a memorized version of it. One could also argue—in conditions in which Gould's account of his life could be generally regarded as untrustworthy because he is a convict, is accused of being a liar, and is a professional forger—that his rather strange and fantastic tale is able to tell more about him and his life than a story striving to tell the "truth," since it conveys his strong desire to pass down a story for posterity.[9]

In a similar way Sid Hammet, the narrator of the frame story, is affected by a book he finds in an antiques shop. Like Gould, he is introduced as a contemporary forger and furniture faker, who furthermore happens to be the "one and only" narrator of *Gould's Book of Fish*, since the book he has found in a Salamanca antiques shop dissolves into a puddle of water once he has reached its conclusion. Therefore he decides to rewrite the book of fish "from memories, good and bad, reliable and unreliable; by using bad transcriptions that I had made, some of complete sections, others only brief notes describing lengthy tracts of the book; and by the useful expedient of reproducing the pictures of the wordless Allport Book of Fish" (Flanagan 2003: 28). In this way the tangible *Gould's Book of Fish*, which readers hold in their hands, is authored by Richard Flanagan and illustrated by William Buelow Gould, whose fish paintings appear on the cover and at the beginning of each chapter. The originals of these paintings remain, as has been neatly recorded on the back cover, in the Allport Library and Museum of Fine Arts, State Library of Tasmania. This establishes a paratext[10] that serves as a threshold between a reality outside of the book and the "reality" accounted for by the novel's diegetic narrative. However, once the story begins, the reader learns that the principal narrator is a certain Sid Hammet, forger and tradesman in stories, who reconstructs from his own unreliable memory what a certain Gould claimed to account for, namely, those perceptual, affective, and perhaps historical events that Gould experienced while making his fish paintings, experiences that may have left their mark on those paintings.

In this mise-en-abyme[11] an author employs a first-person narrator to narrate the story of another first-person narrator, both of whom are professional forgers, notorious liars, and hardly law-abiding persons. This mise-en-abyme stresses that we should not be looking for conventional truth in the story, since none of the narrators seems to place much importance on it. Yet both of them stress the importance of storytelling; Hammet especially, the only "true" narrator who remains after the book of fish has dissolved, reflects extensively on fictionality. In fact one could even claim that he self-reflexively establishes a notion of "the truth of narration," a term that plays a prominent role in my own theoretical framework (see section 1.6). The "truth of narration" attests to the particular powers of storytelling to affect readers. His encounter with the book of fish is already not lacking wonder; when he stumbles upon it in a Salamanca antiques shop under a pile of magazines, he is taken aback by a "mesmeric shimmer," a "gentle radiance," a "phosphorescent marbling" that the book emanates (Flanagan 2003: 1). Once he has it in his hands, he notices not only that it smells of "briny winds that blow from the Tasman seas" (11) but that it was covered with "pulsing purple spots" (13), a color that rubs off on his hands until they glow. As soon as he opens the book, he is so captivated that "the only light that existed in the entire universe was that which shone out of those aged pages" (2). Far from being unimportant, these descriptions mediate the specific infectious quality of the book as object, as well as its tangible, illuminating, and colorful qualities. Yet, above all, it stands in for the experience of a reader who is overwhelmed by the story he reads, a tale that seems to "mirror life" (24) in its uncanny ability to always add new parts and dimensions, adding to the miracle it poses: "Every time I opened the book a scrap of paper with some revelation I had not hitherto read would fall out, or I would stumble across an annotation that I had somehow missed in my previous readings, or I would come upon two pages stuck together that I hadn't noticed and which, when carefully teased apart, would contain a new element of the story that would force me to rethink the whole in an entirely changed light. In this way, each time I opened the Book of Fish what amounted to a new chapter miraculously appeared" (24). The narrative is thus a mirror that reflects the ungraspable quality of life rather than its capturability, therefore showing that a reflection does not need to stabilize the point of view of the reading or viewing subject. It can also unsettle her or him, unhinge her or his preconceived perceptions and opinions by adding a new dimension that, as I want to claim, is enabled by the readerly giving in to a described world in which one is a stranger. As I argued in chapter 1, reading mediates other times, peoples, and worlds; allowing oneself to be haunted by this difference for and in itself makes it possible for one to be othered, thereby creating a time and place from which one might question the knowledge and perceptions one presumably "has." Exactly through Hammet's readerly enactment of wonder, surprise, and astonishment toward the book and its overwhelming and overpowering qualities, it is stressed that fiction is not a model but a form of power (see TI 147): a power that comes into being since it affects its reader and is affected by Hammet's reading.[12]

Which affects overwhelm the reader Hammet, and how is the book affected by him? As I have previously pointed out, Hammet is specifically taken aback by the radiating, fragrant, coloring qualities of the book; furthermore the book seems to be never-ending, since its descriptions continue to gain new dimensions. Yet the evoked enchantment and its sense of wonder are not the sole effects the book of fish has on him. By affecting him in the way it does, it turns him into someone who *invests* in it. He has numerous conversations with his fake-making coworker Mr. Hung and his lover, the Conga, in which he tries to grasp the overpowering qualities of the book. He also tries to convey its worth to "historians and bibliophiles and publishers" (Flanagan

2003: 16), although without success. All of them dismiss the book as a literary fraud and believe his is its author. As mentioned earlier, the attribution of authorship later becomes intradiegetically true when the book of fish dissolves and Hammet starts to rewrite it from memory.[13] Through rewriting the reader Hammet thus becomes the writer of a book that is the memorized version of Gould's memoires, which the latter wrote in an isolation cell while awaiting his death sentence. If one wants to know how the book of fish—and maybe, by extension, *Gould's Book of Fish*—is affected by its reader, "rewriting from memory" becomes an important topos. To delve into that matter, we must scrutinize what exactly the narrator Hammet is memorializing in his book. When reflecting upon the matter, he writes:

> But I must confess to a growing ache within, for these days I am no longer sure what is memory and what is revelation. How faithful the story you are about to read is to the original is a bone of contention with the few people I had allowed to read the original Book of Fish. The Conga—unreliable, granted— maintains there is no difference. Or at least no difference that matters. And certainly, the book you will read is the same as the book I remember reading, and I have tried to be true both to the wonder of that reading and to the extraordinary world that was Gould's. (29)

What the narrator Hammet thus wants to convey is both the affect created by the book—"the wonder of that reading"—as well as its content, "the extraordinary world that was Gould's." And while the wish to account for the way he is affected while reading the book is certainly fulfilled through his manifold self-reflections, they nevertheless induce a further indeterminability into his account. To remember the affects reading creates might not be the same as remembering the content of a book, a difference displayed in his comment that he does not know "what is memory and what is revelation." Affects are, as I have explained elsewhere (see Wiese 2012b), immaterial, since they are situated in time rather than space; they account for becomings evoked by encounters between different forces in an event. These forces effectuate subjectivity rather than being effectuated by a subject, as Deleuze|Guattari have claimed throughout their work (see Deleuze and Guattari 1983, K, TP1, TP2, WP; see Braidotti 2002). As such, affects also point to a different sense of time, since they evoke simultaneous "peaks of the present": "a present of the future, a present of the present and a present of the past, all implicated in the event, rolled up in the event" (TI 97). This means that an affect cannot be represented, since the copresence of its ever-changing relation toward past, present, and future cannot be pinned down and fixed; it evokes becomings that are themselves permanently becoming, even while they are already initially the evoked effect of an event rather than the event itself. Hammet's comment on the undecidability of memory or revelation might in this way hint toward affects with their ever-changing, kaleidoscopic processes. Affect might be induced only "from the forms it develops and the subjects it forms" (TP2 266), which means that its existence is brought into being by a derivation—a derivation whose immateriality, becoming, and ever-changing origins make it impossible to decide what kind of happening it refers to. In other words, it is undecidable whether it could even still be called memory—even the memory of an immaterial, ever-changing event—or if it should be called revelation, since its insights seem to come from a source that cannot be pinned down.

In a similar way, the "content" Hammet evokes, "the extraordinary world that was Gould's," is affected by Gould's strange and fantastic storytelling, which bears no resemblance to conventional representations of historical circumstances. This incongruence is also stressed by staging the voices of historical experts in *Gould's Book of Fish*, most prominently the eminent history professor da Silva, who righteously calls the book of fish a "sad pastiche" in which the location and historical circumstances are accurately described, whereas otherwise "almost nothing in the Book of Fish agrees with the known history of that island hell. Few names mentioned in your curious chronicle are to be found in any of the official documents that survive from that time, and those that take on identities and histories are entirely at odds with what is described" (Flanagan 2003: 20). Yet while Professor da Silva might be right to call the book of fish a pastiche, does that mean that it does not convey a sense of truth? As Gerard Genette (1997a: 15) has claimed, a pastiche is a palimpsestic literary genre,[14] invoking a previous text that it imitates by using the latter's style, only retold through characters that degrade the initial pathos, thereby creating comic effects; a pastiche thus reminds us that "the comic is only the tragic seen from behind." In some ways a pastiche is therefore a text that refers to, hints toward, and comments upon another text, which is simultaneously brought to the mind of its readers as its invisible yet indispensible backside.

In this way *Gould's Book of Fish*—the memorized version of Gould's logbook told by an unreliable narrator—may be said to refer to historical circumstances that it cannot be separated from without being their representation. It employs, in other words, the powers of the false, to evoke not truthful narration but the truth of narration. As a pastiche, it shows the flipside of historical happenings, it sees them "from behind" (Genette 1997a: 15). This vision is generated, I maintain, in a variety of ways, yet most prominently by staging the need to invent the past. In the passage in which Professor da Silva speaks his mind, the difference between historiography and "false" storytelling is dramatized through his attempt to teach Hammet a lesson about the power of history and the futility of fraud. With arguments that are weighed down by the millennia-old tradition from which they stem, he flings a ball and chain upon his desk and asks Hammet to identify the objects, only to claim that they are not what they seem to be: "No, Mr. Hammet, you see nothing of the sort. A fraud, Mr. Hammet, is what you see. A ball and chain made by ex-convicts in the late nineteenth century to sell to tourists visiting the Gothic land of the Port Arthur penal settlement is what you gaze upon. . . . A piece of kitsch that has nothing to do with history" (Flanagan 2003: 18). Yet while da Silva believes that this argument is so incontestable and unassailable that there is no need to further investigate the matter, Hammet suddenly sees himself confronted with the past of "his own noble art" (18). Behind every fraud might be the need to commit it, and the forged balls and chains of former felons show precisely which signs of their suppression and treatment they wanted to communicate. As I argued earlier, this desire to transmit an experience, even by means of the false, should not be regarded as the opposite of history. On the contrary, it shows that something in history has remained hidden: the need to tell a story. This is a desire that literature communicates in another way that does not necessarily claim to be truthful. Hammet's conclusive characterization of da Silva's attitude might in this way defend literature, while giving us reasons to let ourselves be affected and to affect with its powers of the false: "He looked for truth in facts and not in stories. . . . History for him was no more than a rueful fatalism about the present" (20). The affective force of literature, with its potential to open the horizons of time toward an ever-changing eternity,[15] might in this way serve as a counterpoint to any attempt to fix the past by linking it exclusively to those things that are in a positivistic sense "true."

3.5. READERS, WRITERS, NARRATORS:
SHARING PERCEPTIONS AND NARRATIVE DESIRES

In *Gould's Book of Fish*, the desire to give a voice to silenced or silent historical experiences is most prominently articulated by creating a story that accompanies the fish drawings of the real convict-painter Gould. As I have already pointed out, the narrative emphasizes, in numerous reflections of either Hammet or the fictional character and narrator Gould, the importance of these accounts; these contemplations suggest that the stories accompanying the fish drawings "explained the curious genesis of the pictures" (Flanagan 2003: 23). But this "explanation" is understood as an addition to a mystery rather than a clarification. "One," the Salamanca Book of Fish, which is, by way of metalepsis, *Gould's Book of Fish*, "spoke with the authority of words," "and the other," the Allport Library's Book of Fish, which contains the drawings of the "real" convict-painter Gould, "with the authority of silence, and it was impossible to tell which was the more mysterious" (23). This description stresses once more the sense of wonder that the book of fish—either the Salamanca or Allport version—emanates. It also suggests that the historical fish drawings already in themselves pose a problem to historiography, since they convey silence rather than render solely "the Small World of Macquarie Harbour Ichthyology" (126), that is, the fish that populate the waters of Sarah Island. In other words, the Allport Library's Book of Fish already conveys much more than it purports to, namely, the natural history of fish. This surplus of meaning, a speaking silence, is perceptible, even demandingly so, since it makes itself heard with "authority" (24). As we will see, this making-perceptible of silence is closely linked to the intrusion of a materiality whose meaning cannot be pinned down: a materiality that nevertheless can be approached through a sense of wonder and astonishment.

By displaying reproductions of convict-painter Gould's original fish drawings on the novel's cover and at the beginning of each chapter, Flanagan has created two distinct yet interrelated effects. As we will see, the way they are rendered allows the novel's readers to experience the effects produced by the original paintings. Flanagan also creates a narrative knot that ties together different narrative levels. As I have argued throughout this study, a Deleuze|Guattari-inspired understanding of art affirms that "something" of the artist's experiences and/or perceptions will have found its expression in an artwork. However, the relation between the original experience and how it is "taken up"

and expressed in an artwork is never one of straightforward representation—a point of view in which they are perfectly in line with one of
the most shared axioms in literary studies, the incongruence of a piece
of art and its creator's life. To grasp Deleuze|Guattari's suggestions, it
must be kept in mind how they configure the initial encounter between
a subject and an (im)material object of experience and/or perception
that is then transformed into a work of art. As I pointed out in chapter
1, an artist is someone who is overwhelmed by forces that come from
an outside. According to Deleuze|Guattari's definition, these forces are
unrelated, unformed, and uncontained in an era's audiovisual archive
(see section 1.6); these forces create a fold within an artist that is at
once "farther away than any external world . . . [but] closer than any
internal world" (F 97), thereby creating a zone of proximity that is
nevertheless separated by a division between inside and outside, so that
an inappropriable other(ness) is created within subjectivity. Therefore
the initial encounter brings an artistic subjectivity that is other to itself
together with forces uncontained in what can be seen and what can be
said in a given age. Furthermore artworks follow their own intricate
rules and are bound by their own characteristic features, to which end
the artistic experiences and/or perceptions undergo transformations
and metamorphoses that make them virtual instead of actual when
artistically expressed. A perception that belongs to a subjectivity that
is other to itself when confronted with forces uncontained in the audio-
visual archive is configured in a work of art. This perception is further
altered and bound by the very mechanisms of art itself.

Taking these Deleuze|Guattarian configurations as a starting
point, is it impossible to pin down how an artist's experiences and/
or perceptions have entered an artwork? To answer this question, it
is necessary to consider an artwork's mechanisms of transmission.
For Deleuze|Guattari, an artwork incorporates or embodies a virtual
event; "it gives it a body, a life, a universe" (WP 177) without actual-
izing it. In their view, this incorporation or embodiment is achieved
through style[16]: a style through which a virtual event is transmitted
that accounts for an artistic perception affected by uncontained forces.
Taking this definition as a starting point thus means that first of all,
readers of *Gould's Book of Fish* might indeed, as the narrator Hammet
suggests, perceive that something unspeakable and unspoken of
accompanies the pictures that feature on the cover and at the beginning of each chapter. They might sense how the convict-painter Gould,
although not present in the fish paintings as a depicted object, has

transmitted through style a vision that has influenced their expression and expressiveness. He thus has surpassed his work's objective of representing a natural history of Macquarie Harbor's fish by making his own formative experiences and/or perceptions stylistically perceptible alongside the fishy objects he depicts.[17] The point of contact at which an audience might sense the original painter's experiences and/or perceptions consists therefore in his stylistic choices, choices that are not the object of representation but rather the book's singular rendering.[18]

A second effect can be discerned that is triggered by Flanagan's decision to place a reproduction of the fish drawings on the novel's cover and at the beginning of each chapter. As I argued earlier, these reproductions serve as a knot that ties different narrative levels together. On the one hand, there is the narrative level of author and readers—a narrative level that one might call, for lack of a better word, reality.[19] On this narrative level, one faces Gould's unmediated fish drawings, either as a reproduction in *Gould's Book of Fish* or in the Allport Library's Book of Fish. On the other hand, there are metadiegetic and extradiegetic levels on which the narrator Hammet and the narrator William Buelow Gould are situated. Both of them relate to the Allport Library's Book of Fish, either by repainting its content from memory (as in the case of Gould) or by using its paintings on the rewritten version of the narrator Gould's logbook (as in the case of Hammet). This means that, on all narrative levels, a relation to the "original" fish drawings is established, a relation that is shared by author, readers, and narrators alike, although they are situated in different—real or fictional—worlds. This relation is made possible through the paratextual threshold between the inside and the outside that the fish drawings occupy (see section 3.4). This means that the author, readers, and narrators, regardless of whether they are fictional or real, share a common perception of the convict-painter Gould's stylistic influence on the paintings' expression, although this influence does not allow them to deduce substantial background knowledge about his life, his feelings, or his manner of perception. Therefore it can be concluded that the author, readers, and narrators share the same relation to the original fish drawings and their creator. This relation might arouse in them the desire to fabulate a story in which the origins of the fish paintings are explained. While *Gould's Book of Fish* clearly answers this call by inventing a story that accompanies "the curious genesis of the pictures" (Flanagan 2003: 23), the readers might have had the same wish, a desire they see fulfilled by the narrative itself. With the inventive device of placing the original fish drawings on the cover and at the beginning of each chapter, the novel optimally conforms with conditions that evoke the powers of the false. It forms an assemblage that brings "real parties together, in order to make them produce collective utterances" (TI 215). In Flanagan's *Gould's Book of Fish*, these real parties consist of writer, readers, and narrators alike, all of which might share the desire to invent a story based on a perception that is also accessible in reality.

3.6. REFLECTIONS ON FISH DRAWINGS AND THE DRAWING OF FISH

The urge to tell a story that gives Gould's illustrated fish an environment in which they can be rescued from oblivion is most manifestly expressed by Hammet's wish to create a possible world "in which all Gould's fish might be returned to the sea" (Flanagan 2003: 29). This would be a world whose genesis is driven by Hammet's desire to remove the fish-unfriendly conditions in which the original paintings were made, a water world in which fish can thrive rather than die. This wish stands in sharp contrast to the conditions in which, intradiegetically, the original fish paintings were made, conditions that Gould frequently reflects upon in descriptions of the dying fish he is drawing. He gives, for example, the following account of his first impressions and procedures when ordered to paint a fish for the lover of the (unnamed) captain who transports him to Sarah Island:

> The kelpy which he had presented to me to paint was not one that seemed to be cognisant of its fate as an ambassador of romance. Curled in a bucket of seawater, it was still alive &, it seemed, somehow faintly contemptuous of its new role. I took the kelpy out of the bucket for half a minute or so, arranging it on the table in front of me, working quickly, then placing it back in the water so it might breathe & not yet die. This dry table, I realised, was the kelpy's petite noyade, & I his Captain Pinchbeck. Like me, the kelpy was guilty. Like me, it had no idea why. (89)

Strikingly he not only delineates the fish as an innocent creature that will remain unaware of its fate of being transmuted into a token of love, provided it remains in its element; he also describes the fish as a creature whose imminent death comes closer with each attempt to capture its specificities on canvas. Gould's awareness of the kelpy's being given-to-death is furthermore enhanced by parallels he draws between himself and the fish, which are established by memories that surface when he looks at the dying fish: "I found it not so hard to paint a reasonably accurate picture, but the kelpy's eyes followed me as if it knew all our true crimes, just like the machine breaker's eyes had followed me until the moment of his death, but that was not exactly how I painted the fish—as an accusing, horrified eye in a dying body" (89). With this he hints at a number of stories told in the chapter on the kelpy; for example, he refers to the way he has been treated by Pinchbeck, the cruel and tyrannical captain of the ship that transported him to Australia who tortured him by nearly letting him drown in a human "petite noyade," the practice of executing someone by drowning.

Above all, he alludes to the story of a machine breaker from Glasgow with whom he was condemned to operate an instrument called the threadwheel during his first sentence in Tasmania. The threadwheel is also called an "everlasting staircase"; it consisted of "wooden steps built around a cylindrical iron frame" that was powered by as many as forty convicts to grind corn or pump water and forced the prisoners "to continue stepping along the series of planks."[20] The machine breaker from Glasgow slips from the steps and is severely injured by the grinding machine. Moribund, he is plagued by fantasies in which the Kelpy gets him. In this case the Kelpy is the Scottish mystical "water-horse" that can take on any kind of human or animal shape; its only characteristic feature is having wet hair. What unites the Scottish Kelpy and the Tasmanian kelpy is their ability to take on multiple forms and serve multiple functions; they are shape-shifters that can drag their (readerly) victims into their own world, with its own particular conditions. And just as the Scottish Kelpy haunts the machine breaker, threatening to take him to a netherworld, the Tasmanian kelpy haunts Gould with "all our true crimes" while becoming "an ambassador of romance" and subsequently a reminder of a whole range of events in which torture and deliberate extinction were the order of the day. For the associations it triggers feature not only the machine breaker from Glasgow but also Capois Death, purportedly a maroon from Liverpool who tells everyone working at the treadmill stories while the machine breaker is dying. He tells stories of the slave revolt in San Domingo, the island he grew up on, describing not only the slaves' victorious rebellion but also the experience of seeing Negroes being publicly fed to dogs & being burnt alive; of their leader, Toussaint L'Ouverture, the black Napoleon, betrayed by the white Napoleon; of L'Ouverture's cultured black general Maurepas, having to watch his wife & children being drowned before his eyes as the French soldiers nailed a pair of wooden epaulettes into his naked shoulders, taunting him, laughing as they hammered so: A real Bonaparte now! And yet it was also another Frenchman, the sea-captain Mazard, to whom he owed his life, who had refused to drown the one hundred & fifty slaves given to him for that express purpose & instead took them to Jamaica. (Flanagan 2003: 87)

In this way a whole mosaic of stories is built up that pertain to different times and places; a net of associations is woven that does not catch the fish but something entirely different, namely, the wandering mind of the character Gould in his attempt to escape the conditions in which he is caught while writing. His writing takes place retrospectively, when he is placed in solitary confinement in quarters "built at the base of sandstone cliffs below the high water mark" (Flanagan 2003: 43). As a retrospective writer who is no longer situated in his narrative—as a metadiegetic narrator—he announces that he is determined to escape by means of his fish: "But I am William Buelow Gould, party of one, undefinable, & my fish will free me & I shall flee with them" (93). He thereby establishes a notion of writing that brings us back to an observation I made at the beginning of this section. In that context Hammet's wish to "make a vessel—however crude—in which all Gould's fish might be returned to the sea" (29) could be read as an attempt to use the literary machine as a means of preservation and a saving force that is able to simultaneously rescue three different kinds of fish from being forgotten: the real fish that he is painting and that he so vividly describes and remembers; their iconic renderings as naturalistic paintings that appear as reproductions on the cover and at the beginning of each chapter; and his dramatically staged becoming-fish—a becoming that I will scrutinize shortly in more depth. This threefold notion of fish as referring to an object, to an icon, and to a process entails an optimal use of the specificity of literature. When it unfolds its signifiers, it can make us aware of processes of meaning-making by "dissecting and deconstructing our expectations" (Buikema 2009: 315). It can also force an altered consciousness on the readers (see Dillon 1978; Riffaterre 1959, 1960, 1966), which might, I suggest, accept new meanings and new ways of meaning-making. In the case of *Gould's Book of Fish*, this readerly becoming-other bestows upon the signifier ("Gould's fish") the ability to simultaneously signify an object, an icon, and a process, each entailing specific interactions and effects that they create with each other and with the readers. In this way the fish are depicted as having multiple and proliferating meanings. Ultimately they become such slippery beings that any attempt to capture their meaning is once and for all bound to fail. However, this inability is not a defeat but rather allows one to feel the wonder of life. Far from being a determinable, definable, and delimited being, "a fish is a slippery & three-dimensional monster that exists in all manners of curves, whose colouring & surfaces & translucent fins suggest the very reason & riddle of life" (Flanagan 2003: 133). This explains why Gould does not know how to capture the essence of the fish. With its ability to represent the wonder of life itself, the fish also evades the desires of "those cursed Linnaeans of the soul" (93), personified in the character Lemprière, who want to assign "for every plant, a species; for every species, a genus; for every genus, a phylum. No more vulgar folk names for plants based on old witches' tales & widows' remedies, no more ragwort & nightelder & foxglove, but a scientifick Latin name for every living thing, based on a thorough scientifick study of its physical features. No more thinking that the natural & human worlds are entwined, but a scientifick basis for separation of the two, & human advancement on the basis of that scientifick difference forever after" (120–21). In contrast to this endeavor, *Gould's Book of Fish* uses the specificity of the literary machine to multiply meanings rather than contain them, and this multiplication somehow allows for an escape.

What kind of escape is made possible in *Gould's Book of Fish* (Flanagan 2003)? And does this escape evade the numerous captures that the book presents, of fish and convicts alike? On the one hand, already on first sight is it made clear that some kind of substance[21] has been captured and used for determinate means. Gould tells a story of fish "in every which way, even down to the sharkbone quill & the very sepia ink with which I write these words, made from a cuttlefish that squirted me only a few hours ago" (Flanagan 2003: 127), thereby emphasizing the fishy origin of his material means of storytelling. Some hardcover Australian, Dutch, and German editions use a different color of ink for each individual chapter, as described by the extradiegetic firsthand reader—and secondhand writer—Hammet: "Each story is written in a different coloured ink which, as their convict scribe describes, had been made by various ingenious expedients from whatever was at hand: the red ink from a kangaroo's blood, the blue from crushing a stolen stone, and so on" (15). Furthermore the material qualities of the book are enhanced by descriptions that give the book itself qualities that relate it to fish and the sea. It is described as behaving like "a bastard trumpeter caught at night" (13); it smells of "the briny winds from the Tasman Sea" (11); it teems "with words as the ocean did fish" (23); and, most prominently, it dissolves into a puddle after Hammet reads its conclusion. These descriptions not only paint a picture of the substance of *Gould's Book of Fish*; since they become "true" on a diegetic level as well as in the reality of the readers, their rhetorical function changes. A description of a book that smells, looks, and behaves like water is first of all figurative and tropical; the preposition *like* indicates its status as a simile, and for this reason the two entities related to each other will behave approximately like each other but will never be completely interchangeable. However, in *Gould's Book of Fish* the literary and narrative devices are used in such a way that a figurative description situated on the intradiegetic narrative level might become literally "true" on the metadiegetic one—as, for example, the chapters printed in different colored ink, as can be testified by metadiegetic and extradiegetic narrators and "real" readers alike. Figurative descriptions might also transform its rhetorical function on the same narrative level. Narrator Hammet, for example, at the end of the frame story "really" becomes a fish, a pot-bellied seahorse to be precise. In this way the signifier *seahorse* serves as a title for the entire chapter, stands in for a "real" seahorse observed by Hammet, and signifies Hammet after his transformation. In some editions[22] the seahorse even decorates the cover of the book. Furthermore Hammet's metamorphosis into a fish might serve as an allegory for the transformative powers of reading, writing, and the wonders of life, since it is ultimately the book of fish and the fish itself that pave the way for his change.

Gould's Book of Fish allows its readers to puzzle over processes of meaning-making, and interestingly enough, it is specifically its material substance that evades being captured in meaning, as demonstrated by the proliferation of "Gould's fish." Through the intrusion of substance, it shows how meaning is composed of a material carrier—a sound combination, a photograph, a graphic representation, the written word—and a form in which this substance is arranged, such as a syntactic, semantic, or narrative structure. Both material carrier and form need to relate to each other to "make sense." Still the relation between these different components[23] is arbitrary, so that meanings can shift and meaning-making may fail: there is always the possibility that one will be "left without words" before a thing, animal, person, or event. This speechlessness is also described by the Hammet, who characterizes the book as "sometimes . . . so elusive, this book, a series of veils, each of which must be lifted and parted to reveal only another of its kind, to arrive finally at emptiness, a lack of words, at the sound of the sea, of the great Indian Ocean through which I see in my mind's eye Gould now advancing towards Sarah Island, now receding; that sound, that sight, slowly pulsing in and out, in and out" (Flanagan 2003: 32). This is why he believes that his fate is linked to Gould's, since the latter's book of fish conveys to Hammet the conditions of his own life, particularly their elusiveness and ungraspability. What is established by staging "Gould's fish" as a substance in various guises and in ever-changing contexts is therefore a condition of life itself—if we are to take Hammet's suggestion seriously. This condition posits that there is no meaning that can be assigned once and for all, so that life cannot be captured, neither by oneself nor by "those cursed Linnaeans of the soul" who strive to prevent the entanglement of the natural and the human world by applying a scientific vocabulary that assigns each species its name and its place. In some ways, one could claim that it is life itself that escapes, a life that might be able to be captured but that will nevertheless make sense in ways that no one can control. It is a life that goes beyond "social practices of appropriation, perception, and symbolization" (Braidotti 2006: 207), which in Braidotti's theoretical project is called *zoë*, life in its pure, forceful immanence.[24]

For life to escape capture, storytelling itself is a means. For example, when Capois Death tells about the slave rebellion in San Domingo, it seemed "as though there was no escape except in stories" (Flanagan 2003: 88). This impression is further enhanced by Hammet's reflection on Gould's writing. Although the latter is accused of fraud, the book of fish does not seem to admit to the aim of fraudulent behavior: "But as one who knows something of the game of deceit, who knows that swindling requires not delivering lies but confirming preconceptions, the book, if it was a fraud, made no sense, because none of it accorded with any expectations of what the past ought to be" (21). In this quote Hammet not only takes the deed but also its motivation and outcome into account. By expanding the definition of fraud, he is able to differentiate between his own fraudulent behavior of selling fake antique furniture and *Gould's Book of Fish*, which records a world full of wonder and unimaginable cruelties. The furniture he sells to tourists allows them a vision in which the past is romanticized instead of providing a connection "that might prove painful or human" (7). A fraud therefore protects those who are deceived from perceiving reality, which leads Hammet to conclude, "They wanted stories, I came to realise, in which they were already imprisoned, not stories in which they appeared along with the storyteller, accomplices in escaping" (7). This comment also refers back to *Gould's Book of Fish* itself, since, as I have shown, its peculiar metaleptic narration connects different narrative levels with each other, on which the author, the readers, and the fictional narrators are situated. Through this inventive narrative mode, all of these three narrative instances might indeed become "accomplices in escaping" by receiving, perceiving, and enacting the wish to account for experiences of the real convict-painter Gould. These experiences will have to remain untold if they are not fabulated, since there are no historical sources that account for them, apart from the drawings that convict-painter Gould has left behind. Yet to fabulate stories to accompany these pictures means to use the powers of the false; it means to give voice to an impression that is transmitted through a stylistic rendering. What is transmitted to the audiences too is the need to actively transform the effect produced by these images and to engage with their authoritative silence (23). To fabulate a story is a form of engagement: it is a search for possible lines of flight and escape from capture from stabilized and stabilizing processes of meaning-making as practiced, for example, by assigning every living being a place in a chart: "for every plant, a species; for every species, a genus; for every genus, a phylum." The creation of these lines of flight demands active involvement from the audience. The telling of a "false" story adds to the historical record; it provides a point of reference for a collective-to-come that could claim a slippery and speechless—fish-like—historical foundation as its rootless genesis. By engaging with a fabulated story this collective-to-come might reconnect differently to a silent and silenced past, and it might be able to trace the impact of what is missing from the historical record. Yet to do so it has to actively search out processes that transform silences and induce new ways of making sense that do not foreclose difference. This is a form of sense-making that might seek out becomings "from the forms it develops and the subjects it forms" (TP2 266). I will undertake this search in the following section by looking at the particular becomings that the narrator-character Gould undertakes.

3.7. BECOMING-FISH

Gould's Book of Fish describes a movement toward a hyperbolic love for each and everyone, brought about by the encounter of the narrator Gould with the fish he is painting:

> The fish were at the beginning only a job, but to do that job well & keep the undoubted benefits that flowed from it, I had to learn about them. I had to study the manner in which fins passed from the realm of opaque flesh to diaphanous wonder, the sprung firmness of bodies, the way mouths related to oversized heads, heads to expanding bodies, the way scale dewlapped with scale to create a dancing sheen. . . . And I would have to admit that all this painting & repainting began to affect me. (Flanagan 2003: 213–14)

Although Gould first painted the fish solely for survival, already his first encounter with one of his objects, the kelpy, triggers a whole chain of memories and stories that surpass the aim of rendering their life graspable through paintings, to allow for their classification in natural history. This surpassing—which expresses another escape from capture—is brought about by a feeling of wonder *before* a creature, and here, *before* should be understood in a strictly spatial sense.[25] Its "zones of intensity and proximity" (TP2 274) are established through a manner of painting that needs to take into account the singular qualities of the fish, as well as its amazing ability to change its physical functions "from the realm of opaque flesh to diaphanous wonder." In this way the specific situation of painting allows for a perception that is carried along with its object, since neither experience, science, nor habit[26] allows Gould to take in "the sprung firmness of bodies . . . the way scale dewlapped with scale to create a dancing sheen." Rather he has "to learn about them," which might be an entirely different approach. As I have stated elsewhere (Wiese 2011), learning might entail submitting to other epistemological and/or ontological coordinates. It is important to note, however, that in *Gould's Book of Fish* learning is induced by a form of art, painting, which induces a nonhuman becoming of man (see WP 169). Deleuze defines this type of learning as being "essentially concerned with signs. . . . To learn is first of all to consider a substance, an object, a being as it emitted signs to be deciphered, interpreted. . . . Everything that teaches us something emits signs; every act of learning is an interpretation of signs or hieroglyphs"

(P 4). To paint fish means to undergo an apprenticeship of their signs (cf. P 4), which then needs to be actively transformed into an image that surpasses habitual recognition.[27] To understand this process, one has to keep in mind that Deleuze, unlike Kant (1974, 1998), does not separate the receptivity of the senses from the faculties of thinking. Rather being and thinking are "univocal"; there is always "thinking going on in being" (Szafraniec 2007: 120). Nevertheless to go beyond habit and recognition—which are both passive and selective syntheses of worldly encounters, a contemplation-contraction of what affects one—one has to *undo* processes of selection and choice, to *undo* the binding of habit and recognition, aiming at an opening of perception in which "nothing is excluded, all paths of reality are traversed indiscriminately, but also: no identities are produced" (124). In Szafraniec's reading of Deleuze, this third active synthesis of contemplation-contraction consists in the active creation of assemblages that gives one the "common notion" of joy.

Gould's description of his encounter with fish relates to this "undoing" of habit and recognition, because he is affected by them in a way that goes beyond those two contemplation-contractions. By being affected he fails to see the fish solely as an object that needs to be transposed through painterly scrutiny into a biological genus. Gould's close proximity to the fish triggers an affect that he cannot ward off. Being in the grip of its forces, he surrenders himself to the singularity of an encounter with wonderful and miraculous beings. He must render their ever-transforming beauty if he is to be true to the affect that has taken possession of him. Affected by the encounter with these beautiful creatures, he is propelled toward an outside where he sheds the molar form called man to become a multiplicity. This event is described by the narrator Gould as the leaping-over of the fish's soul into his own soul, a leaping-over he cannot avoid but that takes place regardless of whether or not he wants it:

> Perhaps because I spent so long with them, because I had to try to know something of them, they began to interest me, & then to anger me, which was worse, because they were beginning to enter me & I didn't even know that they were colonising me as surely as Lieutenant Bowen had colonised Van Diemen's Land all those years ago. . . .
>
> It was as if it was not possible to spend so long in the company of fish without something of their cold eye & quivering flesh passing across the air into your soul. (Flanagan 2003: 213–14)

For Gould, this event takes place because the fish want "to avoid being consigned to some nether world of lost shapes" (215), an outcome that is avoided precisely by their transposition into a painted object. This transposition does not manage to preserve their life but is at least able to capture their shapes and thus testify to their existence. Nevertheless if Gould's obsession with the fish and the way they take possession of him is to be accounted for by other means besides a painterly style, a transmission of a relation that surpasses a subject-object relation must occur. In other words, he and his fish need to become so inseparable that they are forged into one being forever, an occurrence described by Gould as follows:

> I just had to go back for more fish & why?—for as long as I was charged with the task of painting ever more of these cruel new settlers of my soul, first by an insane Surgeon & then more insanely by myself, there seemed no escape from their insidious invasion, no respite as they commenced swimming towards the backblocks of my heart, of my mind, preparing to take total control of me.
>
> And how could I have known that day . . . that within that huge head of Mr Lempriere's was being born one final tawdry passion, that was to forge fish & me into one forever? (215)

This happening, "[the forging of] fish & me into one forever," surpasses a painterly approach that Gould ascribes to Audubon, which he learns of when he is the latter's apprentice. The mention of Audubon marks another instance in the text in which a historical figure, the naturalist painter of *The Birds of America* (1826–36), finds his way into the novel.[28] In Gould's account, Audubon paints the birds for their "essential humours" (Flanagan 2003: 62), so that their pride, idiocy, or madness comes to the fore. This undertaking needs stories that "distill in a single image the story of a whole life" (62). Yet these stories do not emerge from the birds themselves but originate "in the new American towns & cities . . . in the dreams & hopes of those around him" (63). Ultimately Audubon does not paint birds but "a natural history of the new burghers" (63), which thus reflects *their* trajectory and humor above all else.

In contrast to this approach, the painter Gould lacks a perspective through which the objects he paints can be likened to the history of a civilization:

I could, I suppose, paint the fish in some similar imitation of the schools in which the local free settlers swim. But the fish come to me in the true condition of this life: alone, fearful, with no home, nowhere to run & hide. And if I were to place two of my fish together would I then have a school? . . . No, I would only have two fish: each alone, fearful, united solely in the terror of death I see in their eyes. . . .

Audubon painted the dreams of a new country . . . my fish are the nightmares of the past for which there is no market. . . . It is a natural history of the dead. (Flanagan 2003: 63)

Whereas Audubon has a story to tell that ultimately unites the birds he is drawing in one "natural history of the new burghers," Gould finds an unsettling perspective that posits him and his fish in the same situation, "the true condition of this life: alone, fearful, with no home, nowhere to run and hide." It is a situation in which one cannot find a transcendental aim such as becoming a member of the bourgeoisie, in which one cannot find a transcendental aim at all. Instead one has to face the conditions of "this"—particular—life as such, a life in which fear, homelessness, and death are immanent. It is a life that is particularly bound by being at a certain time in a certain space, yet a life that is nevertheless shared in a most radical sense, namely, by being interconnected, even populated, colonized, and invaded by one's encounters: "They were boring into me, seeping through my pores by some dreadful osmosis. And when within me glimmered the unexpected, somewhat terrifying knowledge that they were taking possession of my daytime thoughts, my night-time dreams, I grew frightened & longed to repel them, to fight back as the blackfellas had" (214). This strange and even violent happening is Gould's account of how the fish take him over. The description makes clear that becoming is not a pleasant surrender of one's selfish interests or desires; rather it is a painful undertaking, which in Gould's case is caused and propelled by even greater violence exerted by colonial agents such as the surgeon Lempriere. Lempriere can order Gould around, and any attempt to disobey his orders might worsen the conditions of Gould's imprisonment. Being Lempriere's servant therefore creates a desperate situation, while his becoming-fish enhances his capability to relate to the world and to feel interconnected with others. When Gould is tried in court for a crime committed on Sarah Island, he describes two discernible becomings:

The more I looked at those sad creatures, still dying, the occasional moral flap of the tail or desperate heave of the gills signalling their silent horror was not yet ended, the more I looked into the endless recesses of their eyes, the more something of them began to pass into me. . . .

And . . . even more peculiar, more shocking: how lately some small part of me, without me willing it, was beginning a long, fateful journey into them! Some small part of me & then more & more was tumbling downwards, falling inwards through their accusing eyes into that spiralling tunnel that was to end only with the sudden awareness that I was no longer falling but rolling ever slower in the sea, not knowing whether I was finally safe or whether I was finally dead. (257–58)

Not only do the fish affect Gould in such a way that he is, first of all, becoming-fish, only to finally arrive at a state in which safety and death are indistinguishable; the fish are also seized in a becoming, which I would describe as a becoming-painting that entails zones of indiscernibility. And although the immanent end of these mutual deterritorializations entails specific kinds of deaths, as we will see, one nevertheless has to note that the line of flight passing in between the fish and Gould realizes an affect too. This affect makes Gould "capable of loving" (TP2 197, 199–200, qtd. in Lawlor 2008: 173), a capability in which a notion of love as a personal feeling is displaced by a notion of love in which "one" is propelled into territories that no longer mark oneself: "My territories are out of grasp, not because they are imaginary, but the opposite: because I am in the process of drawing them" (TP2 199).[29] Such a love is "an exercise in depersonalization" (2), in which multiplicities encounter multiplicities (see TP2 2), until one becomes a world and makes a world. By propelling a subject into unknown situations and constellations such a type of love is an exercise in worlding: an exercise that simultaneously leads to the abolishment of a self, so that an "I" becomes imperceptible since it has become everybody and everything, has become the whole world.[30] In *Gould's Book of Fish*, this deterritorialization first announces itself in the following description of the narrator Gould: "Because of my newfound proximity to what hitherto had been little more than stench wrapped in slime & scale, I began to dream that there was nothing in the extraordinary universe opening in front of me, not a man or woman, not a bird or fish, to which I might be allowed to continue remaining indifferent"

(Flanagan 2003: 258). The first affect produced by becoming is thus the inability to remain "indifferent" to anyone, an "affection" that has the advantage of opening perception to an "extraordinary universe." This ability to be affected is further enhanced when Gould is visited in his cell by his lover, Twopenny Sal. When she turns to say good-bye, he is swept away in a state of delirium in which the borders between "I" and "You," "heaven" and "earth," are finally dissolved in a feeling that embraces the whole universe:

> How I wished to essay the universe I loved which was me also & how I wanted to know why it was that in my dreams I flew through oceans & why when I awoke I was the earth smelling of freshly turned peat. No man could answer me my angry lamentations nor could they hear my jokes why I had to suffer this life. I was God & I was pus & whatever was me was You & You were Holy, Your feet, Your bowels, Your mound, Your armpits, Your smell & Your sound and taste, Your fallen Beauty, I was Divine in Your image & I was You & I was no longer long for this grand earth & why is it no words would tell how I was so much hurting aching bidding farewell? (262)

Dissolving himself into a stream of words, Gould intones the hymn of a world that includes him, that he *is*; a world that his words cannot capture but *for which* he is writing *in favor* of a world that smells, sounds, and tastes; a world in which I and You become inseparably intertwined, a corporeal world in which every bodily inch is saturated by a feeling of holiness. It is a world in which Gould also embodies and encounters pain, treason, torture, and death. But it is also a world he nevertheless loves, as attested to by his "aching bidding farewell," since the same world includes wonder too—since he is able to love and embrace it. Becoming as such therefore makes it possible to transform "negativity into affirmative affects: pain into compassion, loss into a sense of bonding, isolation into care" (Braidotti 2006: 214). The dissolution Gould undergoes might be seen as his own way of disappearing, "a way of dying to and as [a] self. . . , [a] merging with the web of non-human forces that frame him" (252). And while Gould is dissolving, merging, and becoming-imperceptible, he still "conserves" his fish: as a "real" convict-painter by virtue of his fish drawings and as a character and narrator by telling a story that accompanies them and that allows them to be transposed into another form that can testify to their life. As such *Gould's Book of Fish* could indeed be seen as a "vessel—however crude—in which all Gould's fish might be returned to the sea" (Flanagan 2003: 29), although their immanent—and diegetically real—death cannot be prevented but can only be mourned.

> And when I finished the painting & looked at that poor leatherjacket which now lay dead on the table I began to wonder whether, as each fish died, the world was reduced in the amount of love that you might know for such a creature. Whether there was that much less wonder & beauty left to go around as each fish was hauled up in the net. And if we kept on taking & plundering & killing, if the world kept on becoming ever more impoverished of love & wonder & beauty in the consequence, what, in the end, would be left?
>
> And I began to worry, you see, this destruction of fish, this attrition of love that we were blindly bringing about, & I imagined a world of the future as a barren sameness in which everyone had gorged so much fish that no more remained, & where Science knew absolutely every species & phylum & genus, but no-one knew love because it had disappeared along with the fish. (200–201)

Against this destruction of life and love, the only weapon left to Gould is his "sharkbone quill & the very sepia ink with which I write"; he has only his writing, which transmits the ungraspability of materiality and a sense of wonder before the fish whose life—but not whose death—is captured on canvas. *Gould's Book of Fish* invents a story to accompany the story of the making of the fish drawings. It thereby allows its readers to imagine that story and to imagine how the real convict-painter Gould might have experienced affects of love for the world and wonder at the fishes' life. In addition the novel brings the life-threatening and harrowing conditions of Macquarie Harbor Penal Station to the fore, without necessarily merging these conditions with the lives of those who were imprisoned there. It thereby makes it possible to distinguish between life and the conditions of life, showing that the two cannot be lumped together. While transferring the horrors of a world that fundamentally disrespects life, the novel does not adopt this point of view but encourages a notion of respect for life. It hereby fulfills a function that Deleuze (and Guattari) has (have) on numerous occasions accredited to literature: "It is . . . a tool for blazing life lines" (TP2 187); it is there to "liberate life wherever it is imprisoned by and within man, by and with organisms and genera" (Deleuze 1997c: 228). By transferring a sense of wonder before the world, by conjugating its main narrators, Sid Hammet and William Buelow Gould, into the fourth-person singular of becoming—first fish, then imperceptible—the novel conforms optimally to literature's life-preserving function. Yet the novel would not be what it is if it did not run up against destructive forces, forces that Gould wants to escape, once again, yet this time by trying to forge a different future.

It is no surprise that a forger like Gould finds his biggest enemy in an even greater forger who commits the crime of inventing the official truth by keeping the island's records. Gould stumbles by chance one day across a secret entrance to the island's registry, only to discover that the records there have been forged by the settlement's archivist, Jorgen Jorgenson. The world as described by him "was at war with the reality in which we lived" (Flanagan 2003: 284), Gould realizes, concluding that the records' composed order and progress, time rendered as a sequence of events in which the interplay of past and present is absent, "was in these accounts something separate from us—so many equally weighted bricks that together made the wall of the present that denied us any connection with the past, & thus any knowledge of our self" (286).[31] As this kind of representation creates an "eternity of imprisonment" (290), Gould decides to escape—after being accidentally discovered by Jorgensen, who, in the ensuing fight, is in turn accidentally struck dead when a bookshelf falls on him. Gould not only aims to escape his incarceration but also has "an ambition far greater than escape: the intention of once & for all destroying the Convict System" (309). He wants to achieve this by taking a selection of records with him in his flight, which he will then present to the mysterious Matt Brady, a legendary man no one has ever seen, whose physical appearance changes according to the needs of the person describing him (312). In the fantasies of the prisoners and Gould, Brady is going to liberate the prisoners sometime in the future: "And after, Brady would circulate a truthful account that exposed the horror of the settlement for what it truly was, which showed the lie of the official record, of all official records & in doing so inculcate through the length & breadth of Van Diemen's Land a spirit of revolt" (313). But no such thing happens. Gould, now only a shadow of himself, stumbles through a deserted landscape and runs into Twopenny Sal, who burns the evidence that might have put Brady in a position "to organise his vengeance when he came to liberate

Sarah Island" (313). With no strength to follow Twopenny Sal into the future, Gould is once again captured and, in his last attempt at flight, becomes a fish. "I live now in a perfect solitude," he writes. "We fish keep company it is true, but our thoughts are our own & utterly incommunicable" (397). He concludes,

> Sometimes I even want to tap with my long snout on those divers' goggles & say: You want to know what this country will become? Ask me—after all, if you can't trust a liar & a forger, a whore & an informer, a convict murderer & a thief, you'll never understand this country. . . . Everything that is wrong about this country begins in my story: they've all been making the place up, ever since the Commandant tried to invent Sarah Island as a New Venice, as the island of forgetting, because anything is easier than remembering. (401)

If we were to ask the fish Gould, we would find a silence hovering over the past that could be challenged only by our readerly dialogue with ungraspable, slippery, mute, enchanting, lovable, and unrepresentable creatures, with our infinite responsibility of inventing the world by knowing that it is "a world in which man is lost & less but lost & less amidst the marvellous, the extraordinary, the gorgeously inexplicable wonder of a universe only limited by one's own imagining of it" (131).

3.8. A CONCLUSION BEYOND THE NETHERWORLD OF LOST SHADES

In *Gould's Book of Fish* (Flanagan 2003), the main protagonist, Gould, opposes the silencing conditions of the convict system by using writing and painting as means to counter viewpoints that exclude the perspective of those who suffer under it and are exploited and tortured by it. Through its particular assemblage of writing's and painting's specific artistic characteristics, the novel's configurations are able to capture the affective events that have escaped historical documentation. Although the narrative relies heavily on metafictional devices[32] to comment on its own constructedness, and although it constantly alludes to historical "facts" by crafting even its main narrator, Gould, on a historical figure, one can nevertheless claim that it goes beyond historical transmission by developing and deploying the powers of the false. To disclose their forces—specifically their "power to affect and be affected" (TI 147) through which fiction exceeds fixations that aim to contain it within the borders of a model defined by its fictionality—I think it is necessary to ask, as a last step, what new perspective it provides on historical events. This new perspective may allow readers to imagine and relate to stories that could have been part of Tasmania's past. The potentiality of these stories is usually disregarded for the sake of establishing a more heroic image of Australian history in general and Tasmanian history in particular (see Hughes 1987; Jones 2008; Shipway 2003). To trace this "new" perspective, one has to pay close attention to the specific becomings through which the narrator Gould and the narrator Hammet pass while telling their stories, becomings that enable them to be affected by a hyperbolic love for the whole world—an affect that is also stressed in Deleuze|Guattari's concept of becoming (see Lawlor 2008: 173–74). As I have shown, this love is most important to the novel's groundbreaking and enabling vision of life, which offers to its readers a perspective with significant consequences. I will take this love as a point of departure from which to criticize Agamben's notion of "bare life," which has become so influential since its introduction in *Homo Sacer* (1998).

In the understanding of literature inspired by Deleuze|Guattari and elaborated in this study, literature allows for explorations beyond individual memory and recognition and does not listen to "the ontophenomenological demand of Western politics" (Spinks 2001: 33). Literature neither displays "being" nor "experience," but it adds a perspective that reaches beyond being and experience by employing a constellation of signs that have been relieved of their referential functions. If readers submit themselves to the forces of literature, they have to interpret and explicate signs that belong to the created universe of the literary work, which develops its own vision that depends on the possibilities of literary expression. Reading might allow one to explore unworldly and untimely encounters that are enabled by a/the work of literature. Such encounters go beyond "the facility of recognition" (P 27) by suspending the opinions and judgments that hold sway over life and that reduce our ability to explore and to discover what remains unaccounted for, unknown, and new. By staying within processes of memory and/or perception, one participates in a circle in which "we recognize things, but we never know them. What the sign signifies we identify with the person or object it designates. We miss our finest encounters, we avoid the imperatives that emanate from them: to the exploration of encounters we have preferred the facility of recognition" (P 27).

Since literary signs are severed from the world, they allow for encounters that go beyond recognition, thereby setting up a micropolitical constellation that might even shift the terms of politico-discursive power relations. As Lee Spinks (2001) has pointed out, Foucault's notion of biopower has put the regulation of life right into the heart of power as exercised in modern Western nation-states. Going a step further, along with Massumi and Deleuze, Spinks claims that the procedures through which modern power operates are not limited to just regulating knowledge: images and affects especially "compose an investment in 'man'" (24). He therefore asks, "If the meaning of social and political codes originates in the stylistic or affective production of a border between human and inhuman 'life,' to what extent can art and literature help us to rethink the nature of the political limit insofar as the question of style lies at the heart of every aesthetic determination?" (24). To answer this question, Spinks draws on Foucault's view of literature as developed in *The Order of Things: An Archaeology of the Human Sciences* (1992), which closely resembles Deleuze|Guattari's own understanding of literature. For Foucault, from the nineteenth century on, literature is a form of articulation that is impersonal rather than subjective (296–304). Literature's language does not have to conform to linguistic rules. It is singular and expressive and goes beyond the need to resemble so-called reality. Foucault's point of view allows Spinks (2001: 31) to argue that in literature "thought cannot be confined to the perspective of a speaking subject or enclosed within the domain of signification." Literature shows that human beings do not have "a privileged position as the origin of truth and value" (32), since language in literature might be purely self-referential and even meaningless. It thereby points to the precariousness of meaning and the possibility of meaning's breakdown. Literature might disclose how the meaning of being human is constructed, while not necessarily investing in this construction. Therefore, Spinks concludes, literature allows for a model in which "ontology and politics . . . remain irreducible to the biopolitical horizon" (32). Literature might deviate from biopolitically inflected modernity, since it is not a system that mirrors reality. However, it can offer a point of view that allows reflection on the construction of reality.

In the following I will argue that literature's lack of accord with biopolitical encapsulations of life stands in contrast to the propositions of Agamben (1998, 1999a, 1999b, 2000) that have become highly influential in contemporary philosophical and political debates. In my reading

I will focus on *Homo Sacer* (1998), since it is this essay in which Agamben has most extensively elaborated his version of biopolitics. He takes up lines of thought from three different thinkers: Foucault's (1978, 1994) understanding of the intricate link between modern power and biopolitics, Hannah Arendt's (1963, 1958b, 1994) diagnosis of how modernity collapses any separation between politics and life, and Carl Schmitt's (1933, 1974, 1985) proposition of a close link between sovereignty and a state of exemption. Agamben assembles their arguments and hones them by arguing that since antiquity there has been a distinction between political life (*bios*) and a natural—or "bare"—life (*zoë*) in Western societies. The latter also separated the two forms of life and excluded zoë from the political domain. With the advent of the modern nation-state, "bare life" became the former's primary biopolitical object, forming an "excluded inclusion" (Agamben 1998: 7): "It is not possible to understand the 'national' and biopolitical development and vocation of the modern state in the nineteenth and twentieth centuries if one forgets that what lies at its basis is not man as a free and conscious political subject but, above all, man's bare life, the simple birth that as such is in the passage from subject to citizen, invested with the principle of sovereignty" (128). Nativity, rather than political engagement and decision making, becomes the criterion for belonging to a state and being the object—or target—of the state's management, care, control, and use of (bare) life. This politicization of life presents a new threshold and a new decision over "which life ceases to be politically relevant" (139) and can become "sacred life"—a term Agamben uses to qualify the status of a person or a group that can be killed without punishment (see 71–119). The decision that life is "not worthy living," is "socially dead," and the ending of which is not considered a crime marks the exception for the juridical order. Yet, according to Schmitt (1933, 1974, 1985), it is the sovereign who determines the exception, and it is this decision that provides the grounds for sovereignty. Basing his argument on Schmitt, Agamben (1998: 142) therefore argues, "If it is the sovereign who, insofar as he decides on the state of exception, has the power to decide which life may be killed without the commission of homicide, in the age of biopolitics this power becomes emancipated from the state of exception and transformed into the power to decide the point at which life ceases to be politically relevant. . . . Life . . . now itself becomes the place of a sovereign decision." With the advent of the German National-Socialist state in 1933, the state of exception becomes a "new and stable spatial arrangement inhabited by the bare life" (175). This means that the state of exception is no longer temporarily effective through the suspension of law but becomes the permanent rule in a localizable space. For Agamben, the concentration camp is the paradigmatic space in which the exception is spatialized rather than temporalized. Even more, the camp is "the political space of modernity itself" (174), its nomos and hidden ground. It is the space in which modernity's secret tie between power and bare life shows itself, a secret tie that is constitutive for the exercise of (essentially biopolitically exercised) power in modern nation-states. Once such a space has been constituted, "in which bare life and the juridical rule enter into a structure of indistinction, then we must admit that we find ourselves virtually in the presence of a camp" (174). Biopolitics might always become necropolitics, as soon as a location emerges in which the exception becomes the rule. Since the modern nation-state grounds itself upon the care, control, and use of bare life, there is always the possibility that the millennia-old division between political life (bios) and "bare" or "purely biological" life (zoë) emerges. This division might consequently lead to the institution of a place in which a life deemed unworthy of being lived becomes a life that might be taken without punishment. For Agamben, the link between modernity and biopolitics and the distinction between political and bare life is transhistorical and transcultural. Therefore he can conclude that "the camp . . . is the new biopolitical nomos of the planet" (176).

Agamben's thoughts on the biopolitical legacy of modernity have been criticized for a variety of reasons. Most prominently Jacques Rancière (2004: 302) argues that Agamben forecloses the possibility of political contestation, while Slavoj Žižek (2004: 15) sees Agamben's position as an "'ontological trap' in which [the] concentration camp appears as ontological destiny." Jessica Whyte (2009: 159) believes that Agamben provides only a limited basis from which to distinguish between different forms of life, so that the difference between life in a concentration camp and life in a refugee camp is nullified, or Agamben's diagnosis of the collective desubjectification of the working class cannot be distinguished from the "hopeless desubjectification" of concentration camp inmates. In a similar vein Ewa Płonowska Ziarek (2008: 89) criticizes the "negative differentiation of bare life with respect to racial and gender differences." These criticisms are justified insofar as Agamben's transhistorical and transnational analysis indeed does not account for different forms of biopolitical encapsulations of life, nor does it offer a perspective on any kind of power relation that cannot be subsumed under the relation between sovereignty and bare life. Here Agamben can be challenged by a variety of arguments, for example, by a close examination of the major figure he uses to illustrate bare life, the "muselmann" in the concentration camps. The muselmann is a concentration camp inmate who, as Phillipe Mesnard (2004: 145) explains, "suffered from clinical exhaustion and multiple, chronic illnesses and came to embody, in the eyes of fellow deportees, what man, subjected to extreme brutality and deprivation and on the verge of death, could become." Yet, as Mesnard also notes, not every deportee shared the fate of the "muselmänner." There were those who were immediately selected for death by Zyklon B who did not undergo the transformation that the muselmann stands for. Even the muselmänner were not dehumanized from the very beginning, but entered the camp as human beings who probably still had hopes of surviving their incarceration there. Agamben's concept of sovereignty's complete determination of bare life is not able to capture these differences. It is also not his point, since he wants to show that from antiquity to modernity power relations can be accounted for in the same manner. Mesnard's close reading of the different states and modes of dehumanization in concentration camps and Rancière's, Žižek's, Whyte's, and Ziarek's criticisms of Agamben's failure to differentiate between diverse historical events and actors have a number of things in common. Each questions the historical facticity of Agamben's point of view; they object to his theoretical tendency to neglect exceptions in favor of a generalizing, overarching analysis; and they do not agree on his identification of what it means to do politics as a human being.

I also share the concern that it is neither philosophically nor politically desirable to override exceptions to the rule and to fail to differentiate between how the nexus between sovereignty and biopolitical encapsulation varies according to time, place, and population group. In the context of my work, however, I want to advance a slightly different argument. On the grounds of Spinks's suggestions outlined above, I argue that Agamben fails to invest stylistically and affectively in an account of human beings in which they are *not* rendered in a dehumanizing way. This is partly caused by Agamben's specific reading of Foucault (1978, 1983, 1994, 2003a, 2003b, 2007), who posits that power is diffuse, pervasive, and productive and should be understood as an impersonal force that works through discursive practices that limit and regulate subjects. Agamben's rendering of power as the interplay between sovereignty and bare life relies on this depersonalized understanding, which he employs to show how bare life can be captured in full.[33] One strength of Agamben's work is that he shows the total domination of life; here he is in accordance with numerous descriptions of survivors of concentration and death camps. His theory might help to bring to the fore atrocities of colonialism and plantation slavery. However, as Ziarek (2008: 97) shows, Agamben "never considers potentiality from the perspective of bare life—that is, from the perspective of the impossible." She bases her arguments on Patterson's (1982) account of slavery and social death. Although she sees slaves as indeed having been excluded from the polis and having been exposed to a form of violence not defined as criminal, she nevertheless goes along with Patterson's (1982: 342) finding that enslaved people have always struggled for freedom. She therefore argues that Patterson's "insistence on the ongoing struggle for liberation by dominated people points to another legacy of modernity that Agamben sidesteps: the legacy of revolutionary and emancipatory movements" (Ziarek 2008: 97). She believes that Agamben focuses too much on one end of the power relation, sovereignty, and thereby fails to see transformative power, which she defines as "the negation of existing exclusions from the political followed by the unpredictable and open-ended process of creating new forms of collective life—a process that in certain respects more closely resembles an aesthetic experiment rather than an instrumental action" (98). In the understanding of literature inspired by Deleuze|Guattari and developed in this work, literature has transformative powers because it is able to partake in this negation of "new forms of collective life." Its storytelling is a means of calling for "a people to come" (TI 215), able to relate themselves to past events with compassion, sympathy, and solidarity. It prefigures a space for the readers-to-come that might claim a shameful past as its legacy. And it is a space in which bare life might be invested with a narrative voice whose perspective would otherwise be lost, since it cannot be captured in historiographical renderings that rely on passed-down historical sources. In *Gould's Book of Fish*, it is the convict-painter Gould's narrative voice that is invented. This invention counters the exclusion produced by an archive that has not recorded the voices of the dispossessed—in the case of Tasmania, the Aborigines and the lumpenproletarian prisoners. It forges a "false" voice that accounts for a life that is able to escape a dehumanizing colonial prison system, an escape made possible by retaining a loving gaze on the creatures it paints.

Gould's Book of Fish aims for a sense of wonder toward life, despite the fact that the depicted world is full of horror. Yet a world full of horror is nevertheless something that is perceived, and the perception displayed in *Gould's Book of Fish* is one in which the narrator gives the world that he describes certain hues in which the miracle of life still shimmers. The book's ability to shine and to affect with its colorfulness spills over to its (intradiegetic) readers. Hammock gets purple spots on his hands from persistently rubbing the cover of a book of fish that he finds in the antique shop. In this way his hands become an object of wonder to him, "so familiar and yet so alien" (Flanagan 2003: 13). If we take this little story within a story as a self-referential reflection on the possible outcomes of having contact with the book of fish, it is right to claim that Flanagan wants to infect us with the sense of wonder in the face of atrocities. This sense of wonder does not falter before the familiar and spills over into the present time, where it might induce changes similar to the one Hammet undergoes: "It was as if I had already begun a disturbing metamorphosis" (13). In *Gould's Book of Fish*, materiality evades ultimate capture (in a stable meaning), while it nevertheless provokes a sense of wonder. It is this notion of an elusive but wonderful materiality that might be transferred to its readers. The novel therefore allows them to understand how they partake in world-making by engaging with it affectively, by making sense of it and separating it into different hues, "as if the universe was a consequence of colour, rather than the inverse" (13). The book emphasizes that it is necessary to tell stories that would otherwise go untold and to narrate them in a style that can deliver a sensation that is as important as its sense. It thereby calls out, with all its might, for a "people to come" (TI 215) who can claim this possible past as their legacy, however shameful it may be. With a style that gives intensity and consistency to otherwise disparate elements (see Massumi 1996: 7), the novel draws horror and wonder together into one world, by having the most horrendous stories told through the eyes of a narrator who, despite facing atrocities and torture, also encounters the strangest wonders and the most impossible loves.

"Perhaps reading and writing books is one of the last defenses human dignity has left, because in the end they remind us of what God once reminded us before" (Flanagan 2003: 28). The sense that is entangled in the stories that unfold throughout *Gould's Book of Fish* is that one cannot be reduced to the violence that one faces or to the effect this violence produces; persons are more than their deeds alone and are more than the circumstances in which they are caught up. This sense is made possible by literary means. In this way the novel helps to account for those whose lives were lost in a cruel, torturous, and dehumanizing convict system such as the one on Sarah Island in the 1820s. Nevertheless, by depicting convicts and natives as loving and lovable persons, it refrains from reducing them to their conditions. It allows for a vision of life in which the impossible—in the case of Sarah Island, escape—is brought into existence. It thereby allows its readers to imagine "new forms of collective life" that cannot be captured by sovereignty, a "collective life" that *might* have been part of the past. Although it cannot be known what the "real" convict-painter Gould thought and felt while he was painting the fish, the possibility that he was affected by their beauty cannot be excluded. Similarly it would be wrong to assume that he did not include the wonders of life and love in his perception. To invest Gould with these capabilities means to refrain from doubling the violence of a colonial system that had no esteem for the lives of prisoners or natives. *Gould's Book of Fish* supplements historical accounts by giving these bare lives their own perspective, and this perspective, despite being a forgery, is not entirely inconceivable. The novel thereby allows its readers to invest in a "false" vision of life that refrains from dehumanizing it. Here *Gould's Book of Fish* conforms optimally with Ziarek's claim that potentiality should not only be considered as residing on sovereignty's side of power. The novel creates the possibility of claiming a legacy that—although shameful—is nevertheless able to convey a love of life.

CHAPTER 4

Making Time, Undoing Race

Richard Powers's The Time of Our Singing *(2003)*

They stand like giants immersed in time.
—Marcel Proust, *Time Regained*

They would compose and sing as they went along, consulting
neither tune nor time.
—Frederick Douglass, *Narrative of the Life of Frederick Douglass,*
an American Slave

History will never be rid of dates.
—Gilles Deleuze and Félix Guattari, *A Thousand Plateaus*

our fingerprints are
everywhere
on you America, our fingerprints are everywhere, Césaire told
you
—Amiri Baraka (Leroi Jones), "In the Tradition"

4.1. IS LITERATURE A PHONOGRAPH?

The opening sentence of Richard Powers's novel *The Time of Our Singing* (2003) places us at once in medias res. "In some empty hall, my brother is still singing," recounts a first-person narrator, only to continue, "His voice hasn't dampened yet. Not altogether. The rooms still hold an impression, their walls dimpled with his sound, awaiting some future phonograph capable of replaying them" (3). This description entails a certain understanding of time in which the past coexists with the present. The depicted action is defined through a present continuous verb form and the temporal adverb *still*, implying that the act of singing is continuing while the first-person narrator, brother to the singer, writes down the above quoted lines. Usually time is spatialized and imagined as a continuously unfolding line that runs from the past through the present into the future. However, the opening of *The Time of Our Singing* runs counter to this commonsensical understanding. A past action, singing, is depicted as contemporaneous with the present; its acoustic sound waves still reverberate from the walls. With an adequate instrument, this sound could be recorded. This description raises some questions: What kind of temporal understanding is developed in the novel? Where does it come from? What are its causes and effects? Is literature a futuristic machine capable of "writing sound," capable of acting as a phonograph?[1] And if literature can act as a futuristic "writing-sound" machine, is it capable of recording "the time of our singing"?

In this chapter I will look into these questions by offering a temporal-philosophical and literary-political reading of *The Time of Our Singing*, for which a semiotic model of intersubjective memory and a nonlinear time based on reverberations and echoes and hearing and singing is crucial. I will show how the novel establishes a "temporal and aesthetic zone" (English 2009: 362) in which past, present, and future times of individual members of the mixed-race family Strom intermingle with datable historical events. As such the novel recalls events that mostly pertain to a history of "race"[2] and racism in the United States but also social movements and actors that tried and try to counter racism's devastating effects. Most important, the novel shows how a lived, experienced time—one that I will call *durée*, following Bergson (1911a, 1911b, 1919, 1999) and Deleuze (1991 [hereafter B], MI, TI)—constantly changes the meaning of historical as well as personal events. By performing durée, the novel displays how being-in-time and being-of-one's-time can diverge from each other. In short, the novel differentiates between a lived, experienced durée and the datable historical events that can be perceived. One of the most prominent ways in which the novel disturbs naturalizing understandings of "race" is by performing different forms of time.

To help readers grasp these different forms of time, I offer the following example. In *The Time of Our Singing*, the first encounter between the characters David Strom and Delia Daley occurs when they meet and fall in love during a concert of the world-famous contra-alto singer Marian Anderson. This well-known and most influential concert was held at the Lincoln Memorial in Washington in 1939 (see Freedman 2004). This episode establishes the fictive participation of characters in historical events that have been passed down through historiography. However, during the episode in which the concert takes place, David and Delia "travel" into their own "future," so that the plot establishes multiple time lines. As the story develops, the concert and David and Delia's miraculous "time travel" become founding myths of the Strom family and are referred to and remembered in various ways by different family members.

This implies two things. First, it shows how events that take place in one location proliferate, while being situated in different times (the time of the concert and the future time of David and Delia in which the concert is long past). Second, it means that these locatable but temporally diverging events take on different forms of time. They are represented as historically transmitted and datable events, such as Anderson's concert.[3] They are represented as experienced durée, as in the description given about David and Delia's time travel, and in David and Delia's extemporized narrations of their untimely experiences that will have an impact upon various characters who retrospectively hear their story. In the novel's establishment of these different forms of time that are branching out, intersecting, or running parallel to each other, multiple meanings and provisional answers are provided for one crucial question that surfaces again and again in the novel: Will the color line be overcome in some reachable future?

4.2. THE NOVEL'S "MAKING TIME" AND ITS POWERS OF THE FALSE

In the context of this work, the novel's performance of a difference between lived and experienced durée and datable historical events is important for a variety of reasons. For one, it allows me to reflect upon the nature of time—a question that is of fundamental concern for philosophers and natural scientists alike. As Alia Al Saji (2004: 203) has argued, "The ways in which the lines of temporal filiation are conceived, and in which generation and transmission among so-called dimensions of time are understood, are not without consequence for the form of time itself, for the role that memory plays in subjectivity and for the openness of subjects to the future." This statement implies that the form we give to time, how we choose to represent it, will have an influence on the role we allow it to play in the lives of subjects. Concurrently it conveys the idea that the chosen form of time will influence directly the role we grant to memory and how we anticipate the future. Consequently the novel's representation of time is directly connected to the ways readers might conceive the relation of subjects to past, present, and future and how this relation is established.

It is precisely the novel's capability of "making time"[4] that connects it to the overall topic of this work, the powers of the false. As I stated in section 2.4, I see literature as being able to historiographically assemble recounted events anew and to establish new connections between time's different series and dimensions. In *The Time of Our Singing*, this assemblage is guided specifically by currently accepted scientific theories such as Einstein's special relativity theory, as well as ensuing notions of time. In particular I see the novel performing the proposition that "we"—existing creatures—live in a so-called block universe in which past, present, and future coexist (see Dieks 1988; Clifton and Hogarth 1995; Einstein 1961; Gödel 1949; Putnam 1967; Stein 1991). That is, through its use of literary devices as well as its content, the novel stages a notion of time and temporality that is in accordance with current physico-philosophical assumptions about time. In addition to this exposure of the temporality displayed in the novel, I want to discuss what "new" ideas about (social, political) change this form of representation entails. This is important since theories of a prevailing block universe sometimes provoke deterministic understandings of human fate (see Kennedy 2003: 66–71).

Throughout the course of this chapter, I will give a more detailed account of these theories and show how they are made accessible in *The Time of Our Singing*. I will outline the physico-philosophical assumptions that establish the novel's representations of time before showing how the latter is represented. In addition, I will revisit the controversy between Bergson and Einstein regarding their respective notions of time and thoughts about the question of whether physical and philosophical approaches to time can be reconciled. During their lifetime, this question was answered in the negative, despite Bergson's (1999) great efforts to bring the theory of relativity into agreement with his own understanding of time as continuous change. Einstein's (1922: 113) verdict that there is "no philosopher's time; there is only a psychological time that differs from the time of the physicist" determined their debate in 1922, and this has been considered the proper analysis for decades afterward (see Durie 1999; Scott 2006). However, I will argue that contemporary theories of space-time and newer readings of Bergson make it possible to combine Bergson's philosophy with Einstein's special theory of relativity. On the one hand, this concerns propositions about thermodynamics and its implications for space-time, as proposed by Ilya Prigogine or by Prigogine in collaboration with Serge Pahaut or Isabel Stengers (Prigogine 1941, 1947, 1973, 1980, 1993, 1997; Pahaut and Prigogine 1985; Prigogine and Stengers 1985, 1988). On the other hand, Deleuze's reading of Bergson (B, MI, TI), which shifts the understanding of durée from psychological experience to the experience of time's ontology, enables this reconciliation (see Scott 2006; Čapek 1971). It is my thesis that *The Time of Our Singing* is enacting precisely a notion of time that reconciles the philosopher and the physicist. Literature's ability to employ literary means to explore the suggestions of both philosophy and physics is thereby another instance of its powers of the false. In *The Time of Our Singing*, the enabling performance brought about by literature's powers of the false concerns time, and with it, questions of memory and anticipation as well as change, while it challenges the persistence of the notion of "race."

This is to say that the novel's deployment of narrative, rhetorical, and stylistic devices calls an understanding of time into being that contradicts everyday assumptions of its linear, constant, and unchanging nature. Through the forms of temporalization used in the novel, *The Time of Our Singing* is able to do more than just confront readers with a notion of time inspired by Einstein's special theory of relativity and Bergson's concept of durée. Powers's choice of words, his use of the characters' focalizations, the multiple perspectives on one event, and the novel's general composition all combine to enable *The Time of Our Singing* to use different temporalizations to tell a story of a mixed-race family in the United States. By taking miscegenation as a point of departure and by giving mixed-race protagonists a voice, the novel disturbs epidermological evidentialisms in which race becomes a theory of history, as discussed by Tavia Nyong'o (2009), Homi K. Bhabha (1994), and Frantz Fanon (1967). In the conclusion of this chapter, their enabling interventions into conceptualizations of "race" will be constellated with the forms of time that the novel brings into being in its literary world. I will show how *The Time of Our Singing* infects readers with the wish for a possible future in which the unjust and unequal social relations brought about through the notion of "race" are not necessarily overcome but are made questionable through the enabling trope of "racial hybridity."[5]

4.3. "THE PROBLEM OF THE COLOR LINE"

By positing that the novel problematizes a notion of "race," I wish to suggest that it uses literary means to perform W. E. B. Du Bois's (2002: n.p.) famous statement that "the problem of the Twentieth Century is the problem of the color line." Literary characters are an important means to grasp how the notion of "race" shapes and inhibits personal development and cultural achievement over time and space. In *The Time of Our Singing*, the most important characters are members of the extended Daley-Strom family. Delia Daley is the daughter of the highly educated and financially successful doctor William Daley and his energetic wife, Nettie Ellen, who invisibly pulls the strings and manages William's business. Intradiegetically Delia has two brothers and two sisters, Charles, Michael, Lucille, and Lorene, whose children will surface in the story line. David Strom is depicted as a talented physicist from Strasbourg who immigrates to the United States to escape the Nazis' extermination politics. Delia's family is black; her maternal and paternal ancestors are mostly descendants of African slaves. (Although she has white ancestry too, the American "one-drop rule" prescribes this racial alignment.[6] This alignment and its consequences are discussed at length among the different characters.) David's family is white and Jewish; they were persecuted by the Nazis and shared the fate of 6 million European Jews during the reign of German fascism, perishing in a Nazi extermination camp, their precise fate unknown. Delia and David marry in 1940 and have three children, born in 1941, 1942, and late 1945: Jonah, Joseph (often called Joey), and Ruth. Ruth marries Robert Rider, with whom she has two children, Kwame and Robert, who is also called Ode. As the story progresses, all of these characters have to cope with racializations and notions of racial belonging that have an impact on their actions, choices, and decisions. Although everyone in the family is an extremely talented musician and/ or has a strong inclination toward the natural sciences, none is able to see this talent bear fruit without undergoing privations, humiliations, and rejections that might even make it impossible to get adequate musical training or to build a career, as Delia Daley experiences firsthand.

Delia and David's decision to build a family together is based on their conscious decision to counter the color line, brought about by a vision conceived when they get a glimpse of a possible future uninhibited by notions of "race." But their firm conviction of doing the right thing when educating their children in such a manner that they might be able to "go beyond colour" will initially not be fruitful. Any attempt to define oneself and others independently of notions of "race" and "racial belonging" seems bound to fail. Sometimes these attempts fail because racializations hold people of color at bay, securing white privileges and social advantages through terrorizing notions of "white supremacy"; at other times such attempts fail because to "go beyond colour" is seen as a betrayal, an act of disloyalty, or a denial of solidarity with those oppressed by racisms. As such *The Time of Our Singing* stages different notions of "race" that are rooted in the history of black and white "race" relations in the United States. These "race" relations took shape in the enslavement of an estimated 11 million African people (see Eltis 2001) by white European slavers during the Atlantic slave trade (1519–1867). The enslaved Africans were transported to Europe or to colonized territories. By 1860 the number of slaves in the United States, one of the countries that participated in the Atlantic slave trade, increased through population growth to nearly 4 million (see Finzsch, Horton, and Horton 1999: 191).

For *The Time of Our Singing*, historical data are important insofar as they supply background information to many descriptions and discussions about "race" and "racial belonging" that are staged in the novel. As I will discuss at greater length, David and Delia's decision to disregard the color line will be met with suspicion and distrust by other characters. These critical voices are reasonable when considering the historical background of "race" relations in the United States, so that readers familiar with the "black and white" U.S. history might connect with their reservations. As Nyong'o (2009: 5) has pointed out, any sexual relation across the color line is a reminder of "a history utterly commingled with the history of Africans in America, one that structured the slave relations from its very beginning, one that shaped the subsequent, torturous logic of Jim Crow, one that underpins the vexed and enduring dynamics of color consciousness within the black population."[7] In *The Amalgamation Waltz: Race, Performance, and the Ruses of Memory*, Nyong'o is careful to avoid an argumentation in which "racial hybridity" becomes a "depoliticizing catchall" (5) that promises redemption from a heritage of slavery. In his view, the traumas of the past should not be turned into a biopolitical question in which "racial hybridity" becomes the remedy for "centuries of racial domination in the US" (5). But he also points out that "the mongrel past" might be "a historical alternative to overly burdened racial identities bequeathed us by slavery, segregation, and ghettoization" (7). "Racial hybridity" helps to envision a different past and a different future, and as such it can "leverage a critique of the present" (7). It exposes the historicity of the concept of "race" and troubles its underlying teleological temporality. In Nyong'o's view, "race" is not only a historical theory but "a theory of history" whose "assumptions regarding time and temporality" need to be laid bare (11). This means that he refuses to see "race" as an ontological marker; instead it is an epistemological tool that relies on ontology to eternalize itself in dermatological evidentialisms.

4.4. A MULTITUDE OF VOICES FROM DIFFERENT SHEETS OF THE PAST

As I said, *The Time of Our Singing* stages a notion of time that challenges the linear and spatialized representation that makes it objectifiable, measurable, and generalizable. When considering the racialization of historical processes, it now becomes clear how the staging of a tension between lived durée and datable historical events is connected to the topic of "racial hybridity." In some ways "racial hybridity" is a trope that challenges the very existence of "race," with all its historical connotations. It counters the preconception of racial purity, a notion that resurfaces again and again, even in contemporary discourses.[8] The trope of "race" in which it becomes a theory of history is dependent upon clear-cut divisions between differently racialized groups. As Nyong'o (2009: 103) argues, amalgamation offers the possibility of transgressing "the boundaries between blackness and whiteness," making it possible to propose "the performative inhabitation of the nation by a black dignity thriving outside the confines of its dialectical resolution." "Performative time," with its capacity to interpellate the people as a multiplicity, might account for a multitude of voices, whose stories might be contradictory, supportive of each other, or completely unrelated.

In *The Time of Our Singing*, this multitude of voices comes into being because of different first-person narrators with their own point of view. The novel is mostly narrated from a third-person or first-person perspective, either from Delia's point of view or through the narrative voice of her son Joseph. Delia's narrative voice is introduced when she describes Marian Anderson's concert on April 9, 1939, and continues until her sons go to boarding school. Joseph's voice takes up the story line at precisely this point, and the last event he narrates is the (historically transmitted) Million Man March to Washington led by Louis Farrakhan on October 16, 1995. In *The Time of Our Singing*, literary characters are the vehicles that allow readers to grasp how "race" shapes their development over time and space. The characters present a point of view and a voice that orients the narrative perspective and allows characterization. But the characters are also the medium through which readers are able to grasp, as Bakhtin (1981: 84) has argued, how "time, as it were, thickens, takes on flesh, becomes artistically visible." Temporalization is thus one important device for replaying "the problem of the color line," since it allows readers to understand how the characters' engaging, failing, or ignoring interactions with experiences, memories, and histories of racializations come into being. I will come to this important narrative device shortly.

Apart from the multiplication of voices, the novel's challenging of familiar notions of time depicts a situatedness in time that differs from its conventional model as an "irreversible and linear progression of psychological states" (Al Saji 2004: 204). An ontological understanding of time, such as one proposed in Deleuze's reading of Bergson, grants it an "extra-psychological range" (B 55). In fact when the ties between time and psychological states of mind are severed, the past ceases to be solely accessible through individual memories. It is "the whole integral past; it is *all* our past, which coexists with each present" (B 59). Bergson (1911b) and Deleuze (B) argue that it is this "past in general" that accompanies each present moment. For Bergson (and for Deleuze), the present is the most contracted state of the past. Bergson represents the relation between past and present as a cone: the present forms the tip of the cone, and the past fills out its body with different layers that press upon the tip, so that the past colors the present. Every present perception, "however instantaneous, consists . . . in an incalculable multitude of remembered elements; in truth, every perception is already memory. Practically, we perceive only the past, the pure present being the invisible progress of the past gnawing into the future" (Bergson 1911b: 150, qtd. in Al Saji 2004: 208). Furthermore the present moment is split; it propels itself toward its own future while simultaneously becoming its own past (see section 1.4). Memory retains a virtual image of this moment in which the present makes an "image of itself as past" (Al Saji 2004: 210). This virtual image is of particular importance in Alia Al Saji's concept of an intersubjective memory. In "The Memory of Another Past: Bergson, Deleuze and a New Theory of Time," she argues that the virtual image is not only "the image of the passing present" (212). Rather "esprit" (Bergson's term) or memory *adds a reflection* to a perceived object.

To understand Al Saji's (2004) suggestions, it is important to note that for her, the virtual image is a connection between the present moment and *the whole* of the past (see 215). In her interpretation of Bergson and Deleuze, the whole of the past is organized in different planes, in which it is "entangled and coexists at different levels of expansion and contraction. . . . Each plane instantiates a different rhythm of duration, style, speed, configuration and affective coloration, a different perspective" (216). Since the whole of the past is *"all* our past" (B 59), the virtual image reverberates not only with the memory of a particular past. Rather the *whole* of the past, *all* of our past, rings and echoes in the virtual image. This allows Al Saji (2004: 223) to argue, "My pure memory of the present is not strictly mine. It registers interconnections with other affective tonalities and hears other voices, so that each plane of the cone of pure memory is constituted as a 'world-memory,' even while these world-memories come together to form an intersubjectivity within the cone." Since the whole of the past presses upon the present moment, it is possible to perceive different "affective tonalities" (223) and "different perspectives" (216) in its sheets, to attune oneself to different tonalities and colorations, different styles, opening up to a "polyphony of memory" (227). Through Bergson's (1911b) and Deleuze's (B, MI, TI) theory of time, Al Saji (2004: 230) can argue that "memory is not closed in on itself, but opens onto other planes of the past and other affective intensities—onto other memories and lives, different in kind. . . . Time is unhinged by contact with other pasts and memory creates different futures." For Al Saji, this intersubjective and over-personal mode of memory and time is best represented by a model of receptivity that is grounded on hearing rather than seeing. Vision works selectively and differentiates between figure and ground, while sound allows one to hear different voices at once (223).

As I stated earlier, I consider it crucial for a reading of *The Time of Our Singing* to rely on a semiotic model in which echoes and reverberations, hearing and—as we will see—singing are used to describe the novel's staging of a nonlinear time and intersubjective memory. Multiple descriptions of the Daley-Strom family's music-making are given. They allude to important events and protagonists of American music history, especially that of Afro-American provenance. Marian Anderson and her seminal concert at the Lincoln Memorial is just one of many examples. In passing, a multitude of Afro-American performers' and composers' names are mentioned and alluded to, particularly those from classical music. In this way they are called back into remembrance to form an alternative archive. Harry Burleigh, Sissieretta Jones, Elizabeth Taylor Greenfield, Blind Tom, the Fisk and Hampton Jubilees, King Oliver and Empress Bessie, Paul Robeson, Marian Anderson, Dorothy Maynor, Mattiwilda Dobbs, Camilla Williams, Jules Bledsoe, and Robert McFerrin are but a few of the artists who find their way into the story. Already through this naming of Afro-American classical musicians, the novel counters a hegemonic cultural imagination: classical music in particular has become deeply entrenched with a notion of a highbrow culture that seems to be reserved for white middle- and upper-class bourgeois citizens rather than descendants of slaves.[9] This racialization of culture has forced many Afro-American classical music performers into oblivion,[10] a forgetting that is commented upon and countered by numerous remarks of the novel's characters. As such, characters in *The Time of Our Singing* become a medium for transferring knowledge about a forgotten musical history.

However, I argue that these allusions to historical characters and events are not the most influential examples for the use of knowledge about music and sound displayed in the novel. In particular Al Saji's proposal to use hearing and aural effects as enabling metaphors for grasping processes of memorialization and temporalization resonates well with their use in the novel. On the one hand, this concerns narratives that deal with echoes and reverberations of historical and personal events, transmitted and focalized through the voices of its main narrators, Delia and Joseph. On the other hand, these echoes and reverberations make themselves felt in the repetition of historical and personal events in the novel, events that are revisited again and again. These events take on different values and interpretations; they produce different echoes, while retaining their ability to make themselves heard and to reverberate. The novel's form and content relate to the enabling metaphor of sound, so that *The Time of Our Singing* could indeed be described as a phonograph able to catch different sounds, echoes, and reverberations.

Beyond the perception of sound, it is sound-making that displays processes of memorialization and temporalization. *The Time of Our Singing* also effectively shows how one *makes times* by adding voices to one's memories and histories. Going beyond Al Saji's (2004) model, the novel makes use of hearing *and* singing as enabling metaphors for capturing processes of memory-making and time-making. This means that not only are events and their untimely and intersubjective entan-glements passively perceived, but in fact people actively construct times and memories by *participating in the making of sound*, by "singing" times and memories into existence. This enabling metaphor is also pres-ent in the title of the novel, *The Time of Our Singing*. In the following I will analyze how these processes of perceiving and making memories and time are narrated. I will first consider a chapter that introduces and performs a different notion of time; then I will pick up the trail of repetitions that pertain to those echoes and reverberations that resound in the novel. I will pay particular attention to a musical game called Crazed Quotations played often by the family Daley-Strom, a game that might stand in as a *pars pro toto* for the novel's construction of a structure in which interpersonal memories and nonchronological time can appear.

4.5. MAKING TIME

It is David Strom, physicist, who mostly introduces different concepts of time, recounted through the narrative voice of his son Joseph. Tak-ing the chronological order of the story into account, it is in fact the chapter "Spring 1949" that gives initial insight into the novel's rep-resentations of time's ontology. In this chapter David and his two sons, Joseph and Jonah, then age seven and eight, visit the Cloisters, a museum located in Fort Tyron Park, New York City. The Cloisters is an existing branch of the Metropolitan Museum of Art. The "real-life" museum was rebuilt out of five different medieval French cloisters and shows a huge collection of medieval art, including seven tapestries that depict *The Hunt of the Unicorn* (www.metmuseum.org). This series of tapestries shows a hunting party that finds, observes, encircles, tames, and kills a unicorn, whose dead body is brought to a castle. The last tapestry of the series shows the mysterious resurrection of the beast, which is captured and fenced in, showing no resistance to its bond-age. In the novel it is the last tapestry that serves as an example for David's understanding of time, which he wants to relay to his sons. When showing them the tapestry, he insists that they need to answer the question "What is the picture *of?*" if they want to understand time (Powers 2003: 158). The boys are first at a loss; they perceive a picture without seeing its materiality. Only when David gives them the cue that the tapestry is made of knots, "no less than every picture we live in.

Little knots, tied in the clothing of time" (158), is Joseph able to understand his father's vision of time. He is able to see "what he sees. Every now, made from every motion on earth, is a little tied colored thread. And if you can find a place to see it from, all the threads combine, tied in time, into a picture, bound and bleeding in a garden" (159). Joseph's epiphany, recounted by his older self fifty years later (160), might in a nutshell exemplify one way the novel treats time. For the mantras that David intones repeatedly are "The universe has as many metronomes as it has moving things" (151) and "There is no single now . . . and there never was!" (156). All measures for time are "liquid and private" (156); every system's clock runs on its own speed.

David's description (as recounted by Joseph) evokes Einstein's special relativity theory. Einstein claims that in systems of reference moving at different, albeit constant ("inertial"), speeds, measurements will show that the elapsed time measured within one system of reference will differ when compared to the measurements taken in others. In systems of reference that move at a faster speed, time will run slower; it will dilate. The famous twin example illustrates the special relativity theory. A twin boards a spaceship and travels through space at a speed that is nearly as fast as the speed of light. When the space traveler returns to earth after two years ($t1$) have lapsed (as measured by her clock and calendar), her earthbound twin is nearly twenty years ($t2$) older than she is.[11] Since the astronaut has traveled at a very high speed, her time has dilated (see Bassett and Edney 2002; Hawking 1988; Kennedy 2003). Special (and general) relativity theory thereby contradict Isaac Newton's hypothesis that time is absolute and flows "equally without relation to anything external" (Durie 1999: vi), a highly influential theory in modern physics. In Durie's words, "Relativity famously recasts the physical universe as a multiplicity of physical systems of reference in motion relative to each other without absolute frame of reference" (vi).

Physicists maintain that the relativity of time cannot be experienced bodily by earthbound creatures (although it can be measured and observed in other moving systems). The differences in speed that we are able to produce with our bodies or through the usage of mechanical aids like cars, planes, or rockets are still not big enough to produce a measurable or perceptible time dilation. However, the fact that we cannot experience time dilation through our bodies is caused by our inability to move at a constant speed that differs significantly from our current velocity (which in some ways is determined by the speed of the Earth, which moves at an average of 29.78 kilometers per second around the sun, roughly ten thousand times slower than the speed of light). Nevertheless special relativity theory maintains that it is incorrect to see time as a constant and unchangeable phenomenon. Time's slowness or fastness depends on the velocity of the system of reference in which it is measured and on the slowness or fastness of the system of reference to which it is contrasted. David's understanding of time is indebted to special relativity theory in that he simply takes its insights for granted. For him, time is a phenomenon that is relative, and his knowledge and his view of the world are informed by relativity theory's insights.

Joseph's portrayal of David's understanding of time, in which every motion creates a visible trace of its occurrence and becomes like a "tied colored thread" in the fabric of time is thus in congruence with David's constant allusions to Einstein's special relativity theory. But what do we make of Joseph's conclusion that this thread forms part of a much bigger picture, which, if it were seen from afar, would tell the story of suffering and injustice? Joseph claims that time seen through his father's eyes shows more than a conjunction of different moments made by movements: time reveals the image of a being that is "bound and bleeding in a garden," whom Joseph has described earlier as an enslaved being:

> Then I see it: the chain. One end of the chain is clamped to the tree, and the other is fastened to the unicorn's collar. The collar is a cuff, and the unicorn is caught, a prisoner, forever. All over his body are wounds, stab marks I didn't see at first. Spurts of cloth blood pour out of his side.
> "He is captured. The humans got him. He's a slave." I tell Da what the picture is. . . . (Powers 2003: 158)

However, the description of a world-image that would be revealed if one could "find a place to see it from" (158) is no rendition of David's voice. It cannot be considered as either direct speech (David speaks himself) or free indirect speech (David's speech is reported through another intradiegetic or extradiegetic narrator). Rather it is an internal focalizer, Joseph, who renders here his impression of what he would perceive if he were his father and could perceive the state of the world in one image. This means that the passage characterizes first and foremost the literary figure of Joseph, while it simultaneously gives the readers a clue about how Joseph's empathetic telepathy is brought about. In the story line narrated by Joseph, David is mostly shown as a scientist who is chiefly occupied with abstract theories of time that leave no place for the perception of suffering. Primarily occupied as he is with the irreconcilability of mechanics with thermodynamics, and of relativity theory with quantum mechanics, David seems to be unconcerned with worldly events. Joseph recounts the summer in which his brother's voice breaks: "The world is full of snares. The Russians have the bomb. We are at war with China. Jews are executed as spies. Universities refuse my father as a conference speaker. His marriage makes him a criminal in two-thirds of the United States. But this [the irreconcilability between quantum physics and relativity theory] is the crisis in my Da's Zeitgeist: this flaw, this blot on the whole clan of scientist, on all of creation, whose housekeeping they do" (89). In this passage David is described as untouched by (threatening) worldly events. He furthermore seems not to care about societal forms of oppression through anti-Semitism or racism: that he as a Jew cannot speak at some conferences, that his mixed-race marriage is deemed criminal in some U.S. states does not seem to have an effect on him. His Zeitgeist is attuned not to the "spirit of his age" but literally to the "spirit of the time" (the English translation of the German noun *Zeitgeist*) and the mysteries of its being (89). Thoroughly engrossed in his research for the nature of time, he seemingly has no concern for history. Joseph's perception of David's worldview in which suffering dominates is therefore both exceptional and extraordinary.

Nevertheless one could argue that Joseph's perception is brought about by a particular chronotope[12] called "Spring 1949," which he depicts retrospectively, writing from a perspective that is "fifty years" (Powers 2003: 160) later. Furthermore his perception might indeed be justified when aligned with David's viewpoint. Although rarely disclosed in the narrative, there are two chapters in which David's perspective is recounted by an omniscient narrator. In "Easter, 1939" and "August 1963" readers can learn about David's specific way of looking at the world. In "August 1963" David's point of view is given when he and his daughter Ruth participate in the historically well-known and highly influential March on Washington for Jobs and Freedom. I will analyze this chapter later on. David is first introduced as a character in "Easter, 1939." Readers learn about his life story, that he is a Jewish physicist who fled from Berlin to Vienna "just before the Reichstag erupted in flames" (41),[13] only to avoid capture, transportation, and the death camps by escaping to the United States in 1938. David's thoughts allow readers to get a glimpse of his relationship to those datable, historical events in which his character is embedded.

In the chapter "Easter, 1939" David's way of dealing with the imminent Judeocide in Europe is crucial to my reading. David is on the Washington Mall to hear Marian Anderson sing, "the only American singer who can rival the greatest Europeans in tearing open the fabric of space-time" (Powers 2003: 41). In his ensuing train of thought, David establishes a connection between Anderson's concert in 1939 at the Lincoln Memorial and an earlier concert that he heard in the Wiener Konzerthaus in 1935. To him, "each step towards the Mall peels back the four last years, exhuming the day when he first heard this phenomenon" (41). At last, when he has evoked the concert so extensively that its "sound still hangs in his mind" (41), he becomes aware that the time in between those two concerts has created "a temporal rift no theory can mend" (42). While his train of thought jumps back and forth between different theories of time, from Milne and Dirac's dual time scales to Bohr's discovery about fission to the potential existence of tachyons, he can grasp neither the development of history nor his life's story. The difference between 1935 and 1939 is so immense that it defies understanding. While it is the same singer and the same European art songs that he hears, the passage from one "melody" to the other defies his senses, making it "unlistenable": "In between that theme and its recapitulation, only a harrowing development section, jagged, atonal, unlistenable. His parents in hiding near Rotterdam. His sister, Hannah, and her husband, Vihar, trying to reach his country's capital, Sofia. And David himself, a resident alien in the land of milk and honey" (42). What is depicted here is David's feeling of being overwhelmed by a development that changes his world so much that it defies his capacity to grasp it. What has happened remains "jagged, atonal, unlistenable." There is no (musical) theme that has undergone a variation or transformation. The development is disconnected from everything that came beforehand or will come after in David's life. The loss of his family and the uncertainty of their whereabouts, the pressing question of whether all family members are still alive or if one or the other has been captured by the Nazis and transported to a concentration or death camp: there is no way for David to integrate these happenings into a rational or emotional understanding. That he has managed to escape, that he is alive and well-off in "the land of milk and honey" seems a "caprice" (41) of destiny: "David Strom shouldn't be here, free alive. But he is.

Is here, walking across Washington, to hear a goddess sing, live, in the open air" (42).

It is life that has given David an exile, a temporary home. His understanding of the precariousness of his temporal existence is stressed at numerous times in the novel, mostly from Delia's perspective or recounted through the narrative voice of an omniscient narrator: "David Strom never trusted the future enough to own anything that wouldn't fit into a waiting suitcase. Even his appointment in the Physics Department at Columbia seemed a thing so fine, it would certainly be taken away by anti-Semitism, anti-intellectualism, rising randomness, or the inevitable return of the Nazis. That he could afford to rent half a house at all, even in the tidal-pool neighborhood, struck David as beyond luck, given the life he already owned" (Powers 2003: 9). When it comes to his children, however, it seems as if they do not perceive the silent and inexpressible sorrow inflicted on him by the history of European Jewry during Nazi fascism. Although this history is intricately linked to his personal fate and that of his family, it seems ineffable and impenetrable by "theory" (42), which means that it cannot be grasped when looked at. Ruth comes to perceive him as a white man that caused her mother's death; Jonas is too self-concerned to take greater notice of the suffering of others; Joseph is too much an entangled observer to understand his father. This situation changes dramatically in the early 1980s, when Joseph meets a concentration camp survivor in Israel during a concert tour:

> She answered in Russian. . . . She closed her eyes when we told our half of the story, said who we thought she was [David's sister, Hannah]. Hers were my father's closed eyes.
> . . . She smiled and shook her head. The shake was Da's. And in that one tremor, I knew him. Jewish grief. Grief so great, he never had an answer for kinship but to keep it from us. (548)

However, Joseph "knows" (548) about his father only at a later point in his life, when he intuitively grasps the affliction that his father has hidden from his children. Does this temporal delay entail that as a child, in spring 1949, he did not perceive the signs and traces of his father's grief? The narrative suggests the contrary. Joseph perceives his father's vision as one that entails and encompasses the perception of a being that is bound and bleeds, a being that is enslaved and that suffers.

How can we understand this percipience? To answer this question, I would like to draw on Al Saji's (2004) suggestion that we replace a visual model of receptivity with an aural one (see section 4.4). As explained earlier, Al Saji suggests that one make a "virtual image" of each present moment. This virtual image is connected to "the whole of the past," and as such reverberates with "the affective tonalities" of others and with "other voices" (215). If one takes her acoustic model as a starting point, it is possible to see Joseph's perception as reverberating with and echoing his father's. In addition I want to argue that it is most important to pay particular attention to the semiotic model evoked by music and sound, echoes and reverberations, hearing and singing. Theorists of semiotics such as Roland Barthes (1977: 179–90) and Julia Kristeva (1989, 1994) maintain that music differs in important aspects from language. Kristeva (1989: 309) argues, "While music is a system of differences, it is not a system of signs. Its constitutive elements do not have a signified." This means that sounds (of music) do not refer to a stable concept or object. Nevertheless both Barthes and Kristeva maintain that sounds (of music) can refer back to the materiality of the body that produces them. In the context of singing, Barthes speaks of the "grain of the voice" (see 1977: 179–90) that bears along "the materiality of the body speaking its mother tongue; perhaps the letter, almost certainly signifiance" (182).[14] Sounds (of music) do not necessarily need to be arranged in a meaningful syntactic, semantic, or narrative structure. This leaves the listeners in a position to pay attention to the articulating material carrier, to precisely hear "the grain of the voice," without any interference of meaning. A semiotic model of time based on aurality alludes to the possibility of sensing and perceiving sounds, echoes, and reverberations of past events, without necessarily understanding them. However, as I discussed in my reading of *Everything Is Illuminated* and *Gould's Book of Fish*, this failure to include a perception in one's knowledge or habitual recognition should not be seen as a failure. On the contrary, sensing and perceiving something that is "beyond knowledge" forces the self to open up to precisely that which is different, unknown, and/or new.

For my current interpretation of Joseph's perception, this means first of all that Joseph might "hear" his father, "hear" his "affective tonalities" (Al Saji 2004: 215) without making (immediate) sense out of them. Taking up a proposition by Leslie Morris (2001: 372), I suggest viewing Joseph's percipience as having been brought about by an attentive listening "to the very tones that constitute 'unspeakability.'" In *The Time of Our Singing* these tones are brought about by what is "jagged, atonal, unlistenable" and cannot be integrated into a meaningful composition. But if "the very tones that constitute 'unspeakability'" arise from "a temporal rift no theory can mend" (Powers 2003: 42), this means, first of all, that a semiotic model based on visuality cannot restore them. For "theory," as I explained earlier, is derived from the Greek verb *theorein*, which means "to look at" (see "theory" at www.etymonline.com). Aurality, however, includes what goes beyond individual (visual) discernment, what goes beyond knowledge. In addition some aural effects such as echoes and reverberations are by definition able to trace preceding voices, sounds, or noises, although they will repeat them in a distorted manner. It is my thesis that *The Time of Our Singing* assembles not just one notion of time, but several. Next to Einstein's special relativity theory and subsequent physical models of time, it also performs a notion of durée that, following Al Saji's (2004) suggestions, is best guided by an acoustic semiotic model. For my current reading, this means that I need to pay special attention to the ways Joseph performs echoes and reverberations of his father's visions and what model of time the literary rendering of this performance entails.

In the current context I want to argue that "Spring 1949" creates a certain chronotope that establishes David as a survivor of the Holocaust in a very intricate way. First of all, there is a difference between the "narrated time" (the time of the event taking place in "Spring 1949") and the "narrating time" of the story's narrator, Joseph (who tells the story fifty years later, sometime in 1999). This difference between "narrated time" and "narrating time" could hypothetically, for example, indicate that the narrator Joseph knows more than the intradiegetic character Joseph, who experiences the events. This indication is possible because readers can assume that the narrator Joseph, chronologically situated at a later point in time, has more knowledge about the development of the plot. However, "Spring 1949" is not told retrospectively by a first-person narrator. Instead it unfolds in the present tense, thereby creating the immediacy of the experiencing character. Furthermore a complicated relationship is assumed between the retrospective perspective of the narrator who is situated in the narrating time (that is, 1999) and the "prospective" temporal orientation of the narrative "that traces the events as they happened" (Phelan 1994: 227). It seems as if Joseph's (chronologically) future times already bear on his perception of events temporally situated in "Spring 1949." As such the temporality of the novel displays a time in which past, present, and future are stacked up in a misleading "now":

Our Dad watches his old neighbors walk along Bennett Avenue in stunned persistence. The war is four years over. But even now, Da seems unable to figure how we've all been spared. Spring 1949, he and his boys, moored halfway up the steps to Overlook. He shakes his head, knowing something none of his former Washington Heights neighbors would ever believe, now or in a lifetime of Sundays. Everyone is dead. All those names no more than myths to me—Bubbie and Zadie and Tante—everyone we never knew. All of them gone. But all still here, in the shake of our Da's head.

"My boys." Da says the word to rhyme with *voice*. He smiles, lamenting what he must say. "Now is nothing but a very clever lie." (Powers 2003: 151)

David's shake of the head is a gesture that is depicted here as immediately readable. It is a gesture that encrypts "knowing . . . [that] everyone is dead," a knowledge that remains unvoiced and is unbelievable, but which nevertheless is perceivable for Joseph as narrator *and* as character. Wherever the latter is situated, in spring 1949 ("narrated time") or somewhere in 1999 ("narrative time"), the peculiar conjunction of the adverb of time (*still*) and the adverb of place (*here*) attributes the described perception to him as a metadiegetic narrator and also as an intradiegetic character. *Here* indicates a direct situatedness on site, while the temporal *still* relates "two time phases, both of which are characterized by the presence of the same state of affairs" (Michaelis 1993: 197). Bubbie, Zadie, Tante, or his father David could "all still [be] here," present in the narrating time of Joseph in 1999, or in the narrated time of Joseph in spring 1949. Thus it is undecidable if Joseph's description relates how he is experiencing the situation or how he is remembering it. This undecidability is, however, no coincidence. As already stated, it is my firm conviction that the novel performs a "form of time" that is related to the idea of a "block universe" in which past, present, and future coexist. This means that the system of reference, "spring 1949," coexists with the year 1999 and with everything that comes before and after. In such a system "now" is indeed "nothing but a very clever lie." "Now" is a deliberate marker of time, since the past *and* the future are pressing against each moment.

Although my latter conclusion cannot be inferred by a Bergsonian understanding of time, I want to argue here that it can nevertheless be reconciled with it. For this reconciliation, it is crucial to pass through

Deleuze's reading of Bergson (B). As stated earlier, Deleuze shifts Bergson's philosophy of time insofar as he severs the notion of durée from an understanding of it as a psychological experience. For Deleuze, to experience durée means to find one's way into an understanding of time's ontology.[15] In *Cinema 2: The Time-Image*, he expresses his understanding of Bergson in unequivocal terms:

> Bergson has often been reduced to the following idea: duration is subjective, and constitutes our internal life. And it is true that Bergson had to express himself in this way, at least at the outset. But, increasingly, he came to say something quite different: the only subjectivity is time, non-chronological time grasped in its foundation, and it is we who are internal to time, not the other way around. That we are in time looks like a commonplace, yet it is the highest paradox. Time is not interior in us, but just the opposite, the interiority in which we are, in which we move, live, and change. (TI 80)

For Deleuze, Bergson's theory of time has changed over the course of his oeuvre. At the outset, durée was inseparable from "lived experience." With Bergson's notion of intuition, however, it is possible to "enlarge" or even "go beyond" lived experience toward its *condition* (see B 37). Intuition makes it possible to go beyond lived experience because it makes it possible to "state problems and solve them in terms of time rather than of space" (B 31). Through the body, "in the impatience of waiting, for example," intuition facilitates the realization that persons, animals, objects have differing durations that "beat to other rhythms, that differ in kind from mine" (B 32). For Deleuze, this intuitive perception of differing durations is crucial, insofar as it opens to a dimension of time that is single and to which we are internal (see TI 80), although it manifests itself in a multiplicity of lived durations that are accessible through an intuitive grasping of their difference in kind. Intuition proves that "my duration essentially has the power to disclose other durations, to encompass the others, and to encompass itself ad infinitum" (B 80). Intuition first allows the registration of different durations, yet over and above all it causes an affection that might be reflected upon, a reflection that might disclose a knowledge that goes well beyond experience.

Arguably it is precisely this affection that is described in "Spring 1949" and that explains Joseph's perception of his father's grief and his father's vision of history, although David has remained silent about his reasons for going into exile and about his family's fate.

> Jonah yanks Da guide-dog style across the street, toward Frisch's, and further explanation. . . . Jonah races and slows; Da dawdles and speeds up. . . . He has gone a little crazy. This is how we know it's Da. He can look down this length of Sunday street and see no single thing at rest. Every moving point is at the center of some hurtling universe. Yardsticks shrink; weights get heavier; time flies out of the window. He pokes along at his own pace. I try to keep our three hands linked. But there's too much difference. Jonah flies and Da drags, and soon Da's time will run so fast, we'll lose him to the past. He doesn't really need us. He doesn't need any audience at all. He's with Bubbie and Zadie, with his sister and her husband, working on a way to bring them back. (Powers 2003: 153)

In this passage Joseph perceives different durations, how his brother races toward the future and his father turns to the past. This knowledge, however, is transmitted bodily, through the linking of hands. As such it is transmitted through mimesis, a concept explained by Susan Buck-Morss (1992: 14–15): "The three aspects of the synaesthetic system—physical sensation, motor reaction, and psychical meaning—converge in signs and gestures comprising a mimetic language. What this language speaks is anything but the concept. . . . Written on the body's surface as a convergence between the impress of the external world and the express of subjective feeling, the language of this system threatens to betray the language of reason, undermining its philosophical sovereignty." For Buck-Morss, a mimetic understanding is constituted through "a sensory mimesis, a response of the nervous system to external stimuli which [are] 'excessive' because what [is] apprehended [is] *un*intentional, in the sense that it resist[s] intellectual comprehension" (15). As such, Joseph's understanding of the different durations of his father and brother could be interpreted as a "sensory mimesis" that displays a perception able to memorize and preserve a sign or gesture without necessarily transferring it into a linguistic and intellectual explanation. This preservation is brought about by a nonintellectual "sensory mimesis" that has its own durée, a "sensory mimesis" that is able to surface unexpectedly at different moments in time or places in space, linking even distant events with each other in a nonchronological way. In *The Time of Our Singing*, it is not necessary to have personally lived through an event to display a "sensory mimesis." Even events can be linked to each other that pertain to different characters.

Joseph's "knowledge" about the cause of his father's grief when meeting a Jewish survivor of the Holocaust is a point in case. Joseph narrates that he "knew" the cause of his father's grief "in that one tremor" made by the Jewish survivor when she "smiled and shook her head." Here I want to argue that this knowledge is brought about by a "sensory mimesis" that has preserved the gesture of his father's head-shake. However, the transference of this "sensory mimesis" into an intellectual and linguistic explanation needs time. As Gérard Genette points out in *Nouveau discours du récit* (1983: 23), every narrated event needs a duration or speed that Genette discerns on two different levels of the text: "durée d'histoire en longueur de texte, puis de longueur de texte en durée de lecture." This means that a narrated event not only has diegetic "lengths" that are modified by pauses, ellipses, summaries, or descriptions; the reading of a novel needs time too, which is the duration of reading. Taking these two "narrative durations" into account, it takes Joseph (in a reconstructed chronological story line) thirty years to come to terms with his father's grief embodied in a head-shake. Additionally, though, readers have to read 397 pages until they learn about Joseph's interpretation and until the meaning of a gesture is deciphered in such a way that it is translated into an explanation that gives it psychological and narrative depth.

Concerning the aural and temporal semiotic model that I am unfolding in this section, Genette's notion of narrative duration has the following meaning. First of all, I want to align the "sensory mimesis" that Joseph's knowledge entails with Barthes's (1977: 179–90) notion of a "material carrier" that sounds make perceptible, albeit not necessarily understandable. Although the "sensory mimesis" the novel depicts is not about sound in terms of content, it nevertheless hints toward its opposite, a silence that is audible and awaits a linguistic and intellectual coming to words and making sense. This audible silence is enacted in the shaking of heads and is recorded in Joseph's narrative. It is a "sensory mimesis" that reverberates with and records echoes of a gesture, crisscrossing time's different layers, encompassing and embracing different characters' experiences and memories that are encrypted in it. In the diegesis this echo is recorded quite literally in the temporalizations and rhythms brought about by narrative duration, with its pauses and delays, summarizing contractions and descriptive expansions. In the example of Joseph's knowledge about his father's grief, narrative duration shows how a gesture, although inexplicable, might unfold its possible meaning at another point of time, when the context allows for a renewed interpretation. For the transference into an aural model as suggested by Al Saji (2004), it is additionally important to consider that Joseph's knowledge is brought about by a personal gesture that displays an intersubjective memory, insofar as Joseph understands far more than David's life story in it. Joseph grasps in his epiphany different tonalities at once; he is able to hear a polyphony of voices, namely "Jewish grief," in its particular silences and unspeakabilities.

Furthermore Genette's notion of narrative duration is interesting for the aural semiotic model of an intersubjective memory currently under discussion, insofar as it infects the readers quite literally with a Bergsonian notion of durée. Narrative duration implies that readers have to endure greater time spans until literary signs make sense and/or are explicated. During the reading process, readers might have to keep in mind layers of hints, descriptions, characters' actions and reactions before they can reach a conclusion about what meaning they want to assign to a narrative event. Therefore, in some ways the novel constructs a temporal structure in which constant, indivisible change (in the assignment of meaning) is performed by readers, and sometimes by characters too (as shown in the protagonist Joseph).

In the case of *The Time of Our Singing*, however, it is important to notice that Bergson's notion of durée needs to be expanded. As already indicated on several occasions, the novel performs a "form of time" that is related to the idea of a block universe, in which past, present, and future coexist. As we will see in the following, this block universe is staged in the novel by having events resonate with each other that pertain to different points in time. These points in time belong, if considered chronologically, to the past, the present, and the future (if these temporal indicators make sense in a novel that in some way deconstructs their linear ordering). However, if Bergson's understanding of time is extended to *include* the future, it is possible to reconcile his ideas with the astrophysical idea of a block universe. Although Bergson was primarily concerned with the relation between past and present, it is not impossible to integrate a notion of the future into his model of time. If the past presses upon the present moment, coloring perception, it is not inconceivable that the future is, quite literally, pressing upon the present too. As Deleuze proposes, an ontological understanding of Bergson allows for this conclusion: "There is no present that is not haunted by a past and a future, by a past which is not reducible to a former present, by a future which does not consist of a present to come. Simple succession affects the presents which pass, but each present coexists with a past and a future without which it would not itself pass on" (TI 36). In Deleuze's model, there is a future that "coexists" with the past and with the present. However, the future is constantly affected by the passing present. Experiences made and decisions taken in the present will influence future events and cause echoes and reverberations in it. Nor is the past an accumulation of present states, but it changes constantly with each moment in a dynamic interplay with the present. In Deleuze's description, time itself has the potential to change. In fact time is changing "all the time," although it might change in an interaction (or thermodynamic interaction) with we who are making time.

The latter description is of particular importance in clarifying why I believe reconciliation is possible between Bergson's notion of durée—understood through Deleuze's interpretation—and Einstein's relativity theory and ensuing physical research into time, space, and space-time. As Pahaut and Prigogine (1985) have pointed out:

> Both classical and relativistic or quantum physics concentrated on time considered as motion. It seemed as if time as qualitative change lies outside its horizon. From this there results on one side the temptation, which we meet even with Einstein, to deny the existence of time or history, and on the other side there results from this the objections of philosophers like Bergson, Whitehead, Husserl or Heidegger, who see the pauper's oath of the scientific method in this denial. Strangely enough we can today set our sights on the possibility of a synthesis linking these two aspects of time with each other. (qtd. in Sandbothe 2007: 4)

The key to this synthesis lies in Prigogine's proposal of a "participatory universe" (Prigogine and Stengers 1981: 267–88). Prigogine (1993: 267) derives this idea from his own research on thermodynamic "dissipative structures." Dissipative structures occur in chemical fluctuations that are far from entropic equilibrium and are constantly exchanging (energy and matter) with their environment. To understand the importance of Prigogine's discoveries, one needs to know that in thermodynamics research, chemical processes have proven to be irreversible. Over time, element A becomes B, but element B does not become A.

This means that an unfolding of time is involved. In dissipative structures, microevents occur at random and need to be accounted for through a probabilistic approach. However, Prigogine was able to see that over time these random and chaotic chemical microevents gave rise to an order (for example, different gases separating neatly from each other). For Prigogine, this means that there needs to be a dynamic relationship between the microlevel and the macrolevel, which introduces "in a sense 'history' into physics" (273). Past microevents can be "remembered" by the system as a whole and determine the evolution of the system (see Sandbothe 2007: 54). In Prigogine's understanding, time is irreversible, qualitative change occurring in an interaction between microevents and a macrostructure. He argues that his empirical findings and their interpretation by him can give rise "to new theoretical structures" that are applicable "in the microworld of elementary particles or in the macroworld of cosmological dimensions" (264).[16]

Prigogine's "participatory universe" solves some problems of the block universe that have not been accounted for by physicists in favor of this view. The block universe is a logical consequence of Einstein's special relativity theory. If two events happen at a distance from each other in time and space, it is impossible to measure precisely how far the distance and how long the duration is that separate both. In astrophysical terms, neither time nor space is invariant and absolute. It is only a space-time interval that gives their precise position (a geometrical operation invented by Hermann Minkowski to show an absolute and invariant relation in space and time). The space-time interval indicates that we live in a four-dimensional rather than a three-dimensional structure. Einstein proposed that this four-dimensional structure implies that no slice of space-time can represent "now" objectively, for which reason "it appears . . . more natural to think of physical reality as a four-dimensional existence, instead of, as hitherto, the *evolution* of a three-dimensional existence" (Einstein 1961: 150, my emphasis). There are only slices in space-time that coexist, and in consequence past, present, and future are "frozen" in a four-dimensional block universe. Adopting this view means that everything has already happened in some slice of space-time in the block universe, which leads to a deterministic understanding. However, when the block universe is combined with Prigogine's understanding of time, one can conceive of events in space-time that, although occurring randomly and chaotically, will nevertheless influence other space-time events from which they are separate. There only needs to be a superstructure that relates the different events to each other, and this superstructure is time itself. As I will show in the following section, this is precisely the view adopted in *The Time of Our Singing*.

4.6. THE NOVEL AS A BLOCK UNIVERSE AND ITS REVERBERATING TIMES

The question of whether singular actions and events can reverberate with and change a societal structure over the course of time despite occurring at random and seemingly chaotic instants is replayed varyingly in *The Time of Our Singing*. It acquires, however, the most pressing urgency when it comes to the notion of "race." As already stated, racializations are shown to be a means of inclusion and exclusion as well as exploitation, control of resources, and white privilege. Although the determining features of "race" lack any scientific verifiability, as a conceptual category it represents a stalemate version of history, in which everything stays the same when it comes to the distribution of wealth, resources, and access to societal privileges. In this section I will pay close attention to the temporalizations of "race" suggested in the novel. With Fanon (1967), Bhabha (1994), and Nyong'o (2009) as theoretical background I will show how time and history represent two different forces and how the book aims to overcome "race as a theory of history" as diagnosed by Nyong'o.

In *The Time of Our Singing* the story of William and Delia demonstrates most forcefully how the notion of "race" inhibits personal advancement and growth, how it is highly unjust and unfair, how it nourishes hate and humiliation, and how it can lead to arson and murder and elicit the brutality of government agencies. This brutality finds its way into the story line by depicting the political suppression of the Black Panther movement, by linking their history to the character of Ruth, the daughter of David and Delia. However, Delia's story is much more prominent in the novel. Not only is she a narrative voice through which large parts of the story are recounted, but her fate is also decisive in determining the development of the plot. Her sudden death, caused by the explosion of a furnace, gives rise to different interpretations among family members of how it came about. The question of whether the furnace exploded by accident or by arson, if Delia was a victim of unhappy circumstances or if her death was a racially motivated murder will jeopardize the family. In addition to David, Delia is also a narrator and participates in an instance of time traveling that takes place during Marian Anderson's concert at the Lincoln Memorial in 1939. Through her voice and actions, readers learn about the couple's time travel, what it felt like and what kinds of changes were caused by the experience. As a focal point and as a focalizer, Delia is therefore instrumental in determining how the notion of "race" and its effects are depicted in the novel.

It is crucial that Delia is introduced as an outstanding singer. Her father, William, tells her that she "sounds like the angels raised from the dead, if they still bothered with the likes of us down here. A sound like that could fix the broken world" (Powers 2003: 36). The first words that David directs at her are to ask if she is a professional singer (220). Jonah, her first-born son, describes her voice as the "sun coming up on a field of lavender" (295). Yet despite being characterized as an outstanding talent, Delia is not allowed into the Philadelphia Conservatory. When its vocal faculty learns that she is black, they turn her down and leave her without hope of "be[ing] schooled at the upper level of her skills, let alone the lower reaches of her dreams" (88). Through the rejection and dismissal by white characters safeguarding their privileges, Delia is shown to tacitly share this shattering of high hopes with her father. William Daley is a man of outstanding achievements. He trained as a doctor of medicine at Howard and is a certified member of the Talented Tenth of this institution (75). As the plot develops, it is revealed that he, like Delia, has experienced racial hatred and racialized humiliations, but their individual experiences of racism do not lead them to the same conclusions. One evening in August 1945, shortly after the bombing of Hiroshima and Nagasaki, they get into an argument about strategies and tactics against racism that will tear them apart.

The starting point of the argument between William, Delia, and David is the bombing itself. William and Delia know that David has participated in the making of the atomic bomb; at different points in time, David has disclosed to them the secret of his travels to Oak Ridge and his participation in the Manhattan Project, consisting in thinking about neutron absorption and "problems surrounding the implosion" (Powers 2003: 415). However, William comes to see the second blast, the bombing of Nagasaki, as being motivated by racist thinking. He writes his son-in-law with a request for an explanation:

Would this country have been willing to drop this bomb on Germany, on the country of your beloved Bach and Beethoven?

Would we have used it to annihilate a European capital? Or was this mass civilian death meant, from the beginning, to be used only against the darker races? . . . I had in mind a different victor, a different peace, one that would put an end to supremacy forever. We were fighting against fascism, genocide, all the evils of power. Now we've leveled two cities of bewildered brown civilians. . . . You may not understand my racializing these blasts. Maybe you'd have to spend a month in my clinic or a year in the neighborhoods near mine to know what I wanted this war to defeat. (416)

William's standpoint certainly resonates with historical sources and historical investigations into Afro-American views on the bombing of Hiroshima and Nagasaki (see Boyer 1985; Jerome and Taylor 2006; Kearney 1998). As Paul S. Boyer (1985: 199) has pointed out, blacks had their "suspicion that the bomb had been deliberately reserved for use against Asians rather than Europeans." Boyer quotes the newspaper *Washington Afro-American* from August 18, 1945, which reported that the Hiroshima news "'revived the feeling in some quarters that maybe the Allies are fighting a racial war after all.' The editorial suggested that American military planners may have spared the Germans, who, 'after all, represent the white race,' and 'saved our most devastating weapon for the hated yellow men of the Pacific'" (199). The fictional episode thereby establishes itself as "historiographic metafiction" (see Hutcheon 1988), creating a space in which a counterarchive is established that records Afro-American mentalities. The argument between William, Delia, and David replays different strategies of dealing with racism and the question of "race." The historical division between Afro-American and Jewish communities in the United States, last visible in the 1960s, when conflicts arose between the two communities about universities, labor-management relations, housing, welfare systems, and schools (see Harris and Swanson 1970), also plays its part in the novel's construction of metafictional historiographical hints. David's German Jewish roots and the persecution and extinction of his Jewish family are depicted as an important issue in his response to William's remarks, a response that he will describe to Joseph shortly before his death (see Powers 2003: 463–70). However, William's critical stance toward the atomic bomb is shown to be justified, as the military necessity has not been historically proven.[17] One of his sons is drafted into the U.S. Army, suffers under racist structures in the military, and dies a soldier. Thus William can attribute a personal loss to U.S. involvement in World War II. Furthermore his standpoint reflects a commonly held attitude among Afro-Americans, who extensively debated the ethical necessity of U.S. military involvement in that war. Many Afro-Americans, both soldiers and civilians, were trying to wage a "double V campaign": fighting against fascism in military actions abroad, as well as fighting against "racial" injustice and inequality at home (see Cooper 1998). The novel's plot thereby resonates with historiographically recounted developments that are given a fictional setting.

Before I discuss the philosophical implications of the argument between Delia and William, I want to give a short summary of the plot development and the depiction of Delia's and William's standpoints. After announcing his wish to discuss whether the atomic bombings reinforce white supremacy, William arranges a visit with his daughter and her husband when he attends a medical conference in New York. But when he arrives, something has happened that he cannot let go of. His daughter can sense that he is churning inside, embittered by a feeling that he cannot ignore, a feeling that she recognizes from other encounters with him, when he had to struggle with the effects of racial discrimination: "She feels him struggle, with the last scrap of dignity so powerful in him, to bite down his rage and swallow it whole, a cyanide capsule they give to agents caught behind enemy lines. She knows he won't be able to. He'll wrestle and fail, no less spectacularly than the world has failed him" (Powers 2003: 417). It becomes clear that William has not been admitted to the conference, stopped by the hotel detective and escorted out later by a small police force. As the plot unfolds, he can only resort to falling back on identity to counter these humiliations: "His eyes test the extremes of punishment not yet visited on him. Stripped so easily, he knows no bottom. Held and humiliated for an hour: it cost him nothing. Laughable. Dust yourself off and walk away. But if that, why not locked up in the coat check, chained to the shoe-shine stand in Penn Station, kept illiterate, driven out of the polling place, beaten up for turning down the wrong alley, or hung from a ready sumac? Even the most stubborn self in time will be identified" (412). Confronted with his own knowledge about the possible fate every black man might encounter—and in a different way, every black woman, every gender or sexual dissident, every person of color—William embraces his "race." As such he cannot accept the choices his daughter has made, is making, and will make: to marry a white man, to love and sing classical music, and, most of all, to try to raise their children "beyond race" (424). For him, there is no "beyond race" except for those who enjoy the benefit of not seeing the effects of color, for those who cling to the privileges of white supremacy. William considers Delia's wish to raise her children "beyond race" a gesture of nonsolidarity with those oppressed by racism. For William, "beyond race" is synonymous with "beyond me" (426). He and Delia are divided on the question of "race," and after he leaves her and David that evening he never sees them again.

What does Delia make of such accusations? Does she become colorblind after marrying a white man? Does she deny solidarity with those oppressed by racism? The development of Delia's character and the events she encounters do not suggest that she has disengaged herself from the question of "race." Mixed race does not promise redemption from a heritage of slavery. Rather it is a reminder that "race" is a construction, that there is no clear line that separates one "race" from another. As such Delia is much more likely to be a target for racial hatred than a vehicle for progress that could shift the color line:

> Some girlish, unenslaved part of her imagined their marriage might cure the world. Instead, it compounds the crime by assaulting all injured parties. . . . Now even her simplest needs become unmeetable. She'd like to walk down the street with her husband without having to play his hired help. . . . She'd like to sling her baby on her shoulder, take him shopping, and for once not bring the store to a standstill. She'd like to come home without venom all over her. It will not happen in her life-time. But it must happen in her son's. (Powers 2003: 329)

Delia's insistence on a vision that looks "beyond race" is thus brought about by her love for her children; for her, their future should and must look different. It is this possible "future" that she caught a glimpse of when she met David for the very first time. The day after Delia has the argument with her father, she decides that she will not adopt his point of view that she needs to expose her children to the effects of racism. She decides that

> she won't surrender anything. She'll give them warmth, welcome, riffing, the congregation joy of call and response, a dip in that river, deep enough to sport in all their lives. She must give them the riches that are theirs by birth. *Negro. American.*

Of course they must know the long, deadly way those terms have come. But she refuses to give them self by negation. Not the old defeating message that they've already been decided. All she can give them is choice. Free as anyone, free to own, to attach themselves to any tune that catches their inner ear. (479)

For William, turning to "race" as an identificatory marker means to rely on it as a source of belonging, as a signifier that can potentially enable solidarity of the oppressed. For Delia, however, "race" is a marker that prescribes and determines to which "songs" her sons and daughter can have access. She is determined not to submit in advance to the restrictions of "race." Instead of "race," she wants to give them "choice" in the hope that time will offer them a better future and that they might jump into it with both feet. Her actions and choices, which are crucial for the development of the novel's plot, replay the question of whether time can overcome a history in which "race" becomes forever a marker of a racialized identity, whether as a source of belonging and solidarity or one of denial and hatred. Delia's point of view, for which her father considers her guilty, comes down to this:

To think that recognizing means more than its opposite. To think that race is still in motion. That we stand for nothing but what our children might do. That time makes us someone else, a little more free.

Time, she finds, does nothing of the kind. Time always loses out to history. Every wound ever suffered has only lain covered, festering. (329)

Although Delia thinks in the deep of the night that "time loses out to history," it is nevertheless her and David's firm belief that there might be a new choice "beyond race" that their family will invent. As already stated, their hope for a future uninhibited by the notion of "race" comes into being by their time travel and its ensuing vision of future possibilities, whose physico-philosophical implications I will contemplate in the conclusion of this chapter. Yet before looking into David and Delia's time travel, I want to consider the argument Delia has with William in more detail, since it resonates well with discussions and propositions of some black scholars, in particular Fanon (1967), Bhabha (1994), and Nyong'o (2009). They have all contributed to exposing the specific time and temporality of "race" by which it becomes a "theory of history," as Nyong'o has argued.

In the current context, Nyong'o's proposal that we see "racial hybridity" as an enabling tool for unsettling notions of "race" is particularly important to determine what stakes are involved when a long-standing debate among people of color is personified through literary characters. By positing "race" as a theory of history, Nyong'o implicitly and explicitly relies on postcolonial thinking and its critique of Western historiography. In particular Bhabha's differentiation between "pedagogic" and "performative" time is important to his argument. To deploy these terms fruitfully in a discussion of *The Time of Our Singing*, it is important to understand how narratives of "racial hybridity" can unhinge the notion of a linear historical time unfolding teleologically, a notion of time in which human progress is homonymous with racial progress.

To approach Bhabha's postcolonial criticism of Western historiography, I rely on his rereading of Fanon's "The Fact of Blackness" (1967: 109–41). Fanon's famous chapter in *Black Skin, White Masks* begins with the exclamation of a "corporeal malediction" (111): "'Dirty Nigger!' Or simply 'Look, a Negro!'" (109). For Fanon, this malediction is a "historico-racial schema" imposed on the "black man" by "the other, the white man, who had woven me out of a thousand details, anecdotes, stories" (111). This "historico-racial schema" makes any ontology of the black man impossible, since being black never stands for itself but is always already part of a relation, bounded by the role it plays for the white man (110). Fanon performs in his text the impossibility of the black man to be identified with humanist and Enlightenment ideals, "to be a man among other men," "to come lithe and young into the world that was ours and to help it build it together" (112–13). Subsequently he lays bare how the white world's overt or implicit refusal to identify the black man with ideas of continuity, rationality, and progress produces the black man's despair, frustration, anger, and reflexive pride.

In his interpretation Bhabha (1994: 338–68) shows how two different sorts of time rub against each other in Fanon's text and cancel each other out. In Bhabha's view, Fanon not only speaks from a "time-lag of cultural difference" (340) but also refuses to assume the position allocated for the black man in which he has to "occupy the past of which the white man is the future" (341). In Bhabha's reading, Fanon's refusal to accept his place as the white man's belated other constitutes a temporal caesura that opens up an "enunciative space" (339). This "enunciative space" makes the disjunctive temporalities of modernity graspable, while it renders perceptible the active struggle of a postcolonial subject to "make a name for [himself or her]self" (Derrida 1985: 174, qtd. in Bhabha 1994: 347).

Bhabha does not fail to notice that this "name-making" entails the claim to a radical singularity, a position in solidarity with the oppressed. When Fanon (1967: 136) writes that "Negro experience is not a whole, for there is not merely one Negro, there are Negroes," Bhabha (1994: 341) remarks he is *not* performing "a postmodern celebration of pluralistic identities"; rather he "proclaims the oneness of the suffering and the revolt" (342), a performance that goes against the "pedagogical time" of modern nationalism, where to make "out of many one" becomes the formula for a people. In contrast to nationalism's "pedagogical time," which makes one out of many, "performative time" acknowledges "the people as many." In performative time subjects of enunciation emerge to "demonstrate the prodigious, living principles of the people as contemporaneity" (208). The divergent double time of modernity therefore consists in the "signs of a coherent national culture, while the very act of the narrative performance interpellates a growing number of national subjects" (209). Performative time is thus the effect of a narrative's performativity, of narrative's ability to make subject positions available in the narrative process. Performative time enacts the refusal to lump many people together into a single whole, while it displays the urge for connectivity and solidarity.

It is precisely the subaltern's textual, cultural, structural refusal, the subaltern's creation of a caesura, that makes the peculiar double time of modernity visible and that enables an enunciative space which Nyong'o's argumentation takes up. In Nyong'o's (2009: 12) reading of Bhabha, performative time destroys the reproducibility of "docile, useful bodies." This is the case because performative time enacts a moment that is *disjunctive* to the nation's interpellation of a people as one, an interpellation that takes place in a "homogeneous, empty time" (12). In performative time a "disruptive immediacy" emerges, which cannot be lived in the "antechambers of history" (12). "Racial hybridity" is a sign that unsettles narratives of a racialized progress, of a homogeneously developing racialized history, and so destroys "the ability of race to narrativize time" (12). "Racial hybridity" thus unhinges the underlying temporality of "race" in which it acts as a theory of history. It performs the need to "make a name"; it initiates the cathexis to find a story to accompany its unsettling factuality.

It is worth relating *The Time of Our Singing* to Bhabha's suggestions of a performative time that creates a rupture in the empty, continuous time of modernity. As Bhabha shows, this rupture allows for an enunciative space in which "the people as many" can emerge who are in need of connecting in solidarity with each other. Nyong'o, who connects the enabling disruption of performative time to the possibilities of "racial hybridity," warns his readers of uncritically taking on a notion of "reproductive futurity." In Nyong'o's (2009: 171) view, "love, romance and reproduction" are not innocent ways to achieve a just and equal postracial society. In the United States these notions have even been historically proved to maintain racial hierarchies through the "one-drop rule" and the "rule of hypodescent." To see heterosexual reproductive relations as already achieving a postrace society means to yoke heterosexuality "to a vision of politics in which the summum bonum is indefinitely deferred through the figure of the child" (163). Nyong'o points out that any vision that sees racial justice as being achieved through a heterosexual and reproductive "racial mixing" limits "the range of what the future, and by extension, politics, may allow to mean" (171). Most important, he stresses that a turn toward an always deferred futurity of a coming postrace generation too easily abandons the ineffable history of slavery and severs the future from the past.

Here I want to argue that when *The Time of Our Singing* narrates the argument between Delia and William, Nyong'o's (2009: 171) critical viewpoint on "reproductive futurity," achieved by "love, romance and reproduction," is precisely what is made available to readers. Delia's wish for her children to have a future that is just and in which they can choose who they are is countered by William's demand that they need to be introduced to and educated about "history" (Powers 2003: 419). But William's call for history, delivered with a "whip crack of his voice" (419), relies on a notion of "race" in which it becomes not only historical but precisely a "theory of history" in Nyong'o's sense. As William later recounts to Joseph, he was allying himself with "hypodescent" (563), making a social history of "race" into a natural one. This is the case because his need to identify with his "race" is fulfilled only if he accepts the definition with which its essentializing notions have been passed down through history. The identification of "race" enforces the category itself, although it is precisely slavery's cruel and unimaginable exploitation of human beings, as well as its historical continuities in, for example, racial segregation, racial inequality, and racist murder and lynching, that a recourse to "race" in the U.S. context aims to make visible. As Kwame Anthony Appiah and Amy Gutmann (1996: 33) argue, to refer to "race" always means "to identify the things to which it applies, the things we refer to when we speak of 'races.'" To escape essentialist notions of race, they therefore introduce the term *racial identity* to take into account the fact that "individual identities are complex and multifarious" (134). They thereby strengthen a notion that Du Bois (1975: 116) attributes to the "badge of color," a badge he describes as "relatively unimportant save as a badge" and whose real significance is grounded on its ability to ally itself to the "social heritage of slavery." To wear the badge of color means to identify the continuity of racial thinking and racisms, to do the necessary work of "disidentification" (see Muñoz 1999) with essentialist notions of "race." In *The Time of Our Singing*, however, William falls into the trap of essentializing "race" during the argument with his daughter. Because he is identified, stigmatized, and humiliated as whites' fantasized "other," his only escape route is to fall back on a self-definition that takes pride in the category of blackness, while excluding other (strategic, ironic, distant, humorous) identificatory possibilities (as proposed, for example, by Appiah and Gutmann 1996; Du Bois 1975; hooks 1990; Muñoz 1999; Silverman 1996; Spivak 1987, 1993). By essentializing "race" and not allowing his daughter other identificatory options than his own, William indeed "go[es] imperial" (Appiah and Gutmann 1996: 84) in the sense of to essentializing racial notions of collective identities that suppress "the possibility of identification with others," identifications that individuals might also "share with people outside their race or ethnicity" as part of their collective identity (134). Only much later is William able to realize his mistake, while giving his understanding of blackness an inclusive dimension. He tells Joseph his version of the argument with Delia and David:

> "Your parents thought they saw some way out of the rule. The rule of the past." He stares out onto the spring lawn, trying to picture what they saw. "They wanted a place with as many categories as there were cases. But they still had to bring you up here." His voice was desperate, racing the clock. "They wanted a place where everyone was his own tone." He shook his head. "But that's blackness. There is no shade that it doesn't already contain. You weren't any more double than any of us. Your mother should have known that." (Powers 2003: 562)

Blackness here transcends skin color and moves toward a notion of solidarity as proposed in Bhabha's (1994: 342) reading of Fanon, specifically by pronouncing "the oneness of the suffering and the revolt." It acknowledges the singularities of protagonists who are parts of a composition through which a social notion of blackness comes into being. William reaches the conclusion that "we're supposed to take everybody in. All the rest. . . . Everyone. All the half-castes ad quarter-castes and one-thirty-second castes. We should have made room for you" (Powers 2003: 563). All shades are welcome to "become black" and to join a struggle that aims to overcome racism. Not only is the whipping of slaves recalled in the description of the "whip crack of [William's] voice" (419), but its inclusion as a characteristic of his voice also suggests that this recall is spoken in a voice that allows a space to open up, as small as a crack in a wall but nevertheless existent when it separates itself from the whip. While it betrayed William's anger when arguing with his daughter, it becomes in this interpretation what bell hooks (1990: 152) has called the "space in the margin," which she defines as "that inclusive space where we recover ourselves, where we meet in solidarity to erase the category colonized/colonizer." The "whip crack of his voice" becomes an enabling space in which it is possible to be inclusive and to make room for everyone of every possible shade as long as they oppose the reasons for the crack of the whip. As such this opening up of space is a reminder of slavery and a contemporary space for solidarity. It is arguably the same space that Du Bois (1975: 117) described when talking about the source of his solidarity with Africa, for slavery is a "heritage [that] binds together not simply the children of Africa, but extends through yellow Asia and into the South Seas." In this inclusive, nonessential notion of blackness, William recognizes the ideas of his daughter, whom he outlives for so many years, "racing the clock" so that he can still pass his message on to her children.

It would be unjust to the character of Delia to reduce her choices and actions to a naïve belief in a "reproductive futurity" that Nyong'o (2009) has sketched out. In a very important sense, the novel shows that she has to live with the consequences of marrying a white man, and these consequences, as I have already pointed out, are not pleasant. Frequently Delia has only very reduced choices. That she cannot become a professional singer although she is such an outstanding talent is one of many effects of racialization that do not stop after her marriage. Delia struggles to find a livable place for her white Jewish husband and herself, as well as for their mixed-race children. Since she is also one of the principal narrators, *The Time of Our Singing* gives this struggle a personal voice, aligning the readers with her viewpoint. Furthermore, by having a black character marry a white one, the development of the plot is in my view an intimate exploration of the interrelation between race, gender, and sexuality. As Ladelle McWhorter has shown in *Racism and Sexual Oppression in Anglo-America* (2009), race and sexuality do not work merely as analogous or mutually influential forms of self-articulation that allow for forms of societal oppression and exclusion along the axis of normalcy/deviance. Rather, race and sexuality "are mutually codependent and mutually determinative" (14) forms of biopower in a Foucauldian sense.[18] But this does not entail that the category of "race" is conflated into the category of sexuality. In a close reading of Foucault's lectures of 1974–75 at the Collège de France, published in English under the title *Abnormal* (2003a), McWhorter (2009: 35) shows that "modern racism is about racial purification; it defines the abnormalities it identifies as racial impurities or as threats to racial purity. Modern racism is not really about nonwhites; modern racism is really all about white people." For McWhorter, racial thinking provides the means through which "exclusion, oppression, hatred and fear of abnormality" (35) are practiced and perpetuated in society. One important way to accomplish alleged "racial purity," however, is the control and disciplining of sexuality. The effects of myths about the black man being a "sexual predator," "hypersexual," or a "black rapist" and myths about the black woman being a "seductress," the white woman being "pure and virginal," and the white man being "controlled, ordering and morally impeccable," should be analyzed through a Foucauldian lens.[19] For McWhorter, the effects of these stereotypes include terrorizing notions of white supremacy and the biopolitics of state powers that safeguard society's injustices through governmental, social scientific, and legal measures and medical management. She therefore concludes that is it crucial to refuse "to do the work of self- (and other-) policing in the name of the normal" (326). To be able "to perceive any aspect of the power networks that shape our lives other than the narrow face they present to our own group," she sees it as necessary to "stop compartmentalizing oppression on the basis of sociological identity" (327). For McWhorter, to take a stand against biopolitical control and exclusion means to

> [take] up the challenge of inventing what to do in the absence
> of set models and clear precedents and of living with the

uncertainties and unforeseeable consequences that invention entails. . . . Doing [so] . . . is not a guarantee that we shall overcome—or that we shall overcome as agents and conduits in an order we want to resist and dismantle. But it is the only open door, the only possibility. Go forth and do likewise— which means: Listen. Speak. Incite. Invent. And never, ever adjust. (331)

This suggestion resonates well with Delia's agenda, as is perceptible in her actions, perceptions, and descriptions as a character and narrator alike, as well as in those of other characters and narrators. Delia's characterization resonates with McWhorter's suggestion to "take up the challenge of inventing" in the knowledge that what this invention might bring about is unforeseeable. In the terminology I introduced in this chapter, Delia embraces the making of time, of singing it into existence. This is reflected, for example, in her leitmotif about there being nothing but constant modulation, "distant keys always falling back to *do*" (Powers 2003: 331). "Do," however, can indicate the tonic pitch of a scale that calls for harmonic resonance and resolution in major-key pieces of music (see section 1.3), or it can hint at the verb *to do*, stressing that we must work for things to come into being.

At this point I want to connect the double meaning of "falling back to *do*" with my suggestion that the novel makes an enabling use of an aural semiotic model of time and memory that destabilizes "race as theory of history." "Distant keys falling back to *do*" illustrates a notion of time that reconciles Bergson's durée with Einstein's special relativity theory and ensuing notions of a block universe. This reconciliation is made possible through Deleuze's ontological understanding of time and Prigogine's thermodynamic propositions. An aural model of time makes it possible to conceive of time as a superstructure that relates different events to each other that seemingly occur at random and whose exact position in time and space cannot be given in absolute terms (an understanding of time that I advocated in section 4.5). Time is then like a "polytonal cluster" (Powers 2003: 93) that relates different sound-events to each other, even if "melodies" that are formed in that process undergo constant modulations, pertain to "distant keys" (331), or follow their own "intervals, rhythms, durations" (411). This musical understanding of time is displayed at various points in the novel. The following passage should serve to make my description less abstract. Delia relates David's manner of working in the following way, focusing first on his colleagues' astonishment at his ability to solve the strangest physical riddles, while also showing that she agrees with his idea of time:

> "You must learn to listen," he says. If particles, forces, and fields obey the curve that binds the flow of numbers, then they must sound like harmonies in time. "You think with your eyes; this is your problem. No one can see four independent variables mapping out a surface in five or more dimensions. But the tuned ear can hear chords." . . .
>
> Delia, though, believes him, and knows how it is. Her husband hears his way forward. Melodies, intervals, rhythms, durations: the music of the spheres. Others bring him their deadlocks—particles spinning backward, phantom apparitions in two places at once, gravities collapsing on themselves. Even as they describe the hopeless mysteries, her David hears the rich counterpoint coded in the composer's score. (411)

At other times David suggests that "time must be like chords. Not even a series of chords. An enormous polytonal cluster that has the whole horizontal tune stacked up inside it" (93). These descriptions suggest that sound is an enabling semiotic model for understanding a notion of time that is informed by the insights of relativity theory. Taking up a suggestion by Pierre Truchot (2006), I argue that this is the case because music is composed of different and heterogeneous components that human perception does not need to unite into one form of mental representation. As I have shown in my reading of Al Saji (2004), an aural semiotic model of nonlinear, intersubjective, and personal processes of time and memory also unhinges them from their common representation as subjective, personal, and psychological. In the current context that deals with the question of injustice, inequality, and exclusion brought about by "race," this changed understanding of time and memory is important for a number of reasons. It mirrors how the novel uses narrative, figurative, and rhetorical devices to establish precisely this shifted understanding of time and memory. It is also connected to the question of "race" insofar as David and Delia hope to shift its meanings by "inventing" a "fifth choice" for their mixed-race children, beyond a mathematical calculation David did once: "They can be A and not B. They can be B and not A. They can be A and B. Or they can be neither A nor B" (Powers 2003: 287). This invention of a fifth choice is called into being by doing: "their tune together in constant modulation, distant keys falling back to *do*" (331). What "race" means, if a fifth choice is available in the future, is constant modulation called into being by living it differently, minute by minute, day by day, year by year, as recalled in David and Delia's vision: "The future that has led them here. The one they make possible. . . . They can map it slowly, their best-case future. Month by month, child by child. Their sons will be the first ones. Children of the coming age. Charter citizens of the postrace place, both races, no races, *race* itself: blending unblended, like notes stacked up in a chord" (345). This means, however, that the choices that David and Delia want to make available for their children are not a denial of "race," as William had understood his daughter. "Blending unblending, like notes stacked up in a chord" (345) instead suggests that "race" should be *heard*, not seen. To lend one's voice to "race" means to be able to blend with other voices and to enter into a song in which no voice is blended out. A solidarity in singularity, a song to be sung.

4.7. A CONCLUDING TRIP THROUGH TIME VIA "A BRIEF CRACK IN THE SIDE OF SOUND"

As I have shown throughout this chapter, *The Time of Our Singing* establishes a parallelism between time and music that is best captured in the assumption that they exist as a multiplicity of different sounds and events that can nevertheless be integrated into an overall structure. As such the novel's underlying notion of temporality complements Bhabha's (1994) proposition of a performative time very well. This is the case because in performative time, the "people as many" are given multiple subject positions. This multitude of people can come into being through the performativity of narratives that call different subject positions into being. In *The Time of Our Singing*, characters and their development make available different standpoints, resolutions, and conclusions on and about the question of "race." The novel thereby adheres to Bhabha's description of performative time as a rupture in the homogeneous, empty time of modernity with its implicit racializations. The narrative opposes modernity's racialized double time in which the national culture is represented as a dichotomy between white people (signifying continuity, rationality, progress, that is, modernity) and black people (excluded from the assumed teleological unfolding of time and thereby opposed to modernity). However, what Nyong'o (2009: 103) has described as "the performative inhabitation of the nation by a black dignity thriving outside the confines of its dialectical resolution" is best illustrated by David and Delia's journey through time. To conclude, I will suggest a possible reading of this episode.

David and Delia's time travel is narrated, remembered, and referred to at various points in the novel. The first time it is recounted from Delia's point of view, as she remembers it when she tells her parents that she has fallen in love with a white man (Powers 2003: 220–26). The second time, David recalls the incident when he participates with his daughter Ruth in the March on Washington (269–279). The third time, the episode is again told from Delia's perspective, in the final chapter of the book, called "Thee" (627–31). "Thee" refers here to Marian Anderson's opening song, "America," at her Lincoln Memorial concert in 1939, in which she changed the lyrics from "I" to "we". In the chapter "Thee," shortly after she has an epiphany about the doing of "race" that needs undoing, Delia "has this sound everywhere in her. Now it's right in her range: *my country, thee, thee*" (Powers 2003: 630). Laying a claim to the land where her foremothers and forefathers died, directing herself toward an other, Delia suddenly recognizes the boy who brought David and her together. In the earlier chapters dealing with their time travel, David and Delia stumble upon a lost boy who suddenly takes an interest in David, the white foreigner with the strange accent. The boy takes pleasure in having a conversation about astrophysics and enjoys being able to talk about time travel, gravity's bending of space, and the speed of light. But different from the versions previously narrated in the book, "the gravity of the impossible" (225), of a relationship across the color-line, has suddenly undergone a change. In previous versions Delia had always insisted that she could not meet the German again, that a meeting between a black woman and a white man was not possible. Yet in "Thee" "she hears the man answer, not with impossibles, but with the same suspended maybe with which he listened to the impossible contralto" (629). Through this "suspended maybe" she suddenly realizes that "there is nothing but standing change. Music knows that, every time out. Every time you lift your voice to sing" (629). Even sheet music as a form of written musical notation will come to life only through the singularity of a voice that lends itself to its interpretation. Every piece of music needs a voice to sing it into being. Beyond the script and the prescription of musical notation lies the uncapturable "grain of the voice" (Barthes 1977:

179–90) that infects its listeners in an unpredictable, unintelligible, and mysterious manner. However, the uncapturable force of the voice will be realized only if there is someone who listens attentively, for example "to the impossible contralto" (Powers 2003: 629). In the narrative this "impossible contralto" is Delia, who sings sotto voce to herself and is listened to by a white man, David, who on the grounds of this listening starts a conversation "beyond color" with her, a conversation that can take place only in a "suspended maybe." This place is reachable only by time travel. Delia recalls, in conversation with her mother, how she reached that place during Anderson's concert:

> Yet in the last night's rareness, the press of that record-setting crowd, up too close to history, something had turned in her. Some ancient law had split apart. Drunk on the godlike Miss Anderson, the voice of the century, a feather floating on a column of air, Delia made a separate journey, traveled down into the briefest crack in the side of sound. A widening in the day had opened up in front of her, pulling her and her German stranger into it. They'd traveled together down into long time, along a hall without dimension, to a place so far off, it couldn't even really be called the future, yet. . . . She had traveled nowhere. And yet, the man had traveled to that nowhere with her. (135)

It is utopia that David and Delia visit, the land of nowhere, a place that cannot be found on any map of Earth. Their utopia is reachable through "a brief crack in the side of sound," by listening attentively to "the very tones that constitute 'unspeakability'" (Morris 2001: 372), by waiting patiently for a singular interpretation of an all-too-known score. Making time, singing it into existence requires attention to the "affective tonalities" that have come down through history; it also requires attention to possible futures that press upon the present moment, possible futures that shape the present as well as the past. The strength of *The Time of Our Singing* lies in the suggestion that this possible future is reachable, that it is in fact already there, somewhere in cosmic space-time, reverberating not only *in* the present moment but *with* the present choices we undertake. It is Delia who understands this mutual interdependence between present and future, an understanding represented in her epiphany that time, like music, is "nothing but standing change." Past, present, and future are constantly (inter)changing in a block universe that contains all of their dimensions. Time is nothing but "standing change," a change that nevertheless has to be put into practice through decisions and actions whose future outcomes are unknown and unknowable.

Delia decides to trust David and to make a future happen in which her grandson Ode, the son of Ruth, will sit on the steps of the Lincoln Memorial to enjoy a conversation about astrophysics and the secrets of time. He will rap himself into existence by suggesting that not racial mixing but *inventiveness* makes possible what has so far seemed impossible. Invention brings what does not exist into being and provides an answer to the unanswerable question of where the bird and the fish, who have fallen in love, are going to build their nest. "The bird and the fish can make a bish. The fish and the bird can make a fird" (Powers 2003: 631), raps Ode, and David suddenly understands that "the bird can make a nest on the water," and Delia sees that "the fish can fly" (631). David and Delia make "impossible" choices, hoping that the impossible will produce a different echo in the present. If taken by ear, the present may ring with an echo where the prefix *im-* has lost to time.

I am suggesting that we take seriously the development of the plot and the novel's narrative solutions to questions of "race." As I have shown throughout this chapter, temporalizations are an important means for capturing not only the doings of race but also propositions about how "race as a theory of history" can be undone. As Nyong'o (2009) has argued, the dichotomizing double time of modernity that excludes black dignity can be disturbed through the signs of its own multitudinous multiplicities (race, sexuality, gender, class, differently abled). In the novel this multitude is made graspable through the voices and positions of differently racialized characters that interact with each other. Here I want to pay specific attention to the literary descriptions of a game called Crazed Quotations that the family Daley-Strom often play together. I want to suggest that this game functions as a *pars pro toto* for the novel's performance of a multiplicity of interacting voices that perform different standpoints on the question of "race." Crazed Quotations is a competition in which someone picks up a tune to sing, and someone else has to beat the clock and find a countersubject before the singer reaches the double bar (see Powers 2003: 13). In the novel this game is described as a "long conversation of pitches in time" (13) that David takes as a model for his understanding of time: "Our father knew more than any living person about the secret of time, except how to live in it. His time did not travel; it was a block of persisting nows.

To him, the thousand years of Western music might as well have been written that morning. Mama shared the belief; maybe it was why they'd ended up together. Our parents' Crazed Quotations game played on the notion that every moment's tune had all history's music box for its counterpoint" (58). This means that any tune can fit together, as long as someone decides to modify it in such a way that it attunes itself to another and an other's song. To make possible this interaction between different tunes, "all history's music box" (58) can play the counterpart, regardless of where it comes from and when it was composed. Any song chosen to be sung has a countersubject as long as a voice is lifted to enter into a polyphony where no song cancels the other out. "Every stacked sound stayed whole in the changing chord" (611). Music allows different voices to interact with each other so they can follow their own harmonies, rhythms, and durations.

Considering music as a suitable semiotic model to capture the doings and undoings of time means that music can do far more than display different sounds at once and relate them to each other in an unfolding whole. It can also retain traces of past sounds and anticipate future ones that produce echoes and repercussions in a given, present chord. As the game Crazed Quotations shows, these echoes and reverberations can come from "all history's music box." As such, an aural semiotic model as proposed in *The Time of Our Singing* allows reconciliation between different philosophical propositions that deal with the notion of "race." As Du Bois (1975), Fanon (1967), Bhabha (1994), and Nyong'o (2009) have argued, it is important to preserve the history of "race" and its origins in slavery, as well as its (historical) continuities in racial oppression and exclusion, in racist murders and lynching. As I have shown in relation to Appiah and Gutmann's (1996) argument, the notion of "race" is nevertheless a difficult one because it needs a referent to which it applies and therefore is in danger of reifying racist notions that so urgently need to be overcome. Therefore I want to argue that a perception of time that allows a polyphony of voices to compose it, one that sees past, present, and future as a dynamic interplay, makes it possible to integrate these different positions. David suggests that time is like chords, like an "enormous polytonal cluster that has the whole horizontal tune stacked up inside it" (Powers 2003: 93). In the novel's vision, it is not impossible to commemorate an ineffable history of slavery, to perceive historical and contemporary racisms, and to outline a feasible utopia *at once*. The impossible will echo differently in the present when we set out to create a future that is informed by a dream for a better society. As Oscar Wilde (1969: 141) claimed, "A map of the world that does not include Utopia is not worth even glancing at, for it leaves out the one country at which Humanity is always landing. And when Humanity lands there, it looks out, and seeing a better country, sets sail." This means that it is necessary to remember the past, to attune oneself in the best way possible to the songs that compose one's life, while setting sail for an unknown country called Utopia, traveling there through "the briefest crack in the side of sound" (Powers 2003: 135). This crack opens up in the interaction between past, present, and future, when one engages with memories, histories, imaginations, and inventions, endlessly, in unchanging change.

Conclusion

The only historian capable of fanning the spark of hope in the past is the one who is firmly convinced that *even the dead* will not be safe from the enemy if he is victorious. And this enemy has never ceased to be victorious.
—Walter Benjamin, "On the Concept of History"

She told them that the only grace they could have was the grace they could imagine. That if they could not see it, they would not have it.
—Toni Morrison, *Beloved*

When I began this work I set out to determine the stakes involved when a literary writer invents what is missing from a historiographical narrative. I have argued that fictional texts can evoke a literary world that neither corresponds to nor imitates reality. With its use of rhetorical, stylistic, and narrative devices, literature is able to engage its readers in the construction of a story. Readers can make this nonanalogical literary world credible and thereby assume a positionality in which they have to abandon their preconceived perceptions, opinions, and judgments. I have consistently described these processes evoked by literary writing as empowering and enabling different ways for readers and writers to understand the world. Using the image of the brain, I have argued that literature can work like a *faculty of thinking* able to create new perceptions, sensations, thoughts, and even ethical positions. I have used Deleuze's philosopheme of *the powers of the false* to describe these particular capabilities of literature. Through a reading of *Everything Is Illuminated*, *Gould's Book of Fish*, and *The Time of Our Singing* I have shown how and why each of these novels bring something new, such as perspectives, riddles, and sensations, to historiographical representations of the past. Literature can add to such accounts without opposing them dialectically, constituting an addition instead of an opposition. Before I bring this book to a close, I want to address what is at stake in inventing a missing historical narrative. When describing literature's powers of the false as potentially enabling forces, do I not risk concealing the fact that these powers also have a darker and potentially disabling side? Is literature's invention of what is missing from a historical account not also the self-same process and tool that is used for spreading blatant lies and biased propaganda about events of the past? What does it mean if readers get historical occurrences verifiably wrong through a distorted depiction?

The history of literature provides us with numerous examples of literary works that have claimed to be historiographically accurate. Sometimes these claims have been proven wrong, and this deceit has provoked devastating results. A case in point is Binjamin Wilkomirski's *Fragments: Memoires of a Wartime Childhood* (1996). As Froma Zeitlin (2003: 176) recounts, the novel "was taken as a small masterpiece because of the child's-eye view," narrated as a fragmentary recollection that was used to represent a traumatic childhood spent during and after World War II. In 1998 it became known that the author suffered from an identity disorder and had invented the whole story (see Eskin 2002; Lappin 1999; Mächler 2001; Suleiman 2000). Since Wilkomirski's book had passed itself off as the personal testimony of a childhood overshadowed by the Holocaust, the disclosure of its fraudulence had devastating effects on the general credibility of personal testimonies, even those of authentic witnesses (Zeitlin 2003: 177). According to Zeitlin, Wilkomirski's case shows how difficult it is for third parties to distinguish fiction from genuine memoir or verifiable testimony. In fact establishing a clear line between fiction and memoir or testimony seems to depend on the credibility of its authors. Yet this credibility can be misleading, as Wilkomirski's case shows.

In addition literature's technical means of spreading stories is intrinsically linked to the rise of the modern nation-state. As Benedict Anderson (1991) shows, in the eighteenth century the novel was a relatively new form of literary representation that was particularly suited to shaping the kind of imagined community that was discursively equated with the actual inhabitants of the nation. According to Anderson, the novel could also express a time and a space that was imagined as something shared among the nation's population. Taking up Anderson's definition, Ann Rigney (2004) demonstrates how the literariness of Walter Scott's *The Heart of Midlothian* ([1818] 1982) provides a social framework that allows for a dynamic and ongoing formation of cultural memory.[1] Scott's novel makes the character Jeanie Deans memorable (see Rigney 2004: 380), but her depiction in the novel deviates considerably from her historical counterpart, Helen

Walker. Rigney (2004: 391) shows that Scott's depiction is sometimes "even patently false" and therefore concludes that there is a "need for a further elaboration of a 'poetics' of memorability based on the principle of literary form." Through an interdisciplinary and nonlinear approach, scholars can trace how literature becomes "constitutive of memory" (391). This constitutive memory can be inherited by means of cultural artifacts that may pass on a twisted version of historiographically transmitted events.

As the examples from Zeitlin (2003), Anderson (1991), and Rigney (2004) demonstrate, the addition that literature can bring to historiography does not necessarily go against the grain of contemporary mechanisms of historiographical exclusion. Literature can support the ideological formation of the nation-state (see Anderson 1991); it is powerful insofar as it allows cultural memories to circulate that have been crafted by literary rather than historical necessity (see Rigney 2004); and it can even discredit witnesses who have taken upon themselves the impossible deed of passing on memories of events that are too terrible to relate to and whose structure defies representation (see Zeitlin 2003).[2] This is to say that literature is not beyond ideological appropriations, and it can even provide an incorrect, distorted, and delegitimized picture of historical events. But if literature can contribute to a factually incorrect historical image, is this deceitful and deceptive contribution synonymous with the notion of the powers of the false that I have developed? In my reading of the three selected novels, I have frequently argued that their essential qualities are defined by their deployment of rhetorical, stylistic, and narrative devices that *exceed* the aim of historical transmission. This transgression is motivated by the necessity of "an alternative epistemological and ethical space" (Grewal 1998: 10) that, as I have argued, can be evoked through literature.

I argued that literature creates this alternative space that Grewal identifies by connecting not to experience but to a *structure of experience* that enables its readers to learn. This structure of experience originates in literature's dual ability to elicit an attentiveness to singularity and to constitute an openness to perceiving differently. The combination of literature's ability to open perception and to invite different perceptions is the very thing captured by Deleuze's philosopheme of literature's powers of the false. The powers of the false, in other words, are not synonymous with literature's ability to recount historical events. What is transmitted essentially in these novels is *a longing for a narrative space* in which painful or shameful stories can be included. In other words, literature's formative powers consist in using literariness to make a reading position available that evokes the desire (and not necessarily the fulfillment) to include unvoiced or unvoiceable experiences in historical accounts. The selected novels create a reading position that expresses the desire—but not necessarily the fulfillment—of inserting silent or silenced voices into historiographical narratives and processes of cultural remembrance.

In my reading of *Everything Is Illuminated*, I linked Barthes's (1993) arguments about the generic qualities of photography with Anselm Haverkamp's (1993) extrapolation of a specific view on history that ekphrasis allows to emerge. This enabled me to show how the photograph described in Foer's novel changes its generic meaning. In Haverkamp's view, photographs are visual citations from and about history. This is the case because photography, as explained in Barthes's seminal work, indicates a certain relation that objects or persons shown in photographs have to temporality: they are quintessentially captured at a moment that is always already past, so that any knowledge about their limited temporality, their given-to-deathness, is transferred through the medium itself. I have shown how the photograph of Augustine supersedes this quintessential pastness by expressing her survival in the face of an almost certain death at the hands of fascist murderers who invade Trachimbrod. Augustine, it is said, is "the only one still alive" (Foer 2002: 59) of an entire Jewish shtetl. Staged through ekphrasis in a literary work, the photograph of Augustine becomes proof of her being given to life (her survival) and her giving of life (by saving the life of Jonathan's grandfather Safran). The photograph therefore acquires a new meaning that is juxtaposed to photography's generic qualities as diagnosed by Barthes. In this way she transfers the hope for survival (of the Nazi raid) and resistance (by Grandfather Safran's life) against the devaluations of life that are epitomized in the mass murder of a people in Auschwitz. The use of ekphrasis in *Everything Is Illuminated* gives the photograph a new temporality, in which it *does not* capture the being-given-to-death of the person shown. Rather it transfers a notion of hope to characters and readers alike that it is possible to cherish life in the present despite the fact of Auschwitz. In my reading of *Everything Is Illuminated*, I related this notion of hope to the Jewish theologian and philosopher Emil Fackenheim's (1987: 159) diagnosis that a 614th commandment[3] is needed, one which states, "We are forbidden to turn present and future life into death, as the price of remembering death at Auschwitz. And we are equally forbidden to affirm present and future life, at the price of forgetting Auschwitz." With this commandment in mind, it is clear that the novel creates a complicated legacy with a past overshadowed by Auschwitz. Through the characters' choices and loving acts of friendship, a vision of present and past events is established that enables readers and characters alike to appreciate life without forgetting the Shoah. This vision is revealed through, among others, the development of plot, character, and the relationships between characters.

These relationships are quintessentially represented in a letter exchange between the Jewish American Jonathan and his Ukrainian translator Alex. However, I find it particularly interesting that the 614th commandment suggested by Fackenheim is made accessible in the novel through literary devices that are less perceptible as such because they are personified in literary characters and therefore more difficult to detect. For instance, since Alex's choice of words and phrases always seems to miss the target language, readers are asked to retranslate his translation into an idiom that makes sense to them. Readers are thereby directly involved in the production of meaning that is guided by a loving friendship. I have argued that this is the case because readers are asked to surrender to the fraying of meaning in processes of translation. Spivak (1992) defines this surrender to the forces of language as a form of relationality called friendship, since it allows the translator to escape the logic of self-identity. The idiomatic language that Alex uses confronts readers with its selvedges and possible silences, as I have shown by reading it with Spivak's suggestions about translation processes. When readers become translators, they can assume an ethical positionality that allows them to embrace the alterity of language and the fundamental otherness that it can convey. As such, language in *Everything Is Illuminated* incites readers to go beyond their own frame of reference, since they are forced to perceive how meaning can change in the transfer from one idiom to another or that a particular sense cannot be translated. Alex's idiomatic language use is one instance in which the novel develops its powers of the false.

In addition fragments of the past—sentences people have written down, things they have used—surface in the novel's plot again and again in different narrative contexts. Blasted out of their original context, these fragments change their meaning once displaced, thereby stressing the importance of context in establishing meaning. They make it clear why past events cannot always be represented in the way they actually happened. Moreover they inform both readers and characters that an event's meaning can sometimes not be passed on at all. In the face of meaningless death and unfathomable mass murder, it is no longer possible to pass on experience through language and other semiotic systems. This breakdown of meaning is made accessible in the novel in two ways. It is shown that a Jewish writing tradition cannot be passed down, since its content undergoes change. The telling of Jewish lives loses precedence to the telling of how Jewish lives have been taken. Alongside this representation of a rupture in history that makes it impossible to take up the thread of tradition, Jonathan's magical-realist story line establishes a palimpsest in reverse. This not only makes the event of falling silent (see Felman 1999) perceptible, but it also establishes a narrative context in which fragments of the past, although distorted, can resurface. It is the reader's responsibility to make sense of the surfacing bits and pieces, to link fragments, hints, and phrases with each other, and to unravel narrative strands.

The narrative, rhetorical, and stylistic devices used in *Everything Is Illuminated* put readers in an ethical position: because they partake in the construction of the story, they have to assume responsibility for it. As such they are drawn into the construction of a complicated legacy with an unfathomable past, for which they nevertheless provide the grounds (a palimpsest in reverse, a translation without a source language, a form of teleopoiesis cutting and pasting through time and space) for making its unspeakability perceptible and for letting distorted and unrecognizable fragments of the past resurface. The novel's powers of the false consist in the creation of a reading position that urges readers to deal with the past in a way that respects its fundamental nonrepresentability without debasing an unspeakable event. At the same time it urges readers to confront themselves with a past that has repercussions in the present and is close to them in an uncanny and also familiar way. I consider this reading position an urgently needed ethical standpoint for a post-Auschwitz generation. This ethical standpoint is created by a literature that invites readers-to-come to respond to a fictional account that is not opposed to reality but is in fact false.

In my discussion of *Gould's Book of Fish*, I also paid great attention to the usage of rhetorical, stylistic, and narrative devices that, like Foer's novel, transmit the desire to include silenced voices in the historiographical narrative. I have shown that the novel adds a particular vision of life to historiography that contradicts Agamben's highly influential view on "bare life," as developed in *Homo Sacer*. The novel invents what is missing in the historical account, assuming a liminal position that is neither true nor fictional but false.

The false is brought into existence through four different narrative devices: first, the narrative voices of questionably unreliable narrators; second, the paratextual device of placing replicas of the "real" convict-painter Gould's fish paintings on the novel's cover and at each chapter's beginning; third, the magical-realist becoming-fish of its principal narrators and characters; and fourth, a constantly voiced self-reflexivity through which the novel's relation to truth is reflected upon. All these devices are used to suggest that there is a fundamental need to invent the story of Gould and his fish paintings, that there is a need to provide a narrative that explains how and why the drawings were made. To exemplify the novel's use of narrative devices, I examined a number of observations that can be made by scrutinizing the riddles posed through the novel's two unreliable narrators, William Buelow Gould (situated in the 1820s) and Sid Hammet (situated in the present). The former is a professional forger and the latter a dealer of fake antique furniture. Since they admit to being liars and deceivers while also claiming to tell true stories, they create an unsolvable paradox. As in the famous statement "All people from Crete are liars; I am from Crete," forgers confessing to be forgers are not liars. Rather they make it impossible to decide what kind of relation they have to truth. Readers must decide if they believe the unreliable narrators' storytelling. But the readers are implicated in the story as well; they are tied up in a narrative knot created in the story line and therefore might have a less than impartial view on the matter. They could even become "accomplices" in the escape of Gould and his fish (Flanagan 2003: 7), which is made possible by means of the fictional account.

I have argued that the readers' collaboration is facilitated by their inevitable confrontation with reproductions of the convict-painter Gould's original fish drawings. To understand the scope of the narrative knot created in the story line, it is important to remember that not only the readers but also the author and both narrators are implicitly or explicitly aware of the original drawings' existence. Flanagan uses the paintings for the design of his book and as a paratextual device, and the narrators constantly refer to the drawings. Gould claims to reproduce his own paintings from memory while imprisoned; Hammet uses replicas of Gould's original book of fish for his rewritten version of Gould's logbook. This means that author, readers, and narrators, whether they are real or imagined and whether they are situated on extradiegetic, metadiegetic, or intradiegetic levels, share knowledge about, perception of, and experience with the real Gould's paintings. Arguably this perception and experience of the paintings engenders far more than their official objective, namely, to record the natural history of Macquarie Harbor's fish. Through their particular style, the paintings may account for the historical character Gould's vision of his painterly objects. Through their expression and expressiveness, the paintings can provide insights into Gould's perception when drawing his fish. By accompanying the fish drawings with a story about their genesis under the harrowing conditions of indentured convict labor, the novel gives one possible response to a wish that might have arisen when experiencing (reproductions of) the original paintings. This desire may be shared by author, readers, and narrators alike and is enabled by perceiving Gould's style as his way of recording his own history when painting the fish. Admittedly style is too slippery a device for claiming to tell a verifiable story, which is why the historical Gould's experiences cannot be deduced from the paintings themselves and need to be invented. However, it is not inconceivable that what the novel recounts about Gould's vision of the world was in fact the vision he had of himself and the creatures he had to scrutinize so carefully to capture their lifelike resemblance on paper. In other words, the novel uses the powers of the false by inventing a perspective that is missing from the historical account, namely the perspective of those who were imprisoned under inhuman conditions on Sarah Island. I have argued that this invention is false because it is based on perceptions that take place not only in fiction through fictional characters and narrators but also in the world of the author and readers.

Flanagan thereby shows that literature can provide a form of knowledge that differs from historical truth, but without being its dialectical opposite. Literature can construct a nonreferential narrative space in which the unheard-of experiences of convicts imprisoned during Australia's early colonization period take shape. Literature can show the urge and desire to understand historical events that are terrible to relate to, because they bring the gruesome conditions of the convict system to the fore. It can invent a story to account for the consequences of this violent colonial system. Yet, above all, the novel desires to render stories of unspeakable horror through the becoming-fish of its first-person narrator. This desire expresses a hyperbolic love of everyone, which extends so far as to include all the other wonders of this world. By depicting convicts and natives as loving and lovable persons, Flanagan refrains from reducing them to the colonial conditions in which they were caught up. Instead he offers a point of view that differs from Agamben's bare life. I have taken this perspective, in which life and its conditions cannot be lumped together, as a point of departure from which to criticize Agamben's transhistorical and transnational account of biopolitical determinations of life. I have argued that the escape of Gould and his fish is accomplished by the desire of author, readers, and narrators to fabulate a story that accompanies the paintings of the historical Gould. The wish to have insights into the conditions of Gould and his fish paintings, brought into being and fulfilled by the novel itself, means investing affectively and imaginatively in a story that might otherwise be too shameful or too painful to relate to. And while it remains impossible to know with certainty how the real Gould felt when painting his fish, it is nevertheless imaginable that he included the wonders of this world in his perception. *Gould's Book of Fish* provides a story for this possibility, and thereby refrains from doubling the violence of a dehumanizing colonial system that excluded the voices of those dispossessed of their own bodies from their archives. The novel's powers of the false are specifically evident in its move to make a perspective accessible that, despite not having been historically recorded, is nevertheless conceivable and imaginable for those who want to claim this shameful and painful legacy for and in their vision of history.

In my discussion of *The Time of Our Singing*, I connected the novel's specific powers of the false with the temporalizations it offers when dramatizing "the problem of the color line" (Du Bois 2002: n.p.). Nyong'o (2009) posits that "race" holds specific "assumptions regarding time and temporality" (11) that need to be exposed and criticized and that modernity's notions of continuity, progress, and rationality are still identified with white people. The idea of human progress is therefore thoroughly entwined with the idea of racial progress. For my reading of *The Time of Our Singing*, it is important to notice that modernity's notion of "race" is misguided by two leading principles. First, "race" is seen as an existing, clear-cut category despite its lack of scientific verifiability. Racial delineations have varied greatly over time and space and depend on social, historical, and political circumstances that regulate inclusions and exclusions, are exploitative, and control resources. But the idea of "race" arguably persists because it is a social construct that forms and shapes racial identities and senses of belonging. By telling the story of a mixed-race family, Powers's novel dramatizes and makes available the devastating effects of the idea of "race" that is based on its (dermatological) identification. This does not mean, however, that it does not give rise to an idea of solidarity that is able to ally itself with a "social heritage of slavery" (Du Bois 1975: 116) and that identifies the continuity of racism. In Powers's novel, "race" is de-essentialized, while its cruel, exploitative, and murderous social history comes to the fore. Datable historical events that pertain to the history of "race" and racism in the United States intermingle with the story of the Daley-Strom family. Social movements and actors that tried to counter racism and its injustice, violence, and disempowerment are called back into remembrance through the novel's metahistorical fictionality.

The second misleading principle that is thoroughly entrenched with an idea of racial progress is the very notion of time it entails. Its idea of progress takes for granted that time is linear, constant, and unchanging; it assumes that time is a continuously unfolding line that runs from the past through the present into the future. As I have shown, however, contemporary physics sees time as relative, dependent on physical systems in motion, and having no absolute frame of reference (see Durie 1999: vi). Furthermore a spatializing understanding of time (in which time unfolds in a linear fashion) precludes the possibility of envisioning any embedding in time in which a constant interaction between different temporal layers occurs. *The Time of Our Singing* counters this understanding of the nature of time. Instead the novel's temporalizations are guided by currently accepted scientific theories such as Einstein's special relativity theory and ensuing concepts of a block universe in which past, present, and future coexist. However, the temporalizations that are made available in the novel go beyond the implications of special relativity. The novel realizes a notion of time that reconciles Einstein's understanding of its relativity with Bergson's proposition to consider time as ongoing qualitative change, durée. From a theoretical perspective, this reconciliation is made possible by Prigogine and his collaborators' proposition about thermodynamics and its implications on space-time and by Deleuze's readings of Bergson, which shift a philosophical understanding of durée as psychological experience to an experience of time's ontology, bringing physics and philosophy together.

My analysis argued in favor of viewing Powers's novel as a medium that can make the insights of relativity theory accessible. Statements made by Einstein (1924) and Bergson (1999) have prompted Marcio Barreto (2004) to reflect upon relativity theory's provocation to common sense. In contrast to Newton's (1999) conception of time as absolute and unconstrained by exterior influences, Einstein's (1961) special and general relativity theories posit that the velocities of systems of reference determine time's measurements; time cannot be grasped by spatializing it, nor is it intelligible without mediation (see Barreto 2004: 3; Pearson 1999: 31).

Through the temporalizations available in Powers's novel, it performs a form of time that contradicts any suggestion of its linear unfolding, independent of any system of reference. This is achieved by a noncommonsensical deployment of narrative and narrated time, a unique use of temporal and spatial indicators, and a full exploration of the narrative's length and the duration of the reading process. It thereby records "the time of our singing" while showing that an aural semiotic model that is based on echoes, reverberations, hearing, and singing is better suited to capture a nonlinear time and intersubjective memory. By putting an aural semiotic model into practice, the novel corresponds with Al Saji's suggestion to use aurality rather than visuality to capture time and memory's nature. By severing the ties with a common (or commonsensical) representation of memory and time, the novel uses its powers of the false to give its readers access to what cannot be grasped without mediation: a notion of time inspired by relativity theory and by Bergson's durée. Present perceptions of characters are colored by the "affective tonalities" (Al Saji 2004: 223) of others, by a past that is "*all our past*" (B 59), and, I suggest, by a future that is *all* our future. Using the aural semiotic model, the novel can realize a performative time that gives rise to a "people as many" (Bhabha 1994: 209). Characters and their development provide standpoints, resolutions, and conclusions on and about "the problem of the color line," raising their (narrative) voices to partake in a song from which no voice is left out. To remain singular while being in solidarity; to sing into existence, with a multitude of different voices, a song that opposes racism—this is the invention and intervention put into practice by *The Time of Our Singing*. It performs the need to invent "a missing people" while providing a possible model for how this missing people can sing themselves into being. The novel provides a written score for a song still to be sung.

The three novels analyzed here do not employ their powers of the false to tell a verifiable story. Rather they construct a reading position in which readers experience the need and desire to make space for what is missing from particular historical accounts. I maintain that these powers are not intended to be used to misrepresent events of the past. On the contrary, the powers of the false oppose themselves to fictionality by exposing this experience of creating space. The ability to confront what is unfamiliar and new and to make a fictional account credible merge to make up the real experience of readers, which is what literature enables. This potentiality relies on the particular literariness of fictional texts and on their singular use of rhetorical, stylistic, and narrative devices. Reading (and writing) are mediators between different times, peoples, and worlds, so that these "others" can haunt our present. By the close attention paid to language and the surrender to language implied by reading (and writing), these others are called forth (see Wiese 2011: 233). To experience the powers of literature that come into being by attentively and openly reading its fictional suggestions— to experience this structure—means succumbing to the false. It entails encountering oneself as a reader who is simultaneously captivated by literature's powers and pushed to set its propositions free by lending one's opened senses to literature's written score, thereby allowing literature to raise its false but no less real voice.

Notes

INTRODUCTION

1. In *Cinema 1: The Movement Image* (Deleuze 1986, hereafter cited as MI) and *Cinema 2: The Time Image*, Deleuze argues that cinematic forms of expression changed after World War II. In my view, Deleuze's exclusive focus on fascism, Stalinism, and colonialism in his explanation of the changed position of artists after 1945 is brought about by this historical approach. Equally his description of the hope for a revolutionary people is inspired by a historical discourse that was heavily debated by artists belonging to communist and socialist circles just before World War II. Deleuze names Sergei Eisenstein and Diego Vertov as two filmmakers who dedicated their art to a people deemed to be potentially revolutionary. Deleuze assigns a similar political function to the writer of minor literature (see Deleuze and Guattari 1986, hereafter cited as K). I will explain the latter concept in greater detail in section 1.3.

2. The title of a conference, Writing|History, organized by Prof. Dr. Hanjo Berressem and Prof. Dr. Norbert Finzsch, inspired me to use a vertical line, |, as a graphic device in this work. I am particularly interested in its democratic arrangement of space and its ability to simultaneously separate and connect. I cite publications that were written collectively, for example by Deleuze|Guattari, in this way. I want to indicate that collective writing is a process that supersedes the addition of individuals' abilities. Collective writing becomes an endeavor in which individuals establish a collective subject like "Deleuze|Guattari." I also use the vertical line for other entities that have merged with each other but are nevertheless recognizable in their particularity and singularity.

3. My analysis is largely in line with Ronald Bogue's insightful and sensitive reading of the novel as outlined in *Deleuzian Fabulation and the Scars of*

History (2010, 173–232). Bogue shows how the character and narrator Gould displays a worldview that resonates with Australian Aborigines' philosophy of time and their practice of Dreaming and how Dreaming works in conjunction with Deleuzian thoughts on becoming, on fabulation, and on time. Both of us were working on *Gould's Book of Fish* at around the same period, and, as always, I am astonished about the resonances between our respective works.

CHAPTER I

1. Structuralist, poststructuralist, and deconstructionist approaches tend to see the author as a metaphysical concept that does not help to clarify a text's "meaning" or mythically invent one (see, for example, Derrida 1976, 1986b, 1988; Barthes 2002; Genette 1997a; de Man 1988; Moi 1985; Kristeva 1973, 1974; Foucault 2002). In this chapter I will discuss the influential debate on the "death of the author" that radicalized text-oriented methodologies. For an overview on the whole debate, see Irwin 2002, an anthology that features its most debated texts.

2. DeleuzelGuattari's selection of authors testifies to their preference for a modernist canon. I will touch upon the canon as a problematic construction later on in this chapter.

3. "These universes [i.e., 'the art-monument'] are neither virtual nor actual; they are possibles, the possible as an aesthetic category ('the possible or I shall suffocate'), whereas events are the reality of the virtual, forms of a thought nature that survey every possible universe" (WP 178). I will address how DeleuzelGuattari differentiate among real, possible, actual, and virtual at a later point in this chapter.

4. Barthes' polemical essay (2002) in particular plays havoc with an understanding of hermeneutics as developed in the nineteenth century under the influence of German romanticism and idealism. In Friedrich Schleiermacher's (1977, 1998) understanding—which has been formative for later hermeneutic scholars such as Dilthey (1996, 2002), Gadamer (1976, 1986, 1994), Heidegger (1962), Apel and Habermas (1971)—readers should use empathy as a tool for reconstructing the life and historical circumstances of an individual author. According to Schleiermacher, readers might accomplish a higher understanding called divination by interpreting a text. Although his postulations were criticized later for being too idealistic and naïve, his texts nevertheless serve as a useful point of reference and departure. Another influential point of hermeneutical reference has been Martin Heidegger's (1962) understanding of hermeneutics as ontology, displaying sense-making as a fundamental condition of human beings. Heidegger's point of view has been discussed, among others, by Richard Rorty (1979, 1991).

5. In the words of Lawrence Buell (1987: 102), "the very concept of the canon implies a suspect authoritarianism," a point of view that has been shared by writers from a variety of minoritarian positions. To name but a few, canon criticism has been put forward by Appiah and Gates 1992; Bloom 1987; Buikema and Meyer 2003, 2004; Buikema and Meijer 2006; Eagleton 1996; Kolodny 1985; Krupat 1989; McDowell 1985; Meijer 1988; Moers

1977; Ponzanesi 2006a, 2006b; Showalter 1977; Thompkins 1985, 1986; Walker 1983.

6. *Phallogocentrism* is a term coined by Derrida (1978, 1979, 1984, 1985, 1987a, 1990, 1991, 1998b; Derrida et al. 1987), derived from Greek *logos*, meaning "word, speech, discourse, reason" (see "logos," in www.etymonline. com, accessed December 30, 2010) and Greek *phallos*, "carving or image of an erect penis (symbolizing the generative power in nature)" (see "phallus," in www.etymonline.com, accessed December 30, 2010). The term is also used in Lacanian psychoanalysis (see "Phallus" in Laplanche and Pontalis 1996: 385–88; Lacan 1966). It criticizes how "the grammatical Subject has traditionally been figured as a metaphor for the powerful male, who determines reality according to two principles: binary visual distinctions and univocal, 'phallogocentric' naming and language" (Engelbrecht 1990: 87). By determining what signs need to be present to be "central," phallogocentric discourse determines what is "absent," or what and whose meaning needs to be "derived" from its central categories (see Culler 1983; Engelbrecht 1990). Although primarily used in Continental feminist philosophy and literary criticism, the term as such also applies to structures of dominance at work within, for example, post- and neocolonial power structures, in the divide between able and "disabled" bodies, and heteronormativity (see Davis 1999; Netto 2004; O'Rourke 2005).

7. The output of these different streams of criticism and theory-making has been enormous, so it seems impossible to produce an exhaustive reading list. Here I name only a few who have engaged directly with inclusive reading and writing strategies: Appiah and Gates 1992; Boyarin, Itzkowitz, and Pellegrini 2003; Combahee River Collective 1981; Corker and Shakespeare 2002; Parker and the Bolton Discourse Network 1999; Peters and Fendler 2003; Hoogland 1994; Lather 1991; Lorey and Plews 1998; McRuer 2004, 2006; Muñoz 1999; Rodriguez 2003; Sherry 2004; Villarejo 2005.

8. For the text as radical alterity, see Buikema 2009, 2010; Spivak 2005: 238–57.

9. With the term *inject* Deleuze|Guattari bypass discussions about the nature of subject-object relations. This relation has been one of the most discussed problems in political philosophy since Hegel's highly influential *Phenomenology of Spirit* (1977). The inject offers a terminological and theoretical alternative to the dichotomy between the observer and the observed world. Deleuze|Guattari's term—grounded on a Spinozist point of view—suggests that bodies and things intermingle and that some of their forces affect other forces, forming composite relations. The artist not only perceives this interaction and intermingling of forces that happens to her or him but also gives this interplay new artistic form and expression.

10. It is telling how the translation of German *klein*, which means "little, petit, small, tiny," into "minor" already gives a completely new resonance, for example, a musical one, to Kafka's reflections. In the German version this association is not possible, since it is "minor" that refers to tonalities in music, and then only if Italian is used for musical instructions (Italian "minor" is *Moll* in German). However, Kafka does use *minder* as a synonym for *kleiner*

in his description, which means "less" in a qualitative sense (i.e., "von minderer Qualität," "minderwertig"). This resonates with the original French usage of a "littérature mineure" by Deleuze|Guattari, although the French version, while incorporating the musical connotation, loses the "little" one: a good example of the Babylonian condition we are living in, insofar as—far from being a disadvantage—it creates new meanings in the process of translation. In any case, German *klein* is not an adjective that usually works in connection with literature, although its antonym *groß*, which means "big, large" but also "great, grand" would apply. Thus Kafka in fact creates a "new" class of literature that stands in opposition to—and maybe even opposes—"great" ones.

11. The "insular life" has not prevented the existence of a very lively literary community, as the output of the German-speaking minority has been enormous and some of the most famous German-speaking authors were born in Bohemia (in German: Böhmen), as the province was called when it formed part of the Hapsburg and Austrian-Hungarian empires. Among others, Rainer Maria Rilke, Franz Werfel, Egon Erwin Kisch, and Oskar Wiener were born here. All of them—and Kafka—speak an extraordinarily "rich" German, so for literary or journalistic purposes the high coefficient of "artificiality" does not seem to be inhibiting; in fact the contrary is true. Kisch, for example, serves in most journalism classes as a role model for reportage writing, and justifiably so, because of his outstanding richness of precise and to-the-point descriptions; similarly the dream-like and multilayered quality of Rilke's language is, like Kafka's, extraordinarily gripping. As Christian Jäger (2005) has shown, even the "insularity" of German-speaking writers in Bohemia is highly questionable. Major newspapers written in German were available in coffeehouses; the cultural exchange between Berlin, Vienna, and Prague was alive and kicking, especially since Prague is geographically (and at that time also geopolitically) situated between Berlin and Vienna (which until World War I were the residencies of, respectively, the Prussian monarchy and the Austrian-Hungarian Empire). Deleuze|Guattari rely in fact only on one study, Franz Wagenbach's (1958) biography of Kafka, which is a remarkable book but far from being a true sociolinguistic study. As a biography, it relies partly on Kafka's self-perceptions, which are themselves interesting enough, but, as self-descriptions follow their own rules of construction, they are far from applicable to an overarching description. In fact biographical writing might even prevent their application. Nevertheless literary studies tend to repeat Wagenbach's thesis about the poverty of "Prague German," although its presuppositions are hardly sustained historically and in comparison with other minority languages. In general it seems highly questionable whether a distinction between "pure" language (which always seems to be spoken in the so-called center, never a topological description but always linked to power) and some imaginary "margin" can and should be maintained—a differentiation somehow implicit in Deleuze|Guattari's descriptions, although they do not maintain it in other studies, particularly not in "Postulates of Linguistics" (TP1 83–123). The main points of view in the latter chapter will be summarized shortly. For alternative views on "marginal" languages, see, for example, Britton 1999; Derrida 1998a; Glissant 1989, 1997, 2005; Stevens 2004.

12. See Frank 1997.

13. As Adorno (1993) has pointed out, the term *variation* carries different meanings. If it rests on the assumption that structures repeat themselves, it implies *alternation*; if it hints at a differentiation of the material through a work on the material itself, it means *modification*. In music, variation was first understood as the repetition of a theme in, for example, a sonata; with Beethoven's compositions, this understanding was transformed, since he constantly modified musical themes themselves.

14. I am grateful for musicologist Brent Annable's comments on this section.

15. Karg-Elert (1930: 18) has pointed out that while the sound frequencies of a major chord have a ratio of 1:3:5, the frequencies in a minor chord are 10:12:15. The frequencies of a minor chord are not, therefore, a multiple of a prime number.

16. Schönberg (1957: 186) speaks in this context of an emancipation of dissonance.

17. In the French version, Deleuze makes an important distinction between *pouvoir* and *puissance*, a difference that remains untranslatable in English. As the division between both terms derives from Spinoza (and thus from Latin), Braidotti (2002: 21) has suggested using the terms *potestas* and *potentia*, signifying "power that is negative *(potestas)* in that it prohibits and constrains. It is also positive *(potentia)* in that it empowers and enables." See also Braidotti 2006: 28; Negri 1990: xi–xiv.

18. In French *mot d'ordre*, "slogan" and military "password" (see TP1 575).

19. See Deleuze's definition in *Difference and Repetition*: "The virtual is opposed not to the real but to the actual" (DR 260).

20. I am alluding here to Deleuze's description of a certain time-image that works as "a function of remembering, of temporalization: not exactly a recollection but an invitation to recollect" (TI 105).

21. Deleuze|Guattari's notion of becoming-woman (see TP1 272) has been criticized especially by feminists, as it somehow dispossesses minorities of a subject-position that they never were able to claim in the first place. Therefore Braidotti (Braidotti 1994: 111–24; 2002: 84–89) has argued that becoming-minor should be differentiated, depending on the *location* of subjects: it might be useful to engage in identity politics to work for social change, while at the same time changing "structures of the self," working toward a de-subjectification. See Wiese 2000; Möhring, Sabisch, and Wiese 2001: 311–30.

22. In *Proust and Signs*, Deleuze uses violence as a description of these forces: "The mistake of philosophy is to presuppose within us a benevolence of thought, a natural love of truth. Thus philosophy arrives at only abstract truths that compromise no one and do not disturb. . . . Truth is never the product of a prior disposition but the result of a violence in thought" (P 16).

23. The Latin *cogitanda* designates the gerund of Latin *cogere*, which means "to think," and thus translates as "what must be thought." In Latin a gerund construction does not need a subject to which it refers; it might as well express a generality, as in the famous dictum by Cato the Elder (mentioned by Plutarch): "Ceterum censeo Carthaginem esse delendam" (Moreover, I advise that Carthage must be destroyed). In this context the use of the

gerund *cogitanda* is important as it shows a grammatical equivalence to the "diagram" that the "unthought in thought" draws with thinking, since it is an "undefined," "impersonal" subject that is forced to think, a de-individualized subject, that is nevertheless not an object of thought.

24. Braidotti (2002: 24, 28) posits this fundamental openness as being at the heart of living beings. It can be best described as a tendency to become in social networks of power. The social is a web-like field of contradictory forces, in which the subject is actualized; that is, it is relentlessly and endlessly becoming. This becoming is dependent on other embodiments, through which the subject is prompted to change, as intersubjectivity is one of its modes. The subject, in Braidotti's view, is a point of relay and transformation; it consists of intersecting forces and spatiotemporal connections that open up to interstices and in-between spaces of hegemonic power fields and durations. It can best be described through processes, flows, in-between stati, and nonsequential effects (see 62), invested with an a priori desire—its tendency—for connection.

25. Psychoanalytically speaking, the I must be perceived as *moi*: that which belongs to me (see Silverman 1996: 10).

26. Postcolonial critics in particular have stressed the need for narratives that differ. Unanimously they call for a "re-vision of the past" (Ashcroft 2001: 98), for the development of a "new, ex-centric definition of history from the margins" (Davis 1998: 253), for a "prophetic vision of the past" (Glissant 1989: 64), and for "new and better maps of reality" (Rushdie 1992: 100). Similarly postcolonial authors have concluded that historiography is neither truth nor fiction, but rather a method of interpretation and writing within a power|knowledge system in the Foucauldian sense. As they want to challenge this system, they have questioned the disciplinary boundaries of history. For instance, Abdellatif Khayati (1999: 313) has shown in an essay on Toni Morrison's writing that literature can open up "a new space of cultural practice," precisely because it engages in a "historical" act that Morrison (1987, 1991, 1993b) calls "rememory." According to Khayati (1999: 323), rememory engages "discredited knowledge" by its choice of diction, its topics, and the configuration of the text. It conceptualizes difference as a "historical-political choice" (314) and reinvents "traditions and dominant language tropes" (313) in order to enable solidarity and strategic points of identification. For a more detailed elaboration, see Wiese 2009.

27. Although rememory and postmemory pertain to different fields of study, they nevertheless stress the creative endeavor undertaken by the descendents of survivors of historical catastrophes such as slavery and the Shoah. *Rememory* was introduced by Toni Morrison (1987: 199) in her novel *Beloved*, where she tells an ex-slave's story in such a way that her "unspeakable thoughts, unspoken" remain silent but are shaped in their impact, while the narrative performs a longing for the past to become articulated in the lives of the living through the appearance of a haunting yet beloved ghost. As Caroline Rody (1995: 102, my emphasis) has noted, "Rememory . . . functions in Morrison's history as a trope *for the problem* of reimagining one's heritage," and it is exactly this problem of reimagining one's legacy that the narration deals with creatively. And while the impossibilities and distortions of memory are staged

in Morrison's text, at the same time it also performs an affective and passionate cathexis that demands a quest for her people's past. For additional readings, see Davis 1998; Grewal 1998; McDowell 1988; Mohanty 1993.

Postmemory, on the other hand, is a term introduced into cultural theory by Marianne Hirsch (1997, 1999), who argues that postmemory entails "conceiving oneself as multiply interconnected with other of the same, of previous, and of subsequent generations, of the same and of other—proximate or distant—cultures and subcultures" (1999: 9). In her view, postmemory involves "projection, investment, and creation" (8) that children of survivors of cultural or collective trauma generate to approach a "hole of memory": a term that the psychoanalyst Nadine Fresco (1984) used to diagnose the specific relation that children of Holocaust survivors have to their parents' distorted or untold memories. Being divergent from memory through generational distance and from history by personal connection, "postmemory is a powerful and very particular form of memory precisely because its connection to its object of source is mediated not through recollection but though an imaginative investment and creation" (Hirsch 1997: 22).

Prememory is a term that I would like to coin for the particular forms of anticipation of a cultural memory through literature. It is thus "a memory of the future" (see Wiese 2012a).

28. Deleuze appropriated "the time out of joint" from Shakespeare's *Hamlet*, act 1, scene 5, 188 (see Shakespeare 1968: 51).

CHAPTER 2

1. Hannah Arendt's thoughts on *amor mundi*, love for the world, has inspired the title of this section. Amor mundi is a topic that has occupied Arendt throughout her whole life, starting with her dissertation *Der Liebesbegriff bei Augustin* (1929; *Love and Saint Augustine* [1996]) and extending to her later works in political philosophy, such as *The Human Condition* (1958a). Arendt believed that the turn toward the world—the choosing of the world—might allow human beings to unite and to create a common community despite and across differences. For more elaborated readings, see Chiba 1995; Hammer 2000; Miles 2002; Scott 2002. *Hannah Arendt: For the Love of the World* is the title of a book by Elisabeth Young-Bruehl (1982).

2. "Dark times" is a term I have borrowed from Arendt (1968b), which she uses to describe the ethicopolitical events that culminated in the Shoah and also the despair and outrage that accompanied the inadequate political stance of forceful forgetting that one might ascribe to postwar societies in the West. For her, dark times are "not identical with the monstrosity of this century," "which indeed are of an horrible novelty" (ix), but point to a degradation of truth to "meaningless triviality" (viii). See also Bar On 2002: 59–87; Herzog 2000; Luban 1983.

3. The latter is a term used by Deleuze|Guattari to bring about a shift of perception in which not being is taken as a starting point but rather how "one"—a multitude in itself—changes in assemblages, how "one" becomes and explores all the unknown possibilities of what "one" can do (see TP 233–309).

4. Here I rely on Spivak's (2003) description of teleopoiesis as a process of imaging beyond the limits of the already known. It means (literally) to project imaginings to a space far away and into a future perfect. As I point out in "My Dissertation Photo Album: Snapshots from a Writing Tour" (Wiese 2011), teleopoiesis allows one to experience an "othering" of oneself through language, to let oneself be haunted by difference for and in itself.

5. With the term *cracking up*, I allude to Deleuze's (D2) and Deleuze|Guattari's (TP) readings of Fitzgerald's *The Crack-Up, with Other Pieces and Stories* (1965). A crack-up might be understood as a tiny, even imperceptible change in a material—like a plate that cracks (see D2 95)—that causes a radical change, despite its tininess or even its imperceptibility.

6. Gerard Genette (1997a, 2004) defines metalepsis as a stylistic device in which the world of telling and the world told become mutually contaminated, for example, through the intrusion of the extradiegetic narrator into the diegetic world. Thereby the process of telling is exposed, an exposure that asks readers to change the reading contract from a voluntary suspension of disbelief to, for example, complicity with the narrative voice.

7. A palimpsest is a material medium or carrier on which two texts coexist, an old one and a new one. The term's roots are Greek, and it means "to scrub, to make smooth." It points to a medieval practice of manuscript production, in which "scribes . . . re-used sheets of vellum (animal skin such as sheep, calf, or goat) by rubbing or scraping off existing written material" (Cryderman 2002: n.p.). Although the old text has been erased, it might nevertheless be detected by a reader when reading the new text. The erasure might not have been entirely traceless, so that the existence of the old text, readable or not, makes itself felt.

8. Ekphrasis is the rhetorical description of a visual work of art (real or imagined) and has been used in literature since antiquity. One of the earliest examples is in the *Iliad*, where Homer describes in Book 18 how Hephaestus welds a new shield for Achilles (18.468–608). See Heffernan 1993.

9. *Explication* signifies literally unfolding (Latin *ex*, "out of, from within"; Latin *plicare*, "to fold") and should be understood here in this way, since unfolding implies a temporal dimension as well.

10. In some ways this conception is similar to Lacan's (1987: 50) understanding of the task of the psychoanalytic treatment to extract a "full speech" from the "empty speech," where the latter is an articulation in which the subject "loses himself in the machinations of language." Only by working through language's inability to express the subject's truth, by being attentive to language's breakdown and to nonverbal symptoms and repetitions, can one arrive at a "full speech" that paradoxically testifies to exactly this breakdown.

11. As Emma Kafalenos (2005: 259) has argued with regard to Edgar Allan Poe's *The Oval Portrait*, the verbal representation of a visual work of art gives rise to a necessary consideration of two media, if one is to understand "how the embedded artwork is perceived by readers or viewers in our world." Drawing on Tamar Yacobi's (1997) exploration of the interrelation between the arts and media, she argues for their interplay, since on the one hand "there is a medium we would perceive if we could enter the narrative world and experience the

artwork there" (Kafalenos 2005: 259), while on the other hand, this medium can be experienced only via the work of art in which it is represented. In rhetoric this form of intermediality has been considered since antiquity and is called ekphrasis, deriving its meaning from the Greek verb *phrazein*, "to reveal and to manifest," and the prefix *ek* "entirely complete" (see Wandhoff 2003: xx). Ekphrasis signifies a rhetorical strategy that appeals to the mind's eye of the reader or listener by making a vivid description of a time, place, or person. As such it has been closely related to the rhetorical strategy of *energeia* "actualization and vividness," which brings subject matter "vividly [*enargos*] before the eye" (Webb 1999: 11). In the narrower context it entails the description of a visual work of art, be it real or imagined (see Heffernan 1993). Ekphrasis therefore entails the ability of oral or written speech to make something present that is absent in place and/or time, thereby surpassing the verbal characteristics of an utterance (see Graf 1999: 145), since it is said to make viewers out of listeners—a description ascribed to Nicolaus of Myra (see Kennedy 1983: 54–73). The ability of ekphrasis to make something absent vividly present will be theorized in more detail in this chapter.

12. Temporal and spatial distance opens a new horizon—however lunar it might be—in *Everything Is Illuminated*, as symbolized by the first man on the moon: "'I see something,' he says, gazing over the lunar horizon at the tiny village of Trachimbrod. 'There is definitely something out there'" (Foer 2002: 99). That the man on the moon might perceive "something"—that no longer exists when observed—might be caused by his change in perspective from worldly to cosmic. When stars emit their light into the universe, it might take tens of thousands of years until their radiance reaches the human eye. When we see a star, we perceive it as it was in the past, sometimes a very distant past. The coital radiance of the Trachimbroders as the source of light is surely as fantastic as a story can be; in the natural world light will bridge the distance between the moon and the Earth (384.403 km) in only 1.3 light-seconds. In comparison, our galaxy, the Milky Way, has a diameter of 100,000 light-years and it is just one of billions of galaxies in the universe. Therefore, in astrophysical terms, this analogy lacks accuracy. The (lunatic) perspective of the man on the moon might nevertheless be seen as an analogy for the novel's quest for an unworldly point of view that allows one to take in the excessive dimensions of a traumatic event such as the Shoah.

13. This is the case if it is derived from the German verb *aufgeben*.

14. In Wolfgang Iser's (1978: 226) terminology, this vexing absence constitutes a "blank," which involves the readers in the "act of reading": "It [omissions and cancelations that constitute an unformulated background] enables the written words to transcend their literal meaning, to assume a multiple referentiality, and so to undergo the expansion necessary to transplant them as a new experience into the mind of the reader."

15. For a brief history of the shtetl, see www.bet-tal.com/ or http://trochenbrod.com/ (accessed December 30, 2010). The depiction of Ukrainians in the novel has been criticized for being inaccurate. See Ivan Katchanovski, "Everything Is Illuminated, Not!," *Prague Post*, October 7, 2004, http://www.praguepost.com/ (accessed December 30, 2010).

16. A mise-en-abyme (a term derived from French, meaning literally "placing into the abyss") designates the mirroring of a motif or theme within a work of representation, for example, the depiction on a shield of armor. When referring to pictures, it is also called a Droste effect, named after the tins and boxes of Droste cocoa powder, on which the box itself is shown in the picture that depicts it and so on and so forth.

17. The differentiation between the narrative level on which events are told and the events told has been extensively analyzed by Genette 1997a. See section 2.3 for a more detailed account.

18. With the term *incompossible worlds* Leibniz answers the problem of the possible. He suggests that two antithetical events are not mutually exclusive but rather take place in two different, mutually exclusive worlds. Deleuze relates Leibniz's solution of the "possible" as follows: "The naval battle may or may not take place, but this is not in the same world: It takes place in one world and does not take place in a different world, and these two worlds are possible, but are not 'compossible' with each other" (TI 126). With the help of Borges, Deleuze develops this notion further and claims that "nothing prevents us from affirming that incompossibles belong to the same world" (TI 127). The coexistence of incompossible worlds is possible, and this allows for an experience of time as *la durée*, time as becoming, since neither memories of the past nor anticipations of the future can exhaust all incompossible worlds.

19. The splitting up of logic and rhetoric is exploited in Derrida's (1998a: 1) *Monolingualism of the Other*, where he states, "I have only one language, it is not mine." Logically this sentence cannot make sense, because one cannot have something that is not one's own. Yet its rhetoricity, played out through its antinomy, helps to question what kind of ownership language implies, and if its "ownership" and the "belonging" it promises might be permeated by its history and by the geopolitical location of its speakers. Derrida uses his monolingualism to show how his being other—an Algerian Jew speaking French, a language experienced as being spoken "elsewhere"—already infects his sense of the French language, so that a (geo)political location has an important influence on the access to language, which, in the example of Derrida, can be experienced as splitting up. In the context of my argument, I see this as a painful yet interconnecting experience.

20. *Everything Is Illuminated* is a quest without a guide, as is stated in one of the accounts Alex gives to Jonathan that refers to the planning of the tour.

21. To "give ourselves up" hints here at Spivak's (1992) interpretation of the "task of the translator," which is more "sich aufgeben" (to give oneself up) than it is "being defeated."

22. Especially the last sentence of this quotation remains in my view untranslatable. It shifts the meaning of the German verb *hoffen* (to hope) by adding the prefix *ver*: "Das Gedicht verweilt oder *verhofft*—ein auf die Kreatur zu beziehendes Wort—bei solchen Gedanken" (Celan 1990: 53, my emphasis). This neologism changes the meaning of the entire sentence, since *ver* indicates that an action (expressed by the verb) has gone wrong, has ended, or has been done too much or too many times (see "Wortbildung," http://mmtux.idf.uni-heidelberg.de, accessed July 10, 2010). This means that the

hope expressed has gone wrong, has ended, has been felt too much: It is thus *verhoffen* that becomes "a word for living creatures" (Celan 1990: 53). By adding the prefix *ver*—which is such a minor change that one can easily overlook it—Celan connects to a recurrent trope in Holocaust testimonies in which the notion of "impossible" hope is reflected upon, again and again (see Postone and Santer 2003).

23. See note 47. For a brilliant and moving interpretation of Celan's use of dates, see Derrida 2002.

24. Jonathan as an implied author becomes so indistinguishable from the real author, Jonathan Safran Foer, that we can safely assume that we have finally reached the end of a chain of intertwining narrator positions.

25. As Noël Carroll (2007) has argued, "narrative closure" occurs when all questions the narrative evokes are answered and all problems are solved.

26. This description has been inspired by commentators on Benjamin's *Arcade Project* (1999), since Benjamin wanted to create a montage out of his work, in which the "quotation" becomes an important point of departure for a different take on history when considered in conjunction with his "On the Concept of History" (Benjamin 2005b: 389–401). See Buck-Morss 1991: 221; Haverkamp 1993: 275; Rollestone 1989. See also the next section of this work, in which I will delve into a reading of photography as a necessary quotation and its relation to history (see sections 2.16–2.22).

27. Catastrophic difference destroys Nietzsche's philosophical notions of "amor fati" (1974, 1989) and "eternal return" (1961, 1974, 1989), which play such an important role in Deleuze's thought (cf. DR, N, SP). When a traumatic event like genocide occurs, it is, as I will argue in section 2.15, no longer possible to affirm life as such. This is the case because genocide brings into being not the forces of life but rather *the power to take life* when a people are murdered and their way of life threatens to disappear. I am relying here on the definition of genocide agreed upon after World War II by the United Nations (U.N. Doc A/P.V. 179). The term *genocide* was coined by Raphael Lemkin (1944: 79) and describes "the destruction of a nation or ethnic group . . . not only through mass killings, but also through a coordinated plan of different actions aiming at the essential foundations of the life of a national group, with the aim of annihilating the groups themselves." See also Lemkin 1944: 79–95.

28. As Gerald Prince (1997: ix) has pointed out, "Any writing is a rewriting, and literature is always in the second degree." In this understanding, texts are generally transformative or imitative, since they expand or liberate a prior perception of reality or graft themselves onto (an) other preexisting text(s). Genette (1997a)—whose detailed research on different forms of palimpsests has become a point of reference—distinguishes between six different palimpsestic types: transtextuality, paratextuality, intertextuality, metatextuality, architextuality, and hypertextuality. While transtextuality is the superordinate principle, "all that sets the text in relation to other texts," intertextuality is the relation of "co-presence between two or several texts" (1), for example, through quotations or allusions. Paratextuality consists of the nonnarrative elements of a text, such as the title, while metatextuality is an explicit commentary on the text. Architextuality is of a taxonomic nature and refers to the

generic quality of a text, its genre. Hypertextuality—the term that will become prominent in my analysis—is defined through a temporal relation between two texts, in which one text (the hypertext) is "derived from another pre-existent text" (5), called hypotext.

29. This is a past one cannot know, a "general past" that nevertheless presses upon the present—an understanding of time that is explained in section 1.5. and will become prominent in chapter 4.

30. Benjamin's (2005b: 391) Thesis V in "On the Concept of History" reads as follows: "The true image of the past flits by. The past can be seized only as an image that flashes up at the moment of its recognizability, and is never seen again. 'The truth will not run away from us': this statement by Gottfried Keller indicates exactly that point in historicism's image of history where the image is pierced by historical materialism. For it is an irretrievable image of the past which threatens to disappear in any present that does not recognize itself as intended in that image."

31. Here it is important not to forget that this memory-making has as its object not only actuality but also "events"—those incorporeal happenings that evade history, while being born by it, that which becomes, "aternally," when it finds its proper milieu (see section 1.7).

32. Here I am alluding to Deleuze's understanding (F) of language and of light as being the precondition of speaking and seeing. In the context of this chapter, I will theorize about the necessity of a general love as a precondition for ethical actions.

33. Latin *inter* means "amid, in between, while, at"; *fuit* is the third-person indicative active perfect of *esse*, which means "being, existing, being there." *Interesse* translates as "being in between, being there, being different."

34. The Latin noun *infinitivum* is, if taken literally, "the never-ending."

35. The Latin adverb *inter* strongly hints at being "in between" two different parties.

36. *Camera lucida* (illuminated chamber), the original French title of Barthes's work on photography, is a wordplay that hints at the first photographic apparatus, the *camera obscura*, meaning "darkened room." The camera obscura is a predecessor of the camera. Through a hole on one side of a room or a box, the light of an outside scene was transmitted and projected upside down on the opposite wall. Barthes might have chosen the antonym *lucida* to refer to the illumination of the spectators that photographs might invite.

37. *Identity* is etymologically grounded in the Latin *idem*, which means "the same," and Latin *identidem*, "again and again, repeatedly."

38. According to the Online Etymological Dictionary (www.etymonline. com, accessed February 15, 2012), this has been the dominant meaning of *essential* since medieval times.

39. I should also note that the etymological foundation of *science*, that is, the Latin *scientia*, which means "knowledge," is grounded in the Latin *scindere*, "to cut, divide," which in a figurative sense also means "to separate one thing from another, to distinguish" (www.etymonline.com, accessed February 15, 2012). There is another "cut," another "punctum" implied while doing "science."

40. Interestingly enough, this remark includes another hint toward knowledge, since *mathesis singularis*—an invented term, since *mathesis* is not a word—could be composed from Greek *manthanein*, which means "to learn" but also "to think, to have one's mind aroused," while *thesis* derives from Greek, meaning "proposition." That is, *mathesis singularis* could translate as "singular proposition for learning."

41. I owe this insight to Anselm Haverkamp's terrific text "The Memory of Pictures: Roland Barthes and Augustine on Photography" (1993).

42. The catastrophe diagnosed by Barthes is itself a quotation from Benjamin's "Central Park," only the subject of the sentence has been changed. The original sentence is "The concept of progress should be grounded in the idea of catastrophe. That things 'just keep on going' is the catastrophe. Not something that is impending at any particular time ahead, but something that is always given" (Benjamin 2005a: 176) and entails not only a radical critique of historiography but also a new "messianic" conception of history writing that I will consider later on.

43. This notion also connects to Blanchot and Derrida's (2000) understanding of death as a dreamlike and ungraspable presence in human life, a personal and impersonal force that indicates an event that has always already taken place. As Braidotti (2006: 210) has argued, Blanchot's notion of death is useful since it helps to overcome a vision that sees death as the horizon of life rather than an event that takes place in life too, as the "sense of the awareness of finitude, of the interrupted flow of my being there."

44. Literature never represents "reality" but instead, as I would like to suggest, doubles or envelops it. To envelop should be understood literally here; within literature, yet hidden from view, there is reality—albeit a reality that is different in nature from its medium. Similarly I understand doubling strictly in the following sense: to double the play of forces by "folding forces" (Deleuze 1999: 93), creating in this way a fold that is ever-shifting in peristaltic movements.

45. Fackenheim is extending Jewish religious laws (composed of 613 commandments) and therefore states that it is applicable only for Jews. Nevertheless I would like to argue that the moral force of this commandment can be shared by members of other religious or secular groups too.

46. For a more elaborate explanation of the specific twist Celan give to the notion of hope after surviving Auschwitz, see section 2.6.

47. In the English translation, the poem "takes such thoughts for its home" (Celan 2005: 163), while in the German version, the poem "lingers and stays [*verweilen*] with such thoughts": "Das Gedicht verweilt oder verhofft . . . bei diesen Gedanken" (Celan 1990: 53). I consider this to be an important phrasing, since the verb *verweilen* has a primarily temporal dimension of lingering (at a place), of not wanting to part. See *verweilen* in *Deutsches Wörterbuch von Jacob Grimm und Wilhelm Grimm*, 16 Bde. [in 32 Teilbänden] (Leipzig: S. Hirzel 1854–1960), Quellenverzeichnis 1971, Band 25, Spalten 2173–97, http://germazope.uni-trier.de/Projects/DWB/ (accessed February 15, 2012).

48. A very insightful essay about Arendt's "political storytelling" and Benjamin's influence on it has been put forward by Annabel Herzog (2000), as

well as Seyla Benhabib (1990). My own understanding of how storytelling works has been deeply influenced by Arendt, Benjamin, and their reception, and has served numerous times as an inspiration for descriptions, although transferred into the philosophical framework of Deleuze|Guattari. I am deeply thankful for having these thoughts at my disposal.

49. The Greek noun *tele* means literally "far, far off"; in word combinations, it means "far off, afar, at or to a distance" (see *tele* in www.etymonline. com, accessed February 15, 2012).

CHAPTER 3

1. Historians claim that it is exceedingly difficult to estimate the number of Aboriginal deaths or murders by shootings or starvation, as these were often disguised by the casual wording of perpetrators and government officials alike. Due to this, Aborigines' extermination is vulnerable to appropriation by revisionists. A case in point is the debate triggered by Keith Windschuttle's *The Fabrication of Aboriginal History* (2002), which was awarded a Centenary Medal for "services to history" in 2003 by Australian prime minister John Howard. Windschuttle's claim that the Tasmanian Aboriginals were wiped out by disease, ill adaptation, inferior warfare, and population decline due to having sold many of their women, has been disproved thoroughly (see Manne 2003). The debate nevertheless shows how difficult it is for Australian society to acknowledge its guilt in the demise of the Aboriginal population, especially if racism, institutional or otherwise, currently continues to sustain argumentation like Windschuttle's. For devastating statistical evidence of institutional racism and the marginalization of Australian Aborigines, see the Annual Report of the Australian Bureau of Statistics, http://www.abs.gov.au/.

2. Female convicts were less costly and produced more net benefits. In addition the net production was higher once a convict became a free settler (see Lewis 1988).

3. Norbert Finzsch (2005, 2008) has shown how a supremacist racist discourse among colonial settlers discursively prepared the ground for massive killings of Australian (and American) Aborigines.

4. As Linda Ferreira-Buckley (1999: 578–79) has pointed out, there have always been challenges to such a clear-cut understanding of historiographical methods. Herodotus, considered the father of history, was called a prime inventor by Cicero (*De Divinatione* 11: 116; qtd. in Momigliano 1966: 127–28). Leopold von Ranke and Wilhelm von Humboldt's influential faith in historiography's objectivity was challenged by their contemporary Karl Marx (Ferreira-Buckley 1999: 579); Friedrich Nietzsche's interrogation titled "The Use and Abuse of History" (1997) has been taken up, among others, by Karl Popper (Ferreira-Buckley 1999: 580). Historiography as such cannot be seen as a completely unified field: if we take Ferreira-Buckley's insight as a given, there have always been methodological queries.

5. For an overview of the recent developments in queer and postcolonial historiography, see Chiang 2008. For a summary on feminist historiography,

see Tasker and Holt-Underwood 2008. For postcolonial historiography, see Chakrabarty 2000a; Dirlik, Bahl, and Gran 2000.

6. As a number of critics of diverse historical perspectives, such as postcolonial, subaltern, gender studies, postmodern, and metahistory, have argued, the "written history of a people" is far more than the outcome of "a government bureaucracy" (Russell 1993: 300). The rules of evidence—which Carlo Ginzburg (1989) has called "evidentiary paradigms"—pertaining to academic history-writing already inscribe the historic discipline into the Western tradition (cf. Chakrabarty 1992, 2000a), as the required verifiability of sources assume not only their written status but also their storage. This requirement creates internal exclusions: writing is a technology of knowledge production and therefore far from being a transparent medium (cf. Chun 2006; White 1987); furthermore it assumes that writing is a privileged form of knowledge transfer that is accessible in any culture imaginable at any point of time. However, such an assumption excludes oral history-telling as practiced by many peoples; it ignores the fact that prior to emancipation, in several American states it was prohibited by law to teach slaves to read and write (see Appiah and Gates 1992; Span 2002; Goodell 1853); and ignores the fact that, until recently, girls and women were either excluded from education or had access only to different education (cf. Kleinau and Opitz 1996a, 1996b).

7. See Plato 2007; Plato's *Meno, Parmenides, Phaedo, Philebus, Sophist*, and *Timaeus* on http://classics.mit.edu/index.html, accessed February 15, 2012.

8. *Gould's Book of Fish* mentions and stages several books of fish. There is the novel itself, which I will spell with uppercase letters. There is the diegetically rendered book of fish originally written by narrator Gould, written in lowercase letters. There is also the reconstructed version of the book of fish, written by the narrator Sid Hammet. This is called the Salamanca Book of Fish. And finally, there is a book containing the original fish drawings of the real convict-painter William Buelow Gould. This is called the Allport Library's Book of Fish. To avoid confusion, I will refer to these different books accordingly.

9. In this way narratology's understanding of an "unreliable narrator"—a position that Gould claims by confessing self-attribution—is altered. Because Gould differentiates between himself and his storytelling from the start of the book, it is impossible to see him as an unreliable narrator in the sense described by Wayne Booth (1961: 158–59): "I have called a narrator reliable when he speaks for or acts in accordance with the norms of the work (which is to say the implied author's norms), unreliable when he does not"—a definition that has been most influential in narratology. Rather in *Gould's Book of Fish*, the narrator and his narrative can be regarded as separate: the former is a confessed liar and the latter is assuredly true, although we will have to determine in the course of the analysis what kind of truth the novel establishes and how this might relate to the powers of the false that are central in this work. I will argue that there are a number of elements in the novel that sustain the "truthfulness" of his story, for example, the paratextual device of placing the

real Gould's fish drawings on the cover of the book. Devices aiming at a new notion of truthfulness also reflect back on the supposed unreliability of Gould, who is established as someone who lies out of a need to survive the inhuman conditions he is describing.

10. Genette (1997b) understands paratextuality as consisting of paratexts such as titles, prefaces, dedications, notes, and, I would argue, illustrations, and of epitexts that surround a text, like interviews, public statements and discussions, reviews, and criticisms (see Allen 2000: 103). As Genette (1988: 63, qtd. in Allen 2000: 104) has argued, a paratext is the threshold between the inside and the outside of a text and thereby "not only marks a zone of transition between text and non-text ['hors-texte'], but also a transaction." While Derrida (1987b) argues that paratexts therefore frame and constitute a text, Genette is interested in the forms of transaction called into being through paratexts, as for example through their relation to certain hypertexts: in the case of *Gould's Book of Fish*, the fish drawings of the real Gould.

11. As I explained in chapter 2, a mise-en-abyme designates the mirroring of a motif or theme within a work of representation, as in Droste cocoa powder or Quaker Oatmeal, in which the design of the box is repeated by showing the box itself in the picture. For a detailed description, see section 2.6.

12. Here I am paraphrasing Deleuze's definition, which holds that the false has "the power to affect and be affected" (TI 135), a definition that I will flesh out below.

13. Through its use of mise-en-abyme, this novel is extradiegetically Hammet's memorized version of *Gould's Book of Fish*, while "in reality" it is a novel written by Richard Flanagan.

14. As I explained in more detail in chapter 2, a palimpsest is a material medium or carrier in which two texts coexist, an old one and a new one. The term is named after the practice of overwriting old manuscripts with new ones. Genette (1997a) also sees a palimpsest in hypertexts that transform or imitate a text, since they are based on a previous text, which they evoke while telling a story. For a more detailed explanation, see section 2.14.

15. This ever-changing eternity is time as aeon, as infinite-becoming, which is not measured like its counterpart chronos, but rather establishes new connections and intensities within "pure," nonpulsed time (see TP2 262–63; Deleuze 1990: 162–69).

16. In *Proust and Signs*, Deleuze defines style as "the explication of the signs" (P 166), which produces "*effects of resonance and forced movements*" (167). Here "explication," as I explained earlier (see section 2.4), has to be understood literally as the "unfolding" of a sign, the ways its original fold is altered by giving it a literary worlding, by explaining it through a viewpoint that succeeds the writer and precedes the readers-to-come. This is a literary viewpoint that does not collapse back into either writer or reader but is able to reveal "essences," since literature in particular, but also the other arts, allow for the exploration of encounters rendered in a perspective beyond recognition.

17. As Deleuze has maintained in *Cinema 2: The Time-Image*, that which cannot be represented might nevertheless be perceived (see Kawash 1998: 127). Against this background of a possible distinction between the

representable and the perceivable, this means that the reader of *Gould's Book of Fish* might be able grasp that the original painter's experiences and/ or perceptions have been absorbed into his paintings, while accepting that she or he is nevertheless not able to pin them down since they lack their own representation.

18. By understanding "style" as the incorporation of an author's perception, Deleuze|Guattari have established a point of contact with numerous literary theorists. In the wake of structuralism, literary theorists began to understand language quite literally as "the material of the literary artist" (Wellek and Warren 1956: 163), and to develop parameters that might be able to define how an author distinguishes herself or himself through her or his particular use of this linguistic materiality. Structuralist literary scholars such as Roman Jakobson (1971, 1987; Jakobson and Waugh 1979), Michael Riffaterre (1959, 1960, 1966), and George Dillon (1978) were developing models that had been inspired by the differentiation Ferdinand de Saussure (1983) made between the syntagmatic and the paradigmatic axes of language use. Every "word" (a distinction that does not exist in linguistic terminology, where the smallest meaningful unit is a morpheme) competes on the paradigmatic level with a number of synonyms, so that an author's style might be distinguished by her or his particular word choice. Similarly the successive combination of "words" into sequences might also compete with equivalent meanings, for which it is possible to distinguish stylistic choices on the syntagmatic level either. As Taylor (1982) has pointed out, Riffaterre and Dillon have also been interested in considering how literature might urge readers to deviate from their normal linguistic behavior to look only for meaning, which grants literature a specific capability to interrupt and disturb linguistic contexts. For this reason, Buikema (2009: 314) may argue that "deviant linguistic forms make us aware of our conventionally coded ways of dealing with the world," which means that literary styles have repercussions that go beyond the singular artwork, too. Buikema also points this out when she claims that literature is a "performance of the consciousness of alterity, of the other, that which is new, of difference" (315). With Riffaterre and Dillon, one could even claim that an artwork forges an altered consciousness and forces it upon its readers when it disturbs their readerly habit to search for meaning by debasing referentiality. This might also explain why, in Deleuze|Guattari's view, the artwork precedes the readers-to-come: it is already there, waiting for us to become "us" (for a more detailed description, see section 1.5).

19. I consciously do not use the terms *implied author* and *implied reader(s)* here, terms that in narratology define those structural positions of "origin" and "appeal" that can be reconstructed as abstractions from the (literary) text itself (cf. Bal 1985; Booth 1961; Chatman 1990; Fish 1980; Genette 1972; Iser 1974, 1978). Although these terms are valid and highly useful, I want to argue here that the specific use of the materiality of the book itself points toward a physical reality "before" and "beyond" the text itself: a "before" and "beyond" that is also in line with my specific reading of a Deleuze|Guattari–inspired literary machine, as explained in chapter 1.

20. See *treadwheel* in www. britannica.com (accessed February 15, 2012).

21. I am using the terminology of Hjelmslev (1961), since it is foundational for DeleuzeǀGuattari's understanding of linguistics (see TP1 44–123). In Hjelmslev's understanding, *substance* refers to the material transmitter and/ or human/animal content, while *form* relates to language, techniques, style, and semantic/thematic structures (see Chandler 1994–2014). It is advisable to use his ideas in the current context, because, unlike de Saussure, he does not exclude materiality from semiotics.

22. This is the case, for example, in my 2003 British edition, which was published by the aptly named Atlantic Books.

23. Apart from Hjelmslev's (1961) terminology, which uses substance (of expression or content) and form (of expression or content), these are sometimes called signifier and signified (Saussure 1983), sign vehicle, sense, or referent (Peirce 1931–58).

24. Braidotti (2006) proposes understanding the division between *zoë* and *bios* in a completely different way from Agamben (1998, 1999a, 1999b, 2000), whose work is a most important point of reference in contemporary debates on biopolitics. He suggests that from antiquity on, there has been a differentiation between life in its political form (bios) and life as "mere" biological being (zoë), resulting in the exclusion of "mere" biological life from the political sphere. I will scrutinize his philosophical proposals in the conclusion of this chapter. I see *Gould's Book of Fish* as an attempt to create an understanding of life in which its political, polis-making possibilities and its biology are not separated. I have, however, refrained from using a terminological division between bios and zoë, although I understand the need to give corporeal life (zoë) a new value in philosophical thought—an undertaking that in my view is Braidotti's aim. She argues with Deleuze that "it is possible to account for power before its political coding" (2006: 251), and with him, she understands the "politics of zoë to mean a world in which there can be no distinction between the socializing forces of the body politic and the corporeal forces of matter" (251).

25. In the original French version of *A Thousand Plateaus* (TP), it is *devant* that renders this spatial relation (see TP2 275; DR 55). In DeleuzeǀGuattari's understanding, becoming is triggered by direct spatial contact. See Lawlor 2008: 175–76.

26. I am relying here on a description from *A Thousand Plateaus*: "Yes, all becomings are molecular: the animal, flower, or stone one becomes are molecular collectivities, haecceities, not molar subjects, objects, or form that we know from the outside and recognize from experience, through science, or by habit" (TP2 275, qtd. in Lawlor 2008: 175).

27. For a more detailed description of the difference between habitual and attentive recognition, see section 1.4.

28. As Chris Pak has pointed out in The Reader Online (October 6, 2008), Flanagan thereby paints an "alternate picture of history and therefore of the present. He does so to give voice to a type of truth suppressed from the historical record" (www.thereaderonline.co.uk, accessed February 15, 2012).

29. It is important to mention that my insights into DeleuzeǀGuattari's understanding of love are deeply indebted to Leonard Lawlor's reading in "Following the Rats: Becoming-Animal in Deleuze and Guattari" (2008).

30. In the original French version (Deleuze and Guattari 1980), one becomes "tout le monde" (244), which means literally "the whole world" (see Lawlor 2008: 173).

31. In some ways *Gould's Book of Fish* participates in a critique that diverse historians informed by gender studies, queer studies, disabilities studies, or postcolonial studies have argued. What can be qualified as a credible account (Stoler 1992) and what is stored for the future is governed heavily by those in charge of the archives—who, as Derrida (1996: 4) has noted, are exclusively those in political power, which is why Rolph Trouillot (1995) speaks of the unequal distributions of "archival power." If the discipline of history "places a premium on 'archival credibility'" (Featherstone 2000: 169), it seems important to reconsider not the content of the archive but its form, as Ann Laura Stoler (2002b) has argued. The archive is not only a privileged site for retrieving historical knowledge but also a place where this knowledge is created and institutionalized (see Stoler 2002b, 2009), often to sustain the power of the (nation-)state. To circulate and consume this knowledge uncritically might sustain the same implicitly or explicitly racist, sexist, and heteronormative epistemologies and taxonomies that were in place when the archive was created, as is especially the case in the colonial archive (see Arondekar 2005; Bastian 2006; Featherstone 2000; Richards 1993; Russell 1993; Spivak 1985; Stoler 1992). Therefore Stoler (Stoler 2002a: 91) has suggested shifting critical attention from distinguishing fact from fiction "to track[ing] the production and consumption of those 'facts' themselves," whereas the Subaltern Studies Group has made it their aim to retrieve the hidden histories of the subaltern from the official documents. (For an overview of subaltern studies, see Chakrabarty 2000b; Guha 1997.) The colonial records are a good way to get to know a colonial society, even if the sources reflect not the colonized point of view but the colonizers' point of view and interests.

32. Metafiction has been characterized as a group of (post)modern texts that reflect on their own fictive constructedness. Linda Hutcheon (1980: 1) has defined it as "fiction about fiction—that is fiction that includes within itself a commentary on its own narrative and/or linguistic identity." According to *The Routledge Encyclopedia of Narrative Theory* (Herman 2007: 216), "Historiographic metafiction self-consciously explores the status and function of narrative as an ideological construct shaping history and forging identity rather than merely representing the past."

33. Although it is beyond the scope of this work to show how Agamben differs substantially from Foucault, I nevertheless want to stress that especially the deterministic and unilateral point of view of power's influence on subjects deviates from a Foucauldian understanding of power. The latter not only emphasizes that discourses shape subject positions but also shows how subjects resist—and thereby shape—discourses. For Foucault (1978, 1983, 1994, 2003a, 2003b, 2007), power relations are therefore never fixed but are always becoming in a play of multilateral forces. See also section 1.5 of this work. For a critique on Agamben's use of Arendt and Foucault, see Blencowe 2010.

CHAPTER 4

1. The noun *phonograph* is derived from Greek *phono*, which translates as "sound," and *graphos*, "writing, writer."

2. The pseudo-scientific concept of "race" emerged alongside evolutionary theories in the eighteenth and nineteenth century (see Finzsch, Horton, and Horton 1999: 145). In the colonial context it was used to establish a racial hierarchy in which white Europeans were positioned at the top of the evolutionary ladder, while non-Europeans were placed on intermediate rungs (see Malik 1996; Wolpoff and Caspari 1997; Jaimes 1995, all qtd. in Ifekwunigwe 2004: 9). During colonial conquests in Africa, the Americas, Asia, and Australia, racialist thought and racializations helped to divide and conquer native populations and legitimated settler imperialism, colonial wars, genocide, and slavery (American Anthropological Association 2004: 98; Camper 2004: 179). On the European continent it was used to warrant the oppression, social exclusion, and willful murder of poor, homeless, or differently abled persons and Jewish, Sinti, and Romani people (see Bartov 2000). Racialist arguments play a major role in fascist thinking too. The industrial mass murder of 6 million Jews (see Hilberg 1961; Yahil 1998), an estimated 90,000 to 500,000 Sinti and Romani (Margalit 2002; Zimmermann 1996), and the murder of countless differently abled persons would not have been possible without the ideology of race and racial hygiene (Friedlander 1995; Bartov 2000; Essner 2003). The Nazi invasion of Poland and the war against the Soviet Union were equally fueled by a racist ideology that legitimated countless atrocities and the murder of civilians (see Boehler 2006; Mühlhäuser 2010; Pohl 2008).

Today the "scientific" argumentation on race has been thoroughly disproven. Genetically "race accounts for a miniscule 0.012% difference in our genetic material" (Hoffman 1994: 4, qtd. in Ifekwunigwe 2004: 3). The great variation of racial delineations across time and space furthermore strongly suggest that "race" is a social construct and an unstable category. For example, as Sander L. Gilman (2000: 229–37) has pointed out, Jews were considered black in eighteenth- and nineteenth-century Europe; similarly poor Irish immigrants were seen as black in the United States in the nineteenth century (see Roediger 1999, 2005, 2008; Ignatiev 1995). As the seminal historical comparison by Carl Degler (1971) has shown, "race" relations have been constructed very differently in Brazil and the United States, which demonstrates that the idea of "race" depends on historical, social, and political circumstances. I therefore consider "race" a social fiction that is used as a means of inclusion and exclusion, exploitation, and control of resources, and as a social fiction that has proven to be murderous over the course of its existence. My use of quotations marks around the term "race" is indebted to my understanding of its fictionality.

Nevertheless I would also like to acknowledge that "race" marks the life of everyone, whatever their skin color, texture of hair, or shape of eyes, to name but a few phenotypical markers of racial identities. In the words of Gilman (2000: 230), "Race has been a powerful force in shaping how we, at the close the twentieth century, understand ourselves—often in spite of ourselves." One of the topics of *The Time of Our Singing* is how "race" forms and shapes racial identities and belonging and creates inequalities that are not easy to overcome. In this chapter I will explore the performative dimensions of "race," its ability to produce evidence that in turn secures its very existence as a category for the perception of "differences."

3. This "form of time" is conceptualized as measurable, generalizable, and objectifiable. Its very datability implies an understanding of time in which datability follows conventions that account for its succession (one date after another) or its simultaneity (events happening on the same date are understood to take place at the same time). This succession or simultaneity of events is understood to be the same for everyone. Bergson (1919, 1999), calls this form of time "measurable," "spatialized," or "divisible," while Antonio Negri (2003), following Marx, refers to it as "world time" because it coordinates time for everyone on the planet and makes work time the measurement of equivalence.

4. *Making time* is a neologism that I want to introduce in analogy to the concepts of "doing gender" or "doing race." The latter terms express the absence of gender or race prior to their performance. With "making time" I am suggesting that time likewise needs to be enacted.

5. Although the civil rights movement and the black liberation movement in the 1950s, 1960s, and 1970s enforced the demands for equal rights, the social and economic status of the black U.S. population is today still inferior to that of the white population. In 2004 nearly a quarter of all Afro-American families lived below the poverty line (see DeNavas-Walt, Proctor, and Lee 2005). Although the average income of Afro-Americans has increased since the new millennium, in 2004 it was 65 percent that of the income of the white population (see DeNavas-Walt, Proctor, and Lee 2005). New statistical data suggest that Afro-Americans have been hit the hardest by the worldwide economic crisis of 2008. In 2009 their income was 58 percent that of the white population's income, the lowest of all racialized population groups (see DeNavas-Walt, Proctor, and Smith 2010). From 2008 to 2009 the poverty rate for Afro-Americans increased from 24.7 to 25.8 percent; for Hispanics it rose from 23.2 to 25.3 percent (see DeNavas-Walt, Proctor, and Smith 2010). All in all, these data show that the colorism of the U.S. administration and population is far from overcome.

6. In the United States skin color and/or knowledge about family background determined who was a slave and who was a slave owner. Only persons with African heritage could be enslaved, with the occasional exception of Native Americans (see Daniel 2000; Degler 1971: 25; Twine 1998; Winant 1999). To determine who belonged to these groups, the "one-drop rule" and the "rule of hypodescent" were established (see Ifekwunigwe 2004: 10–14). These rules ensured that anyone with one African ancestor—regardless of whether the person had Native American, Pacific Islander, European, and/ or Asian ancestry too—was part of a caste of people that whites could legally enslave until 1865. From 1865 on, the Thirteenth Amendment to the U.S. Constitution abolished slavery. Although interracial marriages were forbidden in several U.S. states until 1967, it is estimated that 75 to 80 percent of the black population has white ancestry (see Degler 1971: 185). Although slave owners often raped female slaves, they were required neither to acknowledge the

"mix-raced" children conceived through these rapes nor to take legal or personal responsibility for their violent deeds. After the abolishment of slavery in 1865, "legal and customary segregation—that is the separation of whites and blacks in activities of daily life" (Degler 1971: 5) became the order of the day. In the southern United States racial apartheid was legally safeguarded by the Jim Crow laws introduced in 1896 and by the "separate but equal" doctrine that held sway between 1876 and 1965. In the northern cities the Afro-American population became ghettoized (see Nyong'o 2009: 7).

7. Although people from a variety of "racial backgrounds" have had sexual and/or conjugal relations, racial apartheid between the perceived black and white population is the matrix upon which race relations are perceived. For an overview, see Root 1992.

8. The lively debate on the U.S. census and its categories is a case in point. For an overview, see Ifekwunigwe 2004: 205–59.

9. The conjunction of classical music with whiteness is, as Lawrence Levin shows in *Highbrow/Lowbrow: The Emergence of Cultural Hierarchy in America* (1988), a fairly recent development. Of particular importance for this development is the rise of the American bourgeoisie in the nineteenth century, when bourgeois forms of conduct and appearance began to set entrance conditions for concert venues. In *The Making of American Audiences: From Stage to Television, 1750—1990*, Richard Butsch (2000: 6) describes how nineteenth-century elites "effectively labeled the working class as rowdy and disreputable." Successively, bourgeois forms of conduct and appearance began to exclude working-class citizens—a large percentage of which was black—from opera houses, concert halls, and other performance venues (see Levin 1988). Numerous examples attest to the fact that, until these forms of conduct and appearance took hold, classical music's audiences were composed of people of diverse colors and classes. Levin (1988) writes that until the end of the nineteenth century classical concerts and operas were often staged in public parks that had a low entry threshold and were not racially segregated. He also describes how opera songs circulated in popular culture, which attests to their availability. Tom Fletcher (1984: 6), a well-known Afro-American performer born in 1873, even records the breakdown of racial segregation in his hometown of Portsmouth in *100 Years of the Negro in Show Business*: "We had a big opera house . . . because Portsmouth was one of the big one-night stands in Ohio. Showboats always stopped there. In that opera house, owned by a man named Mr. H. S. Grimes, we all sat side by side. If there was any prejudice everybody was usually too occupied with the entertainment to take any time to feel it." It is hard to tell if this absence of segregation in an opera house is an exception to the rule, since hardly any research has been done on nineteenth-century *black* American audiences of classical music. Jessica Gienow-Hecht's study *Sound Diplomacy* (2009) is pathbreaking in this respect. Insisting on the popularity and availability of classical music in the long nineteenth century, she shows that organizers undertook directed efforts to enable lower-income classes and women to visit concerts. She mentions photographic evidence of black people in ticket queues and reports that Henry Higginson, the founder of the Boston Symphony Orchestra, was keen on bringing Afro-Americans into

the concert hall. She notes that newspapers reported about Afro-Americans who in 1914 refused to sit in segregated seating areas in a Washington concert hall (132–35). Most research on audiences in the nineteenth and twentieth century seems content to presume the racial segregation of black and white listeners or viewers, but this, as Fletcher's remark and Levin's and Gienow-Hecht's research show, might not be true of all locations.

10. Compared to the multitude of books on "black music" (synonymous with blues, jazz, soul, funk, rap, and hip hop), research on and acknowledgment of Afro-American performers and composers of classical music is infinitely small, with the exception of such outstanding historical figures such as Paul Robeson, Marian Anderson, and Lena Horne. Exceptions to the rule are the seminal works of John Gray (1988) and Eileen J. Southern (1971). This indicates that classical music, although it has always been heavily influenced by Eastern and African music, seems to be perceived as a "pure" European art form. Interestingly enough, this phenomenon also shows how successfully Europe has been racialized. Since colonialism is regarded as having taken place elsewhere, Europe can be imagined as "the place of and for Europeans historically conceived" (Goldberg 2006: 354), and Europeans can be concurrently defined as an exclusively white and Christian population. The myth of a white Christian Europe is maintained by rigorous border policing based on the identification of physical difference (see Goldberg 2006; Wiese 2008).

11. The general formula is $t_1 = t_2/?(1-v^2/c^2)$. If we assume that the velocity (v) of the astronaut's spaceship is 0.995 times the speed of light (c = 299792.458 km/s), then the astronaut's time runs roughly ten times slower than the time of her earthbound twin.

12. The term *chronotope*, which means "space-time," was introduced into literary theory by the early Russian formalist Mikhail Bakhtin (1895–1975) to describe two different relations that a literary work assumes: first, "the intrinsic connectedness of temporal and spatial relationships that are artistically expressed in literature" (Bakhtin 1981: 250, qtd. in Holquist 1990: 109). This means that literature creates meaning by showing a certain place at a certain time or vice versa. Second, as Michael Holquist (1990: 111) has pointed out in his seminal study *Dialogism: Bakhtin and His Work*, "chronotopes are not cut off from the cultural environments in which they arise." Instead literature creates and reflects "chronotopes of the world" (Bakhtin 1981: 253), while necessarily being a representation made out of linguistic and literary signs and conventions. Therefore chronotopes are necessarily "in dialogue with specific, extra-literary historical contexts" (Holquist 1990: 113). This does not mean, however, that Bakhtin considers literature as "mirroring" reality. Rather literature is a representational system following its own rules, while nevertheless remaining connected to and "in dialogue with" extraliterary events.

13. This temporal indicator situates his character in Vienna before February 27, 1933, when the German Reichstag was set on fire.

14. *Signifiance*, in turn, is a term introduced by Barthes (1991: 61) that is "a signifier without a signified. Barthes variously calls signifiance also "the third meaning," which is a "supplement my intellection cannot quite absorb, a meaning both persistent and fugitive, apparent and evasive" (44). The "third

meaning" is obtuse; it defies understanding while encouraging its readers, listeners, or viewers to pay attention to the very materiality of the sign.

15. As David Scott (2006) has pointed out, this interpretation does not agree with that of commentators who rely on Bergson's *Time and Free Will* (1960). In this work Bergson sees durée as inseparable from lived experience, as a time that endures and as such cannot be measured by being made divisible. He defines pure duration as "the form which the succession of our conscious states assumes when our ego lets itself live, when it refrains from separating its present state from its former states" (100, qtd. in Scott 2006: 207). This means that in *Time and Free Will*, durée depends upon a lived experience and therefore belongs to epistemology rather than ontology, as has been noted by Albert Einstein (1961), Ernst Cassirer (1953), and Keith Ansell Pearson (2002).

16. In 1977 Ilya Prigogine won the Nobel Prize for Chemistry "for his contributions to non-equilibrium thermodynamics, particularly the theory of dissipative structures" ("Ilya Prigogine," www.nobelprize.org). I am very grateful to Norbert Finzsch, who advised me to look at Prigogine's fascinating work during a memorable Skype conversation early in the morning of October 26, 2010.

17. See the H-Net debate surrounding Gar Alperovitz's *The Decision to Use the Atomic Bomb* (1995) on http://www.doug-long.com/debate.htm (last visited February 15, 2012).

18. Surprisingly McWhorter (2009) does not include gender in her analysis, probably because she feared that her analysis would otherwise not be as plausible as it is in its current version. However, gender can be integrated into her overall theoretical assumptions and is also called forth by some of her case studies in which stereotyping notions of black masculinity as hypersexual or black femininity as seductive play a crucial role. McWhorter does include heteronormativity in her analysis, another term that in my view, as Judith Butler's (1988, 1990, 1993, 2004) work shows, is inseparable from gender performance.

19. Especially in recent years there has been an enormous output of research that examines the sexualization of "racial" differences. A few examples of insightful and pathbreaking research on the interdependencies of "race" and the regulation of sexuality and gender are Axster 2008; Dyer 1997; McClintock 1995; Morrison 1992; Schneider 2003; Stoler 1995, 2002a; Young 1995, 2008.

CONCLUSION

1. In the words of Ann Rigney (2004: 368), the term *cultural memory* designates "an ongoing elaboration of a collective relationship to the past through the mediation of discourse." I find this term particularly attractive since it is able to capture the continuous formation of memories that can sometimes be passed on only by cultural means. Recently Rigney uses *cultural remembrance* as a term to designate the ongoing negotiations of a culture's relationship to the past. I thank Alana Gillespie for pointing this out to me.

2. The Shoah, for example, is seen as a rupture in history that questions any account of human progress. The implementation of the "final solution" shows,

as Blanchot (1993: 135) has argued, "that there is no limit to the destruction of man." Any rendering of this catastrophic past must therefore take into account that it cannot be integrated into a meaningful whole. For that reason the Shoah poses serious problems for any kind of representation, be it historical or literary. As Primo Levi (1988: 38) has claimed, its structure defies articulation: the "universe concentrationaire" was not only "terrible . . . but also indecipherable: it did not conform to any model." As a result this universe casts a never-ending shadow on language and its ability to refer to a given reality (see Améry 1988: 15–37).

3. Jewish religious laws, as explained earlier, are composed of 613 commandments, which Fackenheim extends by adding a new one to the corpus.

Works Cited

Adorno, Theodor W. 1981. "Cultural Criticism and Society." In *Prisms*, translated by Samuel Weber, 17–34. Cambridge, MA: MIT Press.

———. 1993. *Beethoven: Philosophie der Musik. Fragmente und Texte. Nachgelassene Schriften Bd. I.* Frankfurt am Main: Suhrkamp.

Adorno, Theodor W., and Max Horkheimer. 2002. *Dialectic of Enlightenment: Philosophical Fragments.* Edited by G. S. Noerr. Translated by E. Jephcott. Stanford: Stanford University Press.

Agamben, Giorgio. 1998. *Homo Sacer: Sovereign Power and Bare Life.* Translated by Daniel Heller-Roazen. Stanford: Stanford University Press.

———. 1999a. *The Man without Content.* Translated by Georgia Albert. Stanford: Stanford University Press.

———. 1999b. *Remnants of Auschwitz: The Witness and the Archive.* New York: Zone Books.

———. 2000. *Means without End: Notes on Politics.* Translated by Vincenzo Binetti and Cesare Casarino. Minneapolis: University of Minnesota Press.

Allen, Graham. 2000. *Intertextuality: New Critical Idiom.* London: Routledge.

Allport, Henry. 1931. *Early Art in Tasmania.* Hobart, Australia: Art, Antique and Historical Exhibition.

Alperovitz, Gar. 1995. *The Decision to Use the Atomic Bomb and the Architecture of an American Myth.* New York: Knopf.

Alphen, Ernst van. 1997. *Caught by History: Holocaust Effects in Contemporary Art, Literature, and Theory.* Stanford: Stanford University Press.

Al Saji, Alia. 2004. "The Memory of Another Past: Bergson, Deleuze, and a New Theory of Time." *Continental Philosophy Review* 37: 203–39.

American Anthropological Association. 2004. "American Anthropological Association Statement on 'Race.'" In *Mixed Race" Studies: A Reader,* edited by Jayne O. Ifekwunigwe, 97–100. London: Routledge.

Améry, Jean. 1988. "An den Grenzen des Geistes." In *Jenseits von Schuld und Sühne: Bewältigungsversuche eines Überwältigten,* 15–37. München: Deutscher Taschenbuchverlag.

Anderson, Benedict R. 1991. *Imagined Communities: Reflections on the Origin and Spread of Nationalism.* London: Verso.

Ankersmit, Franklin R. 1983. *Narrative Logic: A Semantic Analysis of the Historian's Language.* The Hague: Martinus Nijhoff.

———. 1989. *The Reality Effect in the Writing of History: The Dynamics of Historiographical Topology.* Amsterdam: Koninklijke Nederlandse Akademie van Wetenschappen.

———. 1994. *History and Tropology: The Rise and Fall of Metaphor.* Berkeley: University of California Press.

———. 1995. *A New Philosophy of History.* London: Reaktion Books.

———. 1996. *De spiegel van het verleden: Geschiedstheorie.* Kampen, Netherlands: Kok Agora.

———. 2005. *Sublime Historical Experience.* Stanford: Stanford University Press.

Apel, Karl-Otto, and Jürgen Habermas, eds. 1971. *Hermeneutik und Ideologiekritik.* Frankfurt am Main: Suhrkamp.

Appiah, Kwame Anthony, and Henry Louis Gates Jr., eds. 1992. *"Race," Writing, and Difference.* Chicago: University of Chicago Press.

Appiah, Kwame Anthony, and Amy Gutmann. 1996. *Color Conscious: The Political Morality of Race.* Princeton, NJ: Princeton University Press.

Arendt, Hannah. 1929. *Der Liebesbegriff bei Augustin.* Berlin: Springer.

———. 1945. "Organized Guilt and Universal Responsibility." *Jewish Frontier* 12: 19–23.

———. 1948. "The Concentration Camps." *Partisan Review* 15 (7): 743–63.

———. 1958a. *The Human Condition.* Chicago: University of Chicago Press.

———. 1958b. *The Origins of Totalitarianism.* New York: Harcourt Brace Jovanovich.

———. 1963. *On Revolution.* New York: Viking.

———. 1968a. *Between Past and Future.* New York: Viking.

———. 1968b. *Men in Dark Times.* Translated by Harry Zorn. New York, Harcourt Brace & World.

———. 1994. *Essays in Understanding, 1930–1954.* Edited by Jerome Kohn. New York: Harcourt & Brace.

———. 1996. *Love and Saint Augustine.* Edited by Joanna Vecchiarelli Scott and Judith Chelius Stark. Chicago: University of Chicago Press.

Arendt, Hannah, and Karl Jaspers. 1992. *Correspondence 1926–1969*. Edited by Lottel Kohler and Hans Saner. New York: Harcourt Brace Jovanovich.

Arondekar, Anjali. 2005. "Without a Trace: Sexuality and the Colonial Archive." *Journal of the History of Sexuality* 14 (1): 10–27.

Ashcroft, Bill. 2001. *Post-Colonial Transformation*. London: Routledge.

Axster, Felix. 2008. "Vom Sinken: Figurationen von Handlungsmacht im kolonialen Diskurs." In *Unmenge—Wie teilt sich Handlungsmacht?*, edited by Ilka Becker, Michael Cuntz, and Astrid Kusser, 321–35. München: Wilhelm Fink Verlag.

Bakhtin, Mikhail Mikhailovich. 1981. "Forms of Time and Chronotope in the Novel." In *The Dialogic Imagination*, edited by Michael Holquist, translated by Caryl Emerson and Michael Holquist, 84–258. Austin: University of Texas Press.

Bal, Mieke. 1985. *Narratology: Introduction to the Theory of Narrative*. Toronto: University of Toronto Press.

Baldwin, James. 1995. *The Evidence of Things Not Seen*. New York: Holt.

Bannear, David. 1991. *King River to Kelly Basin Archaeological Survey*. Occasional Paper No. 29. Department of Parks, Wildlife and Heritage and Forestry Commission, Tasmania.

Baraka, Amiri (LeRoi Jones). 1991. "In the Tradition." In *The LeRoi Jones/ Amiri Baraka Reader*, edited by William Harris, 304. New York: Thunder's Mouth Press.

Bar On, Bat-Ami. 2002. *The Subject of Violence: Arendtean Exercises in Understanding*. Lanham, MD: Rowman & Littlefield.

Barreto, Marcio. 2004. "Bergson et la physique." Paper presented at Colloque international Bergson et la science, Université de Nice, Université de Charles de Gaulles Lille-3, June 25, 2004. http://www.ifch.unicamp.br/cteme/txt/bergson.pdf (accessed February 15, 2012).

Barthes, Roland. 1977. *Image, Music. Text*. Translated by Stephen Heath. New York: Hill and Wang.

———. 1991. "The Third Meaning." In *The Responsibility of Forms*, translated by Richard Howard, 41–62. Berkeley: University of California Press.

———. 1993. *Camera Lucida: Reflections on Photography*. Translated by Richard Howard. London: Vintage.

———. 2002. "The Death of the Author." In *The Death and Resurrection of the Author?*, edited by William Irwin, translated by William Howard, 3–9. Westport, CT: Greenwood.

Bartov, Omar, eds. 2000. *The Holocaust: Origins, Implementation, Aftermath*. London: Routledge.

Bassett, Bruce, and Ralph Edney. 2002. *Introducing Relativity: A Graphic Guide*. London: Icon Books.

Bastian, Jeannette Allis. 2006. "Reading Colonial Records through an Archival Lens: The Provenance of Place, Space and Creation." *Archival Science* 6 (2): 267–84.

Beardsley, Monroe C., and W. K. Wimsatt. 1954. "The Intentional Fallacy." In *The Verbal Icon: Studies in the Meaning of Poetry*, 3–18. Lexington: University of Kentucky Press.

Behlmann, Lee. 2004. "The Escapist: Fantasy, Folklore, and the Pleasures of the Comic Book in Recent Jewish American Holocaust Fiction." *Shofar: An Interdisciplinary Journal of Jewish Studies* 22 (3): 56–71.

Benhabib, Seyla. 1990. "Hannah Arendt and the Redemptive Power of Narrative." *Social Research* 57 (1): 167–96.

Benjamin, Walter. 1969. "The Task of the Translator." In *Illuminations: Essays and Reflections*, edited by Hannah Arendt, translated by Harry Zohn, 69–82. New York: Schocken Books.

———. 1977. "Die Aufgabe des Übersetzers." In *Illuminationen: Ausgewählte Schriften 1*, edited by Siegfried Unseld, 50–63. Frankfurt am Main: Suhrkamp.

———. 1992. "Franz Kafka: Beim Bau der Chinesischen Mauer." In *Benjamin über Kafka: Texte, Briefzeugnisse, Aufzeichnungen*, edited by Herrmann Schweppenhäuser, 39–46. Frankfurt am Main: Suhrkamp.

———. 1999. *The Arcade Project*. Edited on the basis of German volume by Rolf Tiedemann. Translated by Howard Eiland and Kevin McLaughlin. Cambridge, MA: Harvard University Press.

———. 2005a. "Central Park." In *Selected Writing*. Vol. 4: *1938–1940*. Edited by Howard Eiland and Michael W. Jennings, translated by Edmund Jephcott et al., 161–200. Cambridge, MA: Harvard University Press.

———. 2005b. "On the Concept of History." In *Selected Writing*. Vol. 4: *1938–1940*. Edited by Howard Eiland and Michael W. Jennings, translated by Edmund Jephcott et al., 389–401. Cambridge, MA: Harvard University Press.

Benveniste, Emile. 1971. *Problems in General Linguistics*. Coral Gables, FL: University of Miami Press.

Bergson, Henri. 1911a. *Creative Evolution*. Translated by Arthur Mitchell. London: Macmillan.

———. 1911b. *Matter and Memory*. Translated by Nancy Margaret Paul and W. Scott Palmer. London: George Allen and Unwin.

———. 1919. *L'énergie spirituelle*. Paris: Presse Universitaires de France.

———. 1960. *Time and Free Will: An Essay on the Immediate Data of Consciousness*. Translated by Frank Lubecki Pogson. New York: Harper and Row.

———. 1999. *Duration and Simultaneity: Bergson and the Einsteinian Universe*. Translated by Leon Jacobson. Translation of additional material Mark Lewis. Edited and with an introduction by Robin Durie. Manchester, UK: Clinamen.

Bhabha, Homi K. 1994. *The Location of Culture*. London: Routledge.

Blanchot, Maurice. 1993. *The Infinite Conversation*. Translated by Susan Hanson. Minneapolis: University of Minnesota Press.

Blanchot, Maurice, and Jacques Derrida. 2000. *The Instant of My Death*. Translated by Elizabeth Rottenberg. Stanford: Stanford University Press.

Blencowe, Claire. 2010. "Foucault's and Arendt's 'Insider View' of Biopolitics: A Critique of Agamben." *History of the Human Sciences* 23 (5): 113–30.

Bloois, Joost de. 2004. "Bartleby, du Scribe: 'Personage conceptuel' et 'figure esthetique' dans le pensée de Gilles Deleuze." In *Discernements: Deleuzian Aesthetics / Esthetiques deleuziennes*, edited by Joost de Bloois, Sjef Houppermans, and Willem Korsten, 113–31. Amsterdam: Editions Rodopi.

Bloom, Allan. 1987. *The Closing of the American Mind: How Higher Education Has Failed Democracy and Impoverished the Souls of Today's Students*. New York. Simon & Schuster.

Boehler, Jochen. 2006. *Auftakt zum Vernichtungskrieg: Die Wehrmacht in Polen 1939*. Bonn: Schriftenreihe der Bundeszentrale für politische Bildung.

Boes, Tobias. 2008. "Apprenticeship of the Novel: The Bildungsroman and the Invention of History, ca. 1770–1820." *Comparative Literature Studies* 45 (3): 269–88.

Bogue, Ronald. 2007. "Bergsonian Fabulation and the People to Come." In *Deleuze's Way: Essays in Transverse Ethics and Aesthetics*, 91–106. Aldershot, UK: Ashgate.

———. 2010. *Deleuzian Fabulation and the Scars of History*. Edinburgh: Edinburgh University Press.

Booth, Wayne. 1961. *The Rhetorics of Fiction*. Chicago: University of Chicago Press.

———. 1988. *The Company We Keep: An Ethics of Fiction*. Berkeley: University of California Press.

Boyarin, Daniel, Daniel Itzkowitz, and Ann Pellegrini, eds. 2003. *Queer Theory and the Jewish Question*. New York: Columbia University Press.

Boyer, Paul S. 1985. *By the Bomb's Early Light: American Thought and Culture at the Dawn of the Atomic Age*. New York: Pantheon Books.

Braidotti, Rosi. 1994. *Nomadic Subjects: Embodiment and Sexual Difference in Contemporary Feminist Theory*. New York: Pergamon Press.

———. 2002. *Metamorphoses: Towards a Materialist Theory of Becoming*. Cambridge, UK: Polity.

———. 2006. *Transpositions: On Nomadic Ethics*. Cambridge, UK: Polity.

Brand, Ian. 1984. *Sarah Island*. Launceston, Australia: Regal.

Britton, Celia M. 1999. *Edouard Glissant and Postcolonial Theory: Strategies of Language and Resistance*. Charlottesville: University of Virginia Press.

Buck-Morss, Susan. 1991. *The Dialectics of Seeing: Walter Benjamin and the Arcades Project.* Cambridge, MA: MIT Press.

———. 1992. "Aesthetics and Anaesthetics: Walter Benjamin's Artwork Essay Reconsidered." *October* 62 (3): 3–41.

Buell, Lawrence. 1987. "Literary History without Sexism? Feminist Studies and Canonical Reconception." *American Literature* 59 (1): 102–14.

Buikema, Rosemarie. 2009. "Crossing the Borders of Identity Politics: *Disgrace* by J. M. Coetzee and *Agaat* by Marlene van Niekerk." *European Journal of Women's Studies* 16 (4): 309–23.

———. 2010. "Te veel werkelijkheid is dodelijk voor de kunst." *Tijdschrift voor Nederlandse Taal- en Letterkunde* 126 (2): 202–16.

Buikema, Rosemarie, and Maaike Meijer. 2003. *Kunsten in beweging 1900–1980.* The Hague: SDU.

Buikema, Rosemarie, and Maaike Meijer. 2004. *Kunsten in beweging 1980–2000.* The Hague: SDU.

Buikema, Rosemarie, and Lies Wesseling. 2006. *Het heilige huis: De gotieke vertelling in de Nederlandse literatuur.* Amsterdam: Amsterdam University Press.

Butler, Judith. 1988. "Performative Acts and Gender Constitution: An Essay in Phenomenology and Feminist Theory." *Theatre Journal* 40 (4): 519–31.

———. 1990. *Gender Trouble: Feminism and the Subversion of Identity.* New York: Routledge.

———. 1993. *Bodies That Matter: On the Discursive Limits of "Sex."* New York: Routledge.

———. 2004. *Undoing Gender.* New York: Routledge.

Butsch, Richard. 2000. *The Making of American Audiences: From Stage to Television, 1750–1990.* Cambridge, UK: Cambridge University Press.

Camper, Carol. 2004. "Into the Mix." In *"Mixed Race" Studies: A Reader,* edited by Jayne O. Ifekwunigwe, 176–83. London: Routledge.

Čapek, Milič. 1971. *Bergson and Modern Physics: A Reinterpretation and Revaluation.* New York: Humanities Press.

Carroll, Noel. 2007. "Narrative Closure." *Philosophical Studies* 135: 1–15.

Cassirer, Ernst. 1953. *Substance and Function and Einstein's Theory of Relativity.* Translated by William Swabey and Marie Swabey. New York: Dover.

Celan, Paul. 1990. "Der Meridian." In *Der Meridian und andere Prosa,* 40–62. Frankfurt am Main: Suhrkamp.

———. 2005. "The Meridian." Translated by Rosemarie Waldorp. In *Paul Celan: Selections,* edited by Pierre Joris, 154–77. Berkeley: University of California Press.

Chakrabarty, Dipesh. 1992. "Postcoloniality and the Artifice of History: Who Speaks for 'Indian' Pasts?" *Representations* 37 (4): 1–26.

———. 2000a. *Provincializing Europe: Postcolonial Thought and Historical Difference.* Princeton, NJ: Princeton University Press.

———. 2000b. "Subaltern Studies and Postcolonial Historiography." *Nepantla: Views from South* 1 (1): 9–32.

Chandler, Daniel. 1994–2014. *Semiotics for Beginners.* http://www.aber. ac.uk/media/Documents/S4B/ (accessed February 15, 2012).

Chatman, Seymour. 1990. *Coming to Terms: The Rhetoric of Narrative in Fiction and Film.* Ithaca, NY: Cornell University Press.

Chiang, Howard. 2008. "Post-colonial Historiography, Queer Historiography: The Political Spaces of History Writing." *InterAlia: A Journal of Queer Studies* 2. http://www.interalia.org.pl/en/artykuly/2007_2/07_postcolonial_historiography_queer_historiography.htm (accessed February 15, 2012).

Chiba, Shin. 1995. "Hannah Arendt on Love and the Political: Love, Friendship, and Citizenship." *Review of Politics* 57 (3): 505–37.

Chun, Wendy Hui Kyong. 2006. "Introduction: Did Somebody Say New Media?" In *New Media, Old Media: A History and Theory Reader,* 1–11. London: Routledge.

Cixous, Hélène. 1980. *Weiblichkeit in der Schrift.* Translated by Eva Duffner. Berlin: Merve.

———. 1994. *The Hélène Cixous Reader.* Edited and translated by Susan Sellers. New York: Routledge.

Clifton, Rob, and Mark Hogarth. 1995. "The Definability of Objective Becoming in Minkowski Spacetime." *Synthese* 103 (3): 355–87.

Clune, Frank, and Percy Reginald Stephensen. 1962. *Pirates of the Brig Cyprus.* London: Rupert Hart-Davis.

Cocker, Mark. 1998. *Rivers of Blood, Rivers of Gold: Europe's Conflict with Tribal Peoples.* London: Jonathan Cape.

Colebrook, Claire. 2004. "The Sense of Space: On the Specificity of Affect in Deleuze and Guattari." *Postmodern Culture* 15 (1): 1–27.

———. 2006. *Deleuze: A Guide for the Perplexed.* London: Continuum.

Collado-Rodriguez, Francisco. 2008. "Ethics in the Second Degree: Trauma and Dual Narratives in Jonathan Safran Foer's *Everything Is Illuminated.*" *Journal of Modern Literature* 32 (1): 54–68.

Combahee River Collective. 1981. "A Black Feminist Statement." In *This Bridge Called My Back: Writings by Radical Women of Color,* edited by Cherríe Moraga and Gloria Anzaldúa, 210–18. New York: Kitchen Table Women of Color Press.

Cooper, Michael L. 1998. *The Double V Campaign: African-Americans in World War II.* New York: Lodestar Books.

Corker, Mairian, and Tom Shakespeare. 2002. *Disability/Postmodernity. Embodying Disability Theory.* London: Continuum.

Cryderman, Kevin. 2002. "Ghosts in the Palimpsest of Cultural Memory: An Archeology of Faizal Deen's Poetic Memoir *Land without Chocolate* (a.k.a. 'the Art of Writing about Authors before they are Famous')." *Jouvert* 6 (3). http://english.chass.ncsu.edu/jouvert/v6i3/cryder.htm (accessed December 30, 2010).

Culler, Jonathan. 1983. "Reading as a Woman." In *On Deconstruction: Theory and Criticism after Structuralism*, 43–64. London: Routledge.

Daniel, G. Reginald. 2000. "Multiracial Identity in Brazil and the United States." In *We Are a People: Narrative and Multiplicity in Constructing Ethnic Identity*, edited by Paul Spickard and W. Jeffrey Burroughs, 153–78. Philadelphia: Temple University Press.

Davis, Lennard J. 1999. "Crips Strike Back: The Rise of Disability Studies." *American Literary History* 11 (3): 500–512.

Davis, Kimberley Chabot. 1998. "'Postmodern Blackness': Toni Morrison's 'Beloved' and the End of History—Novel by Black Female Author." *Twentieth Century Literature* 44 (2): 242–60.

Degler, Carl. 1971. *Neither Black nor White: Slavery and Race Relations in Brazil and the United States*. New York: Macmillan.

Deleuze, Gilles. 1978–81. *Gilles Deleuze: Lecture Transcripts on Spinoza's Concept of Affect, 24.01.1978–24.03.1981*. Edited by Emilie Deleuze and Julien Deleuze. Translated by Timothy S. Murphy. http://www.gold.ac.uk/media/deleuze_spinoza_affect.pdf (accessed February 15, 2012).

———. 1980. *Les Cours de Gilles Deleuze: Ontology-Ethics, 21.12.1980*. Edited by Emilie Deleuze and Julien Deleuze. Translated by Simon Duffy. http://www.webdeleuze.com/php/texte.php?cle=190&groupe=Spinoza&langue=2n.p. (accessed February 15, 2012).

———. 1986. *Cinema 1: The Movement Image*. Translated by Hugh Tomlinson and Barbara Habberjam. Minneapolis: University of Minnesota Press.

———. 1988b. *Spinoza: Practical Philosophy*. Translated by Robert Hurley. San Francisco: City Lights Books.

———. 1989. *Masochism: An Introduction to Coldness and Cruelty*. Translated by Jean McNeil. New York: Zone Books.

———. 1990. *Logic of Sense*. Edited by Constantine B. Boundas. Translated by Mark Lester. New York: Columbia University Press.

———. 1991. *Bergsonism*. Translated by Hugh Tomlinson and Barbara Habberjam. New York: Zone Books.

———. 1995. *Negotiations, 1972–1990*. Translated by Martin Joughin. New York: Columbia University Press.

———. 1997a. *Differenz und Wiederholung*. Translated by Joseph Vogl. München: Wilhelm Fink Verlag.

———. 1997b. *Essays Critical and Clinical*. Translated by Daniel W. Smith and Michael A. Greco. Minneapolis: University of Minnesota Press.

———. 1997c. "Literature and and Life." Translated by Daniel W. Smith and Michael A. Greco. *Critical Inquiry* 23 (2): 225–30.

———. 1998. "Having an Idea in Cinema." Translated by Eleanor Kaufman. In *Deleuze and Guattari: New Mappings in Politics, Philosophy, and Culture*, edited by Eleanor Kaufman and Kevin Jon Heller, 14–19. Minneapolis: University of Minnesota Press.

———. 1999. *Foucault*. Edited and translated by Séan Hand. London: Continuum.

———. 2000. *Proust and Signs*. Translated by Richard Howard. Minneapolis: University of Minnesota Press.

———. 2004a. *Desert Islands and Other Texts (1953–1974)*. Translated by Mike Taormina. Cambridge, MA: Semiotext(e).

———. 2004b. *Difference and Repetition*. Translated by Paul Patton. London: Continuum.

———. 2005. *Cinema 2: The Time-Image*. Translated by Hugh Tomlinson and Robert Galeta. London: Continuum.

Deleuze, Gilles, and Félix Guattari. 1980. *Mille plateaux*. Paris: Minuit.

Deleuze, Gilles, and Félix Guattari. 1983. *Anti-Oedipus*. Translated by Robert Hurley, Mark Seem, and Helen R. Lane. Preface by Michel Foucault. Minneapolis: University of Minnesota Press.

Deleuze, Gilles, and Félix Guattari. 1986. *Kafka: Toward a Minor Literature*. Translated by Dana Polan. Minneapolis: University of Minnesota Press.

Deleuze, Gilles, and Félix Guattari. 1987. *A Thousand Plateaus*. Translated by Brian Massumi. Minneapolis: University of Minnesota Press.

Deleuze, Gilles, and Félix Guattari. 1994. *What Is Philosophy?* Translated by Paul Patton. New York: Columbia University Press.

Deleuze, Gilles, and Félix Guattari. 2004. *A Thousand Plateaus*. Translated by Brian Massumi. London: Continuum.

Deleuze, Gilles, and Claire Parnet. 2006. *Dialogues II*. Translated by Eliot Ross Albert. London: Continuum.

de Man, Paul. 1986. "'Conclusions': Walter Benjamin's 'The Task of the Translator.'" In *The Resistance to Theory*, 73–106. Minneapolis: University of Minnesota Press.

———. 1988. *Allegorien des Lesens*. Frankfurt am Main: Suhrkamp Verlag.

DeNavas-Walt, Carmen, Bernadette D. Proctor, and Cheryl Hill Lee. 2005. *Income, Poverty, and Health Insurance Coverage in the United States: 2004*. U.S. *Census Bureau, Current Population Reports, P60–229*. Washington, DC: U.S. Government Printing Office.

DeNavas-Walt, Carmen, Bernadette D. Proctor, and Jessica C. Smith. 2010. *Income, Poverty, and Health Insurance Coverage in the United States: 2009*. U.S. *Census Bureau, Current Population Reports, P60–238*. Washington, DC: U.S. Government Printing Office.

Derrida, Jacques. 1976. *Of Grammatology*. Translated by Gayatri Chakravorty Spivak. Baltimore: Johns Hopkins University Press.

———. 1978. *Writing and Difference*. Translated by Alan Bass. Chicago: University of Chicago Press.

———. 1979. *Spurs: Nietzsche's Styles / Éperons: Les Styles de Nietzsche*. Introduction by Stefano Agosti. Translated by Barbara Harlow. Drawings by François Loubrieu. Chicago: University of Chicago Press.

———. 1984. "My Chances / Mes Chances: A Rendezvous with Some Epicurean Stereophonies." Translated by Irene Harvey and Avital Ronell. In *Taking Chances: Derrida, Psychoanalysis, and Literature*, edited by Joseph H. Smith and William Kerrigan, 1–32. Baltimore: Johns Hopkins University Press.

———. 1985. "Deconstruction in America: An Interview with Jacques Derrida." Translated by James Creech. *Critical Exchange* 17 (4): 1–33.

———. 1986a. "Schibboleth." Translated by Joshua Wilner. In *Midrash and Literature*, edited by Geoffrey H. Hartmann and Sanford Budick, 307–47. New Haven, CT: Yale University Press.

———. 1986b. "Structure, Sign and Play in the Discourse of the Human Sciences." Translated by Alan Bass. In *Critical Theory Since Plato*, edited by Hazard Adams and Leroy Searle, 1117–27. Tallahassee: Florida State University Press.

———. 1987a. *The Post Card: From Socrates to Freud and Beyond*. Translated by Alan Bass. Chicago: University of Chicago Press.

———. 1987b. *The Truth in Painting*. Chicago: University of Chicago Press.

———. 1988. *Limited Inc*. Translated by Samuel Weber and Jeffrey Mehlman. Evanston, IL: Northwestern University Press.

———. 1990. "Some Statements and Truisms about Neologisms, Newisms, Postisms, Parasitisms, and Other Small Seismisms." Translated by Anne Tomiche. In *The States of Theory*, edited by David Carroll, 63–94. New York: Columbia University Press.

———. 1991. "'Eating Well,' or the Calculation of the Subject: An Interview with Jacques Derrida." Translated by Peter Connor and Avital Ronell. In *Who Comes after the Subject?*, edited by Eduardo Cadava, Peter Connor, and Jean-Luc Nancy, 96–119. New York: Routledge.

———. 1996. *Archive Fever: A Freudian Impression*. Translated by Eric Prenowitz. Chicago: University of Chicago Press.

———. 1997. "Die Einsprachigkeit des Anderen oder die Prothese des Ursprungs." Translated by Michael Wetzel. In *Die Sprache der Anderen: Übersetzungspolitik zwischen den Kulturen*, edited by Anselm Haverkamp, 15–43. Frankfurt am Main: Fischer.

———. 1998a. *Monolingualism of the Other: Or, The Prosthesis of Origin*. Translated by Patrick Mensah. Stanford: Stanford University Press.

———. 1998b. *Resistances of Psychoanalysis*. Translated by Peggy Kamuf, Pascale-Anne Brault, and Michael Naas. Stanford: Stanford University Press.

———. 2002. *Schibboleth: Für Paul Celan*. Translated by Wolfgang Sebastian Baur. Wien: Passagen Verlag.

Derrida, Jacques, et al. 1987. "Women in the Beehive: A Seminar with Jacques Derrida." *In Men in Feminism*, edited by Alice Jardine and Paul Smith, 189–203. New York: Routledge.

Dieks, Dennis. 1988. "Discussion: Special Relativity and the Fowl of Time." *Philosophy of Science* 55 (3): 456–60.

Dillon, George. 1978. *Language Processing and the Reading of Literature.* Bloomington: Indiana University Press.

Dilthey, Wilhelm. 1996. *Hermeneutics and the Study of History.* Edited by Rudolf A. Makkreel and Frithjof Rodi. Translated by by Garrett Barden and John Cumming. Princeton, NJ: Princeton University Press.

———. 2002. *The Formation of the Historical World in the Human Sciences.* Edited by Rudolf A. Makkreel and Frithjof Rodi. Princeton, NJ: Princeton University Press.

Dirlik, Arif, Vinay Bahl, and Peter Gran, eds. 2000. *History after the Three Worlds: Post-Eurocentric Historiographies.* Lanham, MD: Rowman & Littlefield.

Douglass, Frederick. 1971. *Narrative of the Life of Frederick Douglass, an American Slave, Written by Himself.* Cambridge, MA: Harvard University Press.

Dreyfus, Hubert L., and Paul Rabinow. 1983. *Michel Foucault: Beyond Structuralism and Hermeneutics.* Chicago: University of Chicago Press.

Du Bois, William Edward Burghardt. 1975. *Dusk of Dawn: An Essay toward an Autobiography of a Race Concept.* With an introduction by Herbert Aptheker. Millwood, NY: Kraus-Thomson Organization.

———. 2002. *The Souls of Black Folk: Essays and Sketches.* http://docsouth. unc.edu/church/duboissouls/menu.html (accessed February 15, 2012).

Durie, Robin. 1999. "From Absolute Time to Relative Time." In *Duration and Simultaneity. Bergson and the Einsteinian Universe*, edited and with an introduction by Robin Durie, translated by Leon Jacobson, translation of additional material by Mark Lewis, 202–9. Manchester, UK: Clinamen.

Dyer, Richard. 1997. *White: Essays on Race and Culture.* London: Routledge.

Eagleton, Terry. 1996. *The Illusions of Postmodernism.* Oxford: Blackwell.

Einstein, Albert. 1922. "Reception for Einstein: The Theory of Relativity, Hosted by the Société française de philosophie, on 6th of April, 1922." *Bulletin de la Société française de philosophie* 22 (3): 102–13.

———. 1924. "Meine Relativitätstheorie." Audio recording. Recorded February 6. Deutsches Rundfunkarchiv Wiesbaden, B003852016.

———. 1961. *Relativity: Special and General Theory.* Translated by Robert Lawson. New York: Crown.

Eltis, David 2001. "The Volume and Structure of the Transatlantic Slave Trade: A Reassessment." *William and Mary Quarterly, Third Series (New Perspectives on the Transatlantic Slave Trade)* 58 (1): 17–46.

Engelbrecht, Penelope J. 1990. "'Lifting Belly Is a Language': The Postmodern Lesbian Subject." *Feminist Studies* 16 (1): 85–114.

English, Daylanne K. 2009. "Being Black There: Racial Subjectivity and Temporality in Walter Mosley's Detective Novels." *Novel: A Forum on Fiction* 42 (3): 361–65.

Eskin, Blake. 2002. *A Life in Pieces: The Making and Unmaking of Binjamin Wikomirski.* New York: Norton.

Essner, Cornelia. 2003. *Die Nürnberger Gesetze oder Die Verwaltung des Rassenwahns 1933–1945.* Paderborn, Germany: Ferdinand Schöningh Verlag.

Esty, Jed. 2007. "The Colonial Bildungsroman: The Story of an African Farm and the Ghost of Goethe." *Victorian Studies* 49 (3): 407–30.

Fackenheim, Emil. 1968. *Quest for Past and Future.* Bloomington: Indiana University Press.

———. 1987. *What Is Judaism?* New York: Summit Books.

———. 1994. *To Mend the World: Foundations of Post-Holocaust Jewish Thought.* Bloomington: Indiana University Press.

Fanon, Frantz. 1967. *Black Skin, White Masks.* Translated by Charles Lam Markmann. New York: Grove.

Featherstone, Mike: 2000: "Archiving Cultures." *British Journal of Sociology* 51 (1): 161–84.

Felman, Shoshana 1975. "Women and Madness: The Critical Phallacy." *Diacritics* 5 (4): 2–10.

———. 1981. "Rereading Femininity." *Yale French Studies* 62: 19–41.

———. 1999. "Benjamin's Silence." *Critical Inquiry* 25 (2): 201–34.

Ferreira-Buckley, Linda. 1999. "Rescuing the Archives from Foucault." *College English* 61 (5): 577–83.

Finzsch, Norbert. 2005. "'It Is Scarcely Possible to Conceive That Human Beings Could Be So Hideous and Loathsome': Discourses of Genocide in Eighteenth and Nineteenth-Century America and Australia." *Patterns of Prejudice* 39 (2): 97–115.

———. 2008. "'The Aborigines . . . Were Never Annihilated, and Still They Are Becoming Extinct': Settler Imperialism and Genocide in Nineteenth-Century America and Australia." In *Empire, Colony, Genocide: Conquest, Occupation, and Subaltern Resistance in World History*, edited by A. Dirk Moses, 253–70. New York: Berghahn.

Finzsch, Norbert, James Oliver Horton, and Lois E. Horton. 1999. *Von Benin nach Baltimore: Die Geschichte der African Americans.* Hamburg: Hamburger Edition.

Fish, Stanley E. 1980. "Literature in the Reader: Affective Stylistics." In *Reader-Response Criticism*, edited by Jane P. Tompkins, 70–100. Baltimore: Johns Hopkins University Press, 1980.

Fitzgerald, F. Scott. 1965. *The Crack-Up, with Other Pieces and Stories.* Harmondsworth, UK: Penguin.

Flanagan, Richard. 2003. *Gould's Book of Fish: A Novel in Twelve Fish.* London: Atlantic Books.

Fletcher, Tom. 1984. *100 Years of the Negro in Show Business.* New York: Da Capo Press.

Foer, Jonathan Safran. 2002. *Everything Is Illuminated.* London: Penguin.

Foucault, Michel. 1972. *The Archeology of Knowledge*. Translated by Allan M. Sheridan Smith. London: Routledge.

———. 1977. "Nietzsche, Genealogy, History." In *Language, Counter-Memory, Practice: Selected Essays and Interviews*, edited by D. F. Bouchard, translated by Donald F. Bouchard and Sherry Simoned, 139–64. Ithaca, NY: Cornell University Press.

———. 1978. *History of Sexuality, Volume 1: An Introduction*. Translated by Robert Hurley. New York: Random House.

———. 1983. "Afterword: The Subject and Power." In *Michel Foucault: Beyond Structuralism and Hermeneutics*, edited by Hubert L. Dreyfus and Paul Rabinow, 208–26. Chicago: University of Chicago Press.

———. 1987. "Maurice Blanchot: The Thought from Outside." In *Foucault/Blanchot*, translated by Jeffrey Mehlman, 7–61. New York: Zone Books.

———. 1992. *The Order of Things: An Archaeology of the Human Sciences*. Translated by Alan Sheridan. London: Routledge.

———. 1994. *Dits et écrits*. Vols. 3–4. Paris: Gallimard.

———. 2002. "What Is an Author?" Translated by Donald F. Bouchard and Sherry Simon. In *The Death and Resurrection of the Author?*, edited by William Irwin, 9–23. Westport, CT: Greenwood.

———. 2003a. *Abnormal: Lectures at the College de France 1974–1975*. Translated by Graham Burchell. New York: Picador.

———. 2003b. *"Society Must Be Defended": Lectures at the Collège de France, 1975–1976*. Translated by Graham Burchell. New York: Picador.

———. 2007. *Security, Territory, Population: Lectures at the Collège de France, 1977–1978*. Translated by Graham Burchell. New York: Palgrave.

Frank, Chaim. 1997. "Jiddisch—Die Mameloschn." http://www.hagalil.com/jidish/cf-jid3.htm (accessed December 30, 2010).

Freedman, Russell. 2004. *The Voice That Challenged a Nation: Marian Anderson and the Struggle for Equal Rights*. New York: Clarion Books.

Fresco, Nadine. 1984. "Remembering the Unknown." *International Review of Psycho-analysis* 11 (4): 417–27.

Freud, Sigmund. 1961. "Beyond the Pleasure Principle." In *Standard Edition*, translated by James Strachey, vol. 18, 1–64. New York: Liveright.

Friedlander, Henry. 1995. *The Origins of Nazi Genocide: From Euthanasia to the Final Solution*. Chapel Hill: University of North Carolina Press.

Friedländer, Saul, ed. 1992. *Probing the Limits of Representation: Nazism and the Final Solution*. Cambridge, MA: Harvard University Press.

Gadamer, Hans-Georg. 1976. *Philosophical Hermeneutics*. Translated by David E. Linge. Berkeley: University of California Press.

———. 1986. *The Relevance of the Beautiful and Other Essays*. Edited by Robert Bernasconi. Translated by Nicholas Walker. Cambridge, UK: Cambridge University Press.

———. 1994. *Truth and Method*. Translated by Joel Weinsheimer and Donald G. Marshall. New York: Continuum.

Gatens, Moira. 1996. *Imaginary Bodies: Ethics, Power, and Corporeality.* London: Routledge.

Gatens, Moira, and Genevieve Lloyd. 1999. *Collective Imaginings: Spinoza, Past and Present.* London: Routledge.

Genette, Gérard. 1972. *Figures III.* Paris: Seuil.

———. 1983. *Nouveau discours du récit.* Paris: Seuil.

———. 1988. "The Proustian Paratext." *SubStance: A Review of Theory and Literary Criticism* 17 (2): 63–77.

———. 1997a. *Palimpsests: Literature in the Second Degree.* Translated by Channa Newman and Claude Doubinsky. Foreword by Gerald Prince. Lincoln: University of Nebraska Press.

———. 1997b. *Paratexts: Thresholds of Interpretation.* Translated by Jane E. Lewin. Foreword by Richard Macksey. Cambridge, UK: Cambridge University Press.

———. 2004. *Métalepse: De la figure à la fiction.* Paris: Seuil.

Gearhart, Suzanne, and Paul de Man. 1983. "Philosophy before Literature: Deconstruction, Historicity, and the Work of Paul de Man." *Diacritics* 13 (4): 63–81.

Gienow-Hecht, Jessica C. E. 2009. *Sound Diplomacy: Music, Emotions, and Politics in Transatlantic Relations 1850–1920.* Chicago: University of Chicago Press.

Gilman, Sander. 2000. "Are Jews White?" In *Theories of Race and Racism: A Reader,* edited by Les Back and John Solomons, 229–38. London: Routledge.

Gilroy, Paul. 1993. *The Black Atlantic: Modernity and Double Consciousness.* Cambridge, MA: Harvard University Press.

Ginzburg, Carlo. 1989. *Clues, Myths, and the Historical Method.* Translated by John Tedeschi and Anne C. Tedeschi. Baltimore: Johns Hopkins University Press.

Glissant, Édouard. 1989. *Caribbean Discourse.* Translated by Michael Dash. Charlottesville: University of Virginia Press.

———. 1997. *Poetics of Relation.* Translated by Betsy Wing. Ann Arbor: University of Michigan Press.

———. 2005. *Kultur und Identität: Ansätze zu einer Poetik der Vielheit.* Translated by Beate Thill. Heidelberg: Verlag Das Wunderhorn.

Gödel, Kurt. 1949. "A Remark about the Relationship between Relativity Theory and Idealistic Philosophy." In *Einstein: Philosopher, Scientist. Library of Living Philosophers, Vol. 7,* edited by Paul A. Schilpp, 555–62. Evanston, IL: Northwestern University Press.

Goldberg, David Theo. 2006. "Racial Europeanization." *Ethnic and Racial Studies* 29 (2): 331–64.

Goldstücker, Eduard. 1967. "Die Prager deutsche Literatur als historisches Phänomen." In *Weltfreunde: Konferenz über die Prager deutsche Literatur,* 21–45. Prague: Academia.

Goodell, William. 1853. *The American Slave Code in Theory and Practice.* New York: American and Foreign Anti-Slavery Society.

Graf, Fritz. 1995. "Ekphrasis: Die Entstehung der Gattung in der Antike." In *Beschreibungskunst, Kunstbeschreibungen—Ekphrasis von der Antike bis zur Gegenwart*, edited by Gottfried Boehm and Helmut Pfotenhauer, 143–55. München: Bild und Text.

Gray, John. 1988. *Blacks in Classical Music. A Bibliographical Guide to Composers, Performers, and Ensembles.* New York: Greenwood.

Greene, Gayle, and Coppélia Kahn. 1985. "Feminist Scholarship and the Social Construction of Woman." In *Making a Difference: Feminist Literary Criticism*, edited by Gayle Greene and Coppélia Kahn, 137–45. London: Routledge.

Grewal, Gurleen. 1998. *Circles of Sorrow, Lines of Struggle: The Novels of Toni Morrison.* Baton Rouge: Louisiana State University Press.

Guha, Ranajit, ed. 1997. *Subaltern Studies Reader, 1986–1995.* Minneapolis: University of Minnesota Press.

Habermas, Jürgen. 1980. "The Hermeneutic Claim to Universality." Translated by Josef Bleicher. In *Contemporary Hermeneutics*, edited by Josef Bleicher, 245–72. London: Routledge.

Hammer, Dean. 2000. "Freedom and Fatefulness: Augustine, Arendt and the Journey of Memory." *Theory, Culture & Society* 17 (2): 83–104.

Harris, Louis, and Bert E. Swanson. 1970. *Black-Jewish Relations in New York City.* New York: Praeger.

Häsner, Bernd. 2005. *Metalepsen: Zur Genese, Systematik und Funktion transgressiver Erzählweisen.* http://www.diss.fu-berlin.de/2005/239/kap1.pdf (accessed December 30, 2010).

Haverkamp, Anselm. 1993. "The Memory of Pictures: Roland Barthes and Augustine on Photography." *Comparative Literature* 45 (3): 258–79.

Hawking, Stephen William. 1988. *A Brief History of Time.* New York: Bantam Press.

Heffernan, James W. A. 1993. *The Museum of Words: The Poetics of Ekphrasis from Homer to Ashbery.* Chicago: University of Chicago Press.

Hegel, Friedrich. 1977. *Phenomenology of the Spirit.* Translated by Arnold V. Miller. Oxford: Oxford University Press.

Hegel, Georg Wilhelm Friedrich. 1978. *Religionsphilosophie.* Edited by Karl-Heinz Ilting. Naples: Bibliopolis.

———. 1984. *Mythologie der Vernunft: Hegels ältestes Systemprogramm des deutschen Idealismus.* Edited by Christoph Jamme and Helmut Schneider. Frankfurt am Main: Suhrkamp.

———. 1986. *Jenaer kritische Schriften.* Edited by Hans Brockard and Hartmut Buchner. Hamburg: Meiner.

———. 1993. *Einleitung in die Geschichte der Philosophie: Orientalische Philosophie.* Edited by Walter Jaeschke. Hamburg: Meiner.

Heidegger, Martin. 1962. *Being and Time.* Translated by John Macquarrie and Edward Robinson. San Francisco: Harper.

Herman, David. 2007. *The Routledge Encyclopedia of Narrative Theory*. London: Routledge.

Herzog, Annabel. 2000. "Illuminating Inheritance: Benjamin's Influence on Arendt's Political Storytelling." *Philosophy & Social Criticism* 26 (5): 1–27.

Hilberg, Raul. 1961. *The Destruction of the European Jews*. London: W. H. Allen.

Hirsch, Marianne. 1997. *Family Frames: Photography, Narrative, and Postmemory*. Cambridge, MA: Harvard University Press.

———. 1999. "Projected Memory." In *Acts of Memory: Cultural Recall in the Past*, edited by Mieke Bal, Jonathan W. Crewe, and Leo Spitzer, 3–24. Hanover, NH: University Press of New England.

Hjelmslev, Louis. 1961. *Prolegomena to a Theory of Language*. Translated by Francis J. Whitfield. Madison: University of Wisconsin Press.

Hobbs, James. 1830. "James Hobbs to Aborigines Committee, 9 March 1830." In *House of Commons Parliamentary Papers*, 50. National Library of Australia. http://www.nla.gov.au/app/eresources/item/1642 (accessed March 6, 2014).

Hoffman, Paul. 1994. "The Science of Race." *Discover* 15 (2): 4.

Holquist, Michael. 1990. *Dialogism: Bakhtin and His World*. London: Routledge.

Holt, Jason. 2002. "The Marginal Life of the Author." In *The Death and Resurrection of the Author?*, edited by William Irwin, 65–79. Westport, CT: Greenwood.

Hoogland, Renee C. 1994. *Elizabeth Bowen: A Reputation in Writing*. New York: New York University Press.

hooks, bell. 1990. "Marginality as a Site of Resistance." In *Out There: Marginalization and Contemporary Culture*, edited by Russell Ferguson, Martha Gever, Trinh Minh-ha, and Cornel West, 341–43. Cambridge, MA: MIT Press.

Hooper, Frederic C. 1966. "Booth, Charles O'Hara (1800—1851)." In *Australian Dictionary of Biography*, vol. 1, 125. Melbourne: Melbourne University Press.

Hughes, Robert. 1987. *The Fatal Shore*. New York: Knopf.

Hurley, Robert. 1988. Preface to *Spinoza: Practical Philosophy*, translated by Robert Hurley, i–iii. San Francisco: City Light Books.

Hutcheon, Linda. 1980. *Narcissistic Narrative: The Metafictional Paradox*. Waterloo, Canada: Wilfrid Laurier University Press.

———. 1988. *A Poetics of Postmodernism: History, Theory, Fiction*. London: Routledge.

Ifekwunigwe, Jayne O., ed. 2004. *"Mixed Race" Studies: A Reader*. London: Routledge.

Ignatiev, Noel. 1995. *How the Irish Became White*. London: Routledge.

Irigaray, Luce. 1974. *Spéculum de l'autre femme*. Paris: Minuit.

———. 1977. *Ce sexe qui n'en est pas un*. Paris: Minuit.

———. 1979. *Et l'une ne bouge pas sons l'autre*. Paris: Minuit.

———. 2002. *The Way of Love.* Translated by Heidi Bostic and Stephen Pluhácek. London: Continuum.

Irwin, William, ed. 2002. *The Death and Resurrection of the Author?* Westport, CT: Greenwood.

Iser, Wolfgang. 1970. *Die Appellstruktur der Texte: Unbestimmtheit als Wirkungsbedingung literarischer Prosa.* Konstanz, Germany: Universitätsverlag.

———. 1974. *The Implied Reader: Patterns of Communication in Prose Fiction from Bunyan to Beckett.* Baltimore: Johns Hopkins University Press.

———. 1978. *The Act of Reading: A Theory of Aesthetic Response.* Baltimore: Johns Hopkins University Press.

Jackson, Rosemarie. 1981. *Fantasy: The Literature of Subversion.* London: Methuen.

Jäger, Christian. 2005. *Minoritäre Literatur: Das Konzept der kleinen Literatur am Beispiel prager- und sudetendeutscher Werke.* Wiesbaden: Deutscher Universitäts-Verlag.

Jaimes, M. Annette. 1995. "Some Kind of Indian: On Race, Eugenics and Mixed Blood." In *American Mixed Race*, edited by Naomi Zack, 133–53. London: Rowman and Littlefield.

Jakobson, Roman. 1971. "Quest for the Essence of Language." In *Selected Writings*, vol. 2: *Word and Language*, edited by Roman Jakobson, 345–59. The Hague: Mouton.

———. 1987. *Language in Literature.* Edited by Krystyna Pomorska and Stephen Rudy. Cambridge, MA: Harvard University Press.

Jakobson, Roman, and Linda R. Waugh. 1979. *The Sound Shape of Language.* Bloomington: Indiana University Press.

Jameson, Frederic. 1986. "On Magic Realism in Film." *Critical Inquiry* 12 (2): 301–25.

Jerome, Fred, and Rodger Taylor. 2006. *Einstein on Race and Racism.* New Brunswick, NJ: Rutgers University Press.

Jones, Jo. 2008. "'Dancing the Old Enlightenment': *Gould's Book of Fish*, the Historical Novel and the Postmodern Sublime." "The Colonial Present." Special issue of *Journal of the Association for the Study of Australian Literature*: 114–29.

Kafalenos, Emma. 2005. "Effects of Sequence, Embedding, and Ekphrasis in Poe's 'The Oval Portrait.'" In *A Companion to Narrative Theory*, edited by James Phelan and Peter J. Rabinowitz, 253–69. Malden, MA: Blackwell.

Kafka, Franz. 1948. *The Diaries 1910–1923.* Translated by Joseph Kresh. New York: Schocken Books.

———. 1977. Letter to Oskar Pollak, January 27, 1904. In *Letters to Friends, Family, and Editors*, translated by by Richard and Clara Winston, 15–16. New York, Schocken Books.

———. 2005a. *Metamorphosis*. Translated by David Wyllie. Project Gutenberg Ebook. http://www.gutenberg.org/files/5200/5200.txt.

———. 2005b. *The Trial*. Translated by David Wyllie. Project Gutenberg Ebook. http://www.gutenberg.org/ebooks/7849.

Kant, Immanuel. 1964. *Vorlesungen über die Metaphysik*. Darmstadt: Wissenschaftliche Buchgesellschaft.

———. 1967. *Was ist Aufklärung? Aufsätze zur Geschichte und Philosophie*. Edited and with an introduction by Jürgen Zehbe. Göttingen: Vandenhoeck and Ruprecht.

———. 1974. *Kritik der Urteilskraft*. Frankfurt am Main: Suhrkamp.

———. 1998. *Kritik der reinen Vernunft*. Edited by Jens Timmermann. With a bibliography by Heiner Klemme. Hamburg: Meiner.

Kao, Karl S. Y. 1997. "Self-Reflexivity, Epistemology, and Rhetorical Figures." *Chinese Literature: Essays, Articles, Reviews* 19 (4): 59–83.

Karafilis, Maria. 1998. "Crossing the Borders of Genre: Revisions of the 'Bildungsroman' in Sandra Cisneros's 'The House on Mango Street' and Jamaica Kincaid's 'Annie John.'" *Journal of the Midwest Modern Language Association* 31 (2): 63–78.

Karg-Elert, Sigfrid. 1930. *Polaristische Klang- und Tonalitätslehre*. Leipzig: CMF Rothe.

Kawash, Samira. 1998. "415 Men: Moving Bodies, or, The Cinematic Politics of Deportation." In *Deleuze and Guattari: New Mappings in Politics, Philosophy, and Culture*, edited by Eleanor Kaufman and Kevin Jon Heller, 127–45. Minneapolis: University of Minnesota Press.

Kearney, Reginald. 1998. *African American Views of the Japanese: Solidarity or Sedition?* Albany: State University of New York Press.

Kennedy, George A. 1983. *Greek Rhetoric under Christian Emperors*. Princeton, NJ: Princeton University Press.

Kennedy, John Bernhard. 2003. *Space, Time and Einstein: An Introduction*. Chesham, UK: Acumen.

Khayati, Abdellatif. 1999. "Representation, Race, and the 'Language' of the Ineffable in Toni Morrison's Narrative." *African American Review* 33 (2): 313–24.

Kleinau, Elke, and Claudia Opitz, eds. 1996a. *Geschichte der Mädchen- und Frauenbildung: Vom Mittelalter bis zur Aufklärung*. Frankfurt am Main: Campus Verlag.

Kleinau, Elke and Claudia Opitz, eds. 1996b. *Geschichte der Mädchen- und Frauenbildung: Vom Vormärz bis zur Gegenwart*. Frankfurt am Main: Campus Verlag.

Kolodny, Annette. 1985. "The Integrity of Memory: Creating a New Literary History of the United States." *American Literature* 57 (2): 291–307.

Kristeva, Julia. 1973. "The Ruin of a Poetics." In *Russian Formalism*, edited by Stephen Bann and John E. Bowlt, translated by Vivienne Mylne, 111. Edinburgh: Scottish Academic Press.

———. 1974. *La révolution du langage poétique*. Paris: Seuil.

———. 1977. "Un nouveau type d'intellectuel: Le dissident." *Tel Quel* 74 (4): 3–8.

———. 1980. *Desire in Language: A Semiotic Approach to Literature and Art*. Edited by Léon S. Roudiez, translated by Thomas Gora, Alice Jardine, and Leon S. Roudiez. Oxford: Blackwell.

———. 1989. *Language: The Unknown. An Initiation into Linguistics*. Translated by Anne M. Menke. London: Harvester.

———. 1994. *Revolution in Poetic Language*. Translated by Margaret Waller. New York: Columbia University Press.

Krupat, Arnold. 1989. *The Voice in the Margin: Native American Literature and the Canon*. Berkeley: University of California Press.

Lacan, Jacques. 1966. "La signification du phallus." In *Ecrits*, 685–95. Paris: Seuil.

———. 1987. *The Seminar of Jacques Lacan*. Book 1: *Freud's Papers on Technique, 1953–4*. Cambridge, UK: Cambridge University Press.

———. 1991. "Über die Bedeutung des Phallus." In *Schriften II*, edited by Norbert Haas, translated by Hans-Dieter Gondek, 121–32. Berlin: Quadriga Verlag.

Lamarque, Peter. 2002. "The Death of the Author: An Analytical Autopsy." In *The Death and Resurrection of the Author?*, edited by William Irwin, 79–93. Westport, CT: Greenwood.

Lampriere, T. J. 1954. *The Penal Settlements of Early Van Diemen's Land*. Hobart: Royal Society of Tasmania.

Lang, Berel. 2007. "Evil, Suffering, and the Holocaust." In *The Cambridge Companion to Modern Jewish Philosophy*, edited by Michael L. Morgan and Peter Eli Gordon, 277–300. Cambridge, UK: Cambridge University Press.

Laplanche, Jean, and Bertrand Pontalis. 1996. *Das Vokabular der Psychoanalyse*. Translated by Emma Moers. Frankfurt am Main: Suhrkamp.

Lappin, Elena. 1999. "The Man with Two Heads." *Granta* 66 (Summer): 9–65.

Lather, Patti. 1991. *Getting Smart: Feminist Research and Pedagogy with/in the Postmodern*. New York: Routledge.

Lawlor, Leonard. 2008. "Following the Rats: Becoming-Animal in Deleuze and Guattari." *SubStance* 37 (3): 169–87.

Lawrence, D. H. 1971. "Fish." In *Lawrence's Collected Poems*, edited by Vivian de Sola Pinto and F. Warren Roberts, 334–40. London: Penguin.

Leibniz, Gottfried, and Sir Isaac Newton. 2007. *Über die Analysis des Unendlichen–Abhandlung über die Quadratur der Kurven*. Ostwalds Klassiker der exakten Wissenschaften, Band 162. Frankfurt am Main: Harri Deutsch.

Lemkin, Raphael. 1944. *Axis Rule in Occupied Europe: Laws of Occupation, Analysis of Government, Proposals for Redress*. Washington, DC: Carnegie Endowment for International Peace, Division of International Law.

Levi, Primo. 1988. *The Drowned and the Saved*. New York: Summit Books.

Levin, Lawrence. 1988. *Highbrow/Lowbrow: The Emergence of Cultural Hierarchy in America*. Cambridge, MA: Harvard University Press.

Lewis, Frank. 1988. "The Cost of Convict Transportation from Britain to Australia, 1796–1810." *Economic History Review* 41 (4): 507–24.

Lorey, Christoph, and John L. Plews. 1998. *Queering the Canon: Defying Sights in German Literature and Culture*. Studies in German Literature, Linguistics and Culture. Elizabethtown, NY: Camden House.

Luban, David. 1983. "Explaining Dark Times: Hannah Arendt's Theory of Theory." *Social Research* 50 (1): 215–48.

Mächler, Stefan. 2001. *The Wilkomirski Affair: A Study in Biographical Truth*. Translated by John E. Woods. New York: Random House.

Madley, Benjamin. 2008. "From Terror to Genocide: Britain's Tasmanian Penal Colony and Australia's History Wars." *Journal of British Studies* 47 (1): 77–106.

Malik, Kenan. 1996. *The Meaning of Race*. London: Macmillan.

Manne, Robert, ed. 2003. *On Keith Windschuttle's Fabrication of Aboriginal History*. Melbourne: Black.

Margalit, Gilad. 2002. *Germany and Its Gypsies: A Post-Auschwitz Ordeal*. Madison: University of Wisconsin Press.

Massumi, Brian. 1996. *A User's Guide to Capitalism and Schizophrenia: Deviations from Deleuze and Guattari*. Cambridge, MA: MIT Press.

———. 2002. *Parables for the Virtual: Movement, Affect, Sensation*. Durham, NC: Duke University Press.

Maxwell-Steward, Hamish. 2006. "Macquarie Harbour Penal Station." In *The Companion to Tasmanian History*. http://www.utas.edu.au/library/companion_to_tasmanian_history/ (accessed Jan 15, 2010).

———. 2008. *Closing Hell's Gates: The Death of a Convict Station*. Sydney: Allen and Unwin.

Mbembe, Achille. 2002. "The Archives and the Political Imaginary." In *Refiguring the Archive*, edited by Carolyn Hamilton and Verne Harris, 20–37. Cape Town: David Phillip.

McClintock, Anne. 1995. *Imperial Leather: Race, Gender and Sexuality in the Colonial Contest*. London: Routledge.

McDowell, Deborah E. 1985. "New Directions for Black Feminist Criticism." In *The New Feminist Criticism: Essays on Women, Literature and Theory*, edited by Elaine Showalter. New York: Pantheon.

———. 1988. "'The Self and the Other': Reading Toni Morrison's *Sula* and the Black Female Text." In *Critical Essays on Toni Morrison*, edited by Nellie McKay, 77–90. Boston: Hall.

McRuer, Robert. 2004. "Compulsory Able-Bodiedness and Queer/Disabled Existence." In *Disability Studies: Enabling the Humanities*, edited by Sharon L. Snyder, Brenda Jo Brueggemann, and Rosemarie

Garland Thomson, 88–99. New York: Modern Language Association of America.

———. 2006. *Cultural Signs of Queerness and Disability*. New York: New York University Press.

McWhorter, Ladell. 2009. *Racism and Sexual Oppression in Anglo-America: A Genealogy*. Bloomington: Indiana University Press.

Meijer, Maaike. 1988. *De lust tot lezen: Nederlandse dichteressen en het literaire systeem*. Amsterdam: Sara/Van Gennep.

Melville, Herman. "We Fish." In *Mardi and a Voyage Thither*, edited and with an introduction by Tyrus Hillway, 144. Lanham, MD: Rowman and Littlefield.

Mesnard, Phillipe. 2004. "The Political Philosophy of Giorgio Agamben: A Critical Evaluation." Translated by Cyrille Guiat. *Totalitarian Movements and Political Religions* 5 (1): 139–57.

Michaelis, Laura A. 1993. "'Continuity' within Three Scalar Models: The Polysemy of Adverbial *Still*." *Journal of Semantics* 10 (3): 193–237.

Miles, Margaret. 2002. "Volo ut sis: Arendt and Augustine." *Dialog* 41: 221–30.

Moers, Ellen. 1977. *Literary Women: The Great Writers*. Oxford: Oxford University Press.

Mohanty, Satya. 1993. "The Epistemic Status of Cultural Identity: On *Beloved* and the Postcolonial Condition." *Cultural Critique* 24 (2): 41–80.

Möhring, Maren, Petra Sabisch, and Doro Wiese. 2001. "'Nur war es ihr manchmal unangenehm, dass sie nicht auf dem Kopf gehen konnte': Szenarien zur Textur des Körpers." In *Jenseits der Geschlechtergrenzen*, edited by Ulf Heidel, Stefan Micheler, and Elisabeth Tuider, 311–30. Hamburg: Männerschwarmskript.

Moi, Toril. 1985. *Sexual/Textual Politics: Feminist Literary Theory*. London: Routledge.

Momigliano, Arnaldo. 1966. "The Place of Herodotus in the History of Historiography." In *Studies in Historiography*, edited by Arnaldo Momigliano, 127–42. London: Weidenfeld and Nicolson.

Morgan, Michael. 2007. "Emil Fackenheim, the Holocaust, and Philosophy." In *The Cambridge Companion to Modern Jewish Philosophy*, edited by Michael L. Morgan and Peter Eli Gordon, 256–77. Cambridge, UK: Cambridge University Press.

Morris, Leslie. 2001. "The Sound of Memory." *German Quarterly* 74 (4): 368–78.

Morrison, Toni. 1977. *Song of Solomon*. New York: Plume.

———. 1984. "Rootedness: The Ancestor as Foundation." In *Black Women Writers, 1950–1980: A Critical Evaluation*, edited by Mari Evans, 339–45. New York: Doubleday.

———. 1987. *Beloved*. New York: Plume.

———. 1991. Lecture. Frederick G. Melcher Book Award. Unitarian Universalist Association. Cambridge, MA, October 12, 1988. Cambridge Forum. Broadcast on WVTF, Roanoke, VA, April 5, 1991.

———. 1992. *Playing in the Dark: Whiteness and the Literary Imagination.* Cambridge, MA: Harvard University Press.

———. 1993a. *The Bluest Eye.* New York: Penguin.

———. 1993b. "The 1993 Nobel Prize in Literature Speech." In *Dictionary of Literary Biography: Yearbook 1993*, edited by James W. Hipp. New York: Random.

Mühlhäuser, Regina. 2010. *Eroberungen: Sexuelle Gewalttaten und intime Beziehungen deutscher Soldaten in der Sowjetunion 1941–1945.* Hamburg: Hamburger Edition, HIS.

Muñoz, José Esteban. 1999. *Disidentifications: Queers of Color and the Performance of Politics.* Cultural Studies of the Americas. Minneapolis: University of Minnesota Press.

Muresan, Maria. 2004. "Belated Strokes: Lyotard's Writing of the Confession of Augustine." *Romanic Review* 95 (1–2): 151–69.

Negri, Antonio. 1990. *Savage Anomalie: The Power of Spinoza's Metaphysics and Politics.* Minneapolis: University of Minnesota Press.

———. 2003. *Time for Revolution.* London: Continuum.

Netto, Priscilla. 2004. "Postcolonial Phallogocentrism and the Challenge of Radical Alterity." Paper presented at the annual meeting of the International Studies Association, Le Centre Sheraton Hotel, Montreal, March 17.

Newton, Isaac. 1999. *The Principia: Mathematical Principles of Natural Philosophy.* Translated by I. Bernard Cohen, Anne Whitman, and Julia Budenz. Berkeley: University of California Press.

Nietzsche, Friedrich. 1961. *Thus Spoke Zarathustra: A Book for Everyone and No One.* Translated and with an introduction by R. J. Hollingdale. London: Penguin.

———. 1968. *The Will to Power.* Edited by Walter Kaufmann. Translated by Walter Kaufmann and R. J. Hollingdale. New York: Vintage Books.

———. 1974. *The Gay Science: With a Prelude in Rhymes and an Appendix of Songs by Friedrich Nietzsche.* Edited and translated by Walter Kaufmann. New York: Vintage Books.

———. 1989. *Ecce Homo.* Translated by Walter Kaufmann. In *On the Genealogy of Morals and Ecce Homo*, edited and commentary by Walter Kaufmann, translated by Walter Kaufmann and R. J. Hollingdale, 210–339. New York: Vintage Books.

———. 1994. *On the Genealogy of Morality.* Edited by Keith Ansell-Pearson. Translated by Carol Diethe. Cambridge, UK: Cambridge University Press.

———. 1997. "On the Uses and Disadvantages of History for Life." In *Untimely Meditations*, edited by Daniel Breazeale, translated by R. J. Hollingdale, 57–125. Cambridge, UK: Cambridge University Press.

———. 2002. *Beyond Good and Evil*. Edited by Rolf-Peter Horstmann. Translated by Judith Norman. Cambridge, UK: Cambridge University Press.

Nobles, Melissa. 2000. *Shades of Citizenship: Race and the Census in Modern Politics*. Stanford: Stanford University Press.

Nyong'o, Tavia. 2009. *The Amalgamation Waltz: Race, Performance, and the Ruses of Memory*. Minneapolis: University of Minnesota Press.

O'Rourke, Michael. 2005. "On the Eve of a Queer-Straight Future: Notes toward an Antinormative Heteroerotic." *Feminism & Psychology* 15 (1): 111–16.

Pahaut, Serge, and Ilya Prigogine. 1985. "Die Zeit wiederentdecken." In *Zeit, die vierte Dimension in der Kunst*, edited by Michel Baudson, 22–33. Weinheim, Germany: Acta Humaniora.

Parker, Ian, and the Bolton Discourse Network. 1999. *Critical Textwork: An Introduction to Varieties of Discourse and Analysis*. Buckingham, UK: Open University Press.

Patterson, Orlando. 1982. *Slavery and Social Death: A Comparative Study*. Cambridge, MA: Harvard University Press.

Pearson, Keith Ansell. 1999. *Germinal Life*. London: Routledge.

———. 2002. *Philosophy and the Adventure of the Virtual: Bergson and the Time of Life*. New York: Routledge.

Peirce, Charles Sander. 1931–58. *Collected Writings*. 8 vols. Edited by Charles Hartshorne, Paul Weiss, and Arthur W. Burks. Cambridge, MA: Harvard University Press.

Peters, Susan, and Lynn Fendler. 2003. "Disability, Flanerie, and the Spectacle of Normalcy." In *Dangerous Encounters: Genealogy and Ethnography*, edited by Maria Tamboukou and Stephen J. Ball, 111–31. New York: Peter Lang.

Phelan, James. 1994. "Present Tense Narration, Mimesis, the Narrative Norm, and the Positioning of the Reader in *Waiting for the Barbarians*." In *Understanding Narrative*, edited by James Phelan and Peter J. Rabinowitz, 222–45. Columbus: Ohio State University Press.

Plato. 1994–2009a. *Meno*. Translated by Benjamin Jowett. The Internet Classics Archive, edited by Daniel C. Stevenson and Web Atomics. http://classics.mit.edu/Plato/meno.html (accessed February 15, 2012).

———. 1994–2009b. *Paremenides*. Translated by Benjamin Jowett. The Internet Classics Archive, edited by Daniel C. Stevenson and Web Atomics. http://classics.mit.edu/Plato/parmenides.html (accessed Feb 15, 2012).

———. 1994–2009c. *Phaedo*. Translated by Benjamin Jowett. The Internet Classics Archive, edited by Daniel C. Stevenson and Web Atomics. http://classics.mit.edu/Plato/phaedo.html (accessed February 15, 2012).

———. 1994–2009d. *Philebus*. Translated by Benjamin Jowett. The Internet Classics Archive, edited by Daniel C. Stevenson and Web Atomics. http://classics.mit.edu/Plato/philebus.html (accessed February 15, 2012).

———. 1994–2009e. *Sophist*. Translated by Benjamin Jowett. The Internet Classics Archive, edited by Daniel C. Stevenson and Web Atomics. http://classics.mit.edu/Plato/sophist.html (accessed February 15, 2012).

———. 1994–2009. *Timaeus*. Translated by Benjamin Jowett. The Internet Classics Archive, edited by Daniel C. Stevenson and Web Atomics. http://classics.mit.edu/Plato/timaeus.html (accessed February 15, 2012).

———. 2007. Book X. In *The Republic*, translated by Desmond Lee, 335–54. London: Penguin.

Plomley, Norman J. P., ed. 1990. *Weep in Silence: A History of the Flinders Island Aboriginal Settlement with the Flinders Island Journal of George Augustus Robinson, 1835–1839*. Hobart, Australia: Blubber Head Press.

Pohl, Dieter. 2008. *Die Herrschaft der Wehrmacht: Deutsche Militärbesatzung und einheimische Bevölkerung in der Sowjetunion 1941–1944*. München: Oldenbourg.

Ponnesi, Sandra. 2006a. "Boutique Postcolonialism: Literary Awards, Cultural Value and the Canon." In *Fiction and Literary Prizes in Great Britain*, edited by Holger Klein and Wolfgang Görtschacher, 107–34. Vienna: Praesens.

———. 2006b. "Under Erasure: The Commercial Sustainability of Minority Literatures and Cultures." In *Perspectives on Endangerment*, edited by Graham Huggan and Stephan Klasen, 137–49. New York: Olms.

Postone, Moise, and Eric Santner, eds. 2003. *Catastrophe and Meaning: The Holocaust and the Twentieth Century*. Chicago: University of Chicago Press.

Powers, Richard. 2003. *The Time of Our Singing*. New York: Farrar, Straus and Giroux.

Pretyman, E. R. 1970. *Some Notes on Maria Island and Its Penal Settlements*. Hobart, Australia: Tasmanian Museum and Art Gallery.

Prigogine, Ilya. 1941. "Modération et transformations irréversibles des systèmes ouverts." *Bulletin de la Classe des Sciences, Academie Royale de Belgique* 31: 600–606.

———. 1947. *Etude thermodynamique des phénomènes irreversibles*. Paris: Dunod.

———. 1973. "Time, Irreversibility and Structure." In *The Physicist's Conception of Nature*, edited by Jagdish Mehra, 561–93. Dordrecht: Reidel.

———. 1980. *From Being to Becoming: Time and Complexity in the Physical Sciences*. San Francisco: Freeman.

———. 1993. "Nobel Lecture." In *Nobel Lectures, Chemistry 1971–1980*, edited by Tore Frängsmyr and Sture Forsén, 263–85. Singapore: World Scientific.

———. 1997. *The End of Certainty: Time, Chaos, and the New Laws of Nature*. New York: Free Press.

Prigogine, Ilya, and Isabelle Stengers. 1981. *Dialog mit der Natur: Neue Wege naturwissenschaftlichen Denkens*. München: Piper.

Prigogine, Ilya, and Isabelle Stengers. 1985. *Order out of Chaos: Man's New Dialogue with Nature*. New York: Bantam.

Prigogine, Ilya, and Isabelle Stengers. 1988. *Entre le temps et l'éternité*. Paris: Fayard.

Prince, Gerald, 1997. Foreword to *Palimpsests: Literature in the Second Degree*, by Gérard Genette. Translated by Channa Newman and Claude Doubinsky, ix–xiii. Lincoln: University of Nebraska Press.

Proust, Marcel. 2009. *Time Regained*. http://ebooks.adelaide.edu.au/p/proust/marcel/p96t/chapter3.html (accessed February 15, 2012).

Putnam, Hilary. 1967. "Time and Physical Geometry." *Journal of Philosophy* 64 (8): 240–47.

Pybus, Cassandra. 1991. *Communities of Thieves*. Port Melbourne: Heinemann Australia.

Rancière, Jacques. 2004. "Who Is the Subject of Human Rights?" *South Atlantic Quarterly* 103 (2–3): 297–310.

Reeds, Kenneth. 2006. "Magical Realism: A Problem of Definition." *Neophilologus* 90 (2): 175–96.

Richards, Thomas. 1993. *The Imperial Archive: Knowledge and the Fantasy of Empire*. London: Verso.

Ricoeur, Paul. 1984. *Time and Narrative*. 3 vols. Translated by Kathleen McLaughlin and David Pellauer. Chicago: University of Chicago Press.

———. 2000. *La mémoire, l'histoire, l'oubli*. Paris: Édition du Seuil.

Riffaterre, Michael. 1959. "Criteria for Style Analysis." *Word* 15 (1): 154–74.

———. 1960. "Stylistic Context." *Word* 16 (2): 207–18.

———. 1966. "Describing Poetic Structures—Two Approaches to Baudelaire's 'Les Chats.'" *Yale French Studies* 36–37 (October): 200–242.

Rigney, Ann. 2004. "Portable Monuments: Literature, Cultural Memory, and the Case of Jeanie Deans." *Poetics Today* 25 (2): 361–96.

Roberts, David Andrew. 2009. "Bearing Australia's 'Beloved Burden': Recent Offerings in Australian Convict History." *Journal of Australian Studies* 33 (2): 227–36.

Robertson, Ritchie. 1985. *Kafka: Judaism, Politics, and Literature*. Oxford: Clarendon.

Robinson, George Augustus. 1966. *Friendly Mission: The Tasmanian Journals and Papers of George Augustus Robinson, 1829–1834*. Edited by Norman J. B. Plomley. Hobart, Australia: Kingsgrove.

Rodriguez, Clara E. 2000. *Changing Race: Latinos, the Census and the History of Ethnicity*. New York: New York University Press.

Rodriguez, Juana Maria. 2003. *Queer Latinidad: Identity Practices, Discursive Spaces, Sexual Cultures*. New York: New York University Press.

Rody, Caroline. 1995. "Toni Morrison's *Beloved*: History, 'Rememory,' and a 'Clamor for a Kiss.'" *American Literary History* 7 (1): 92–119.

Roediger, David R. 1999. *The Wages of Whiteness: Race and the Making of the American Working Class*. London: Verso.

———. 2005. *Working toward Whiteness: How America's Immigrants Became White. The Strange Journey from Ellis Island to the Suburbs*. New York: Basic Books.

———. 2008. *How Race Survived U.S. History: From Settlement and Slavery to the Obama Phenomenon*. New York: Verso.

Rollestone, James. 1989. "The Politics of Quotation: Walter Benjamin's Arcades Project." *PMLA* 104 (1): 13–27.

Root, Maria P. P. 1992. *Racially Mixed People of America*. Thousand Oaks, CA: Sage.

Rorty, Richard. 1979. *Philosophy and the Mirror of Nature*. Princeton, NJ: Princeton University Press.

———. 1991. *Essays on Heidegger and Others*. Cambridge, UK: Cambridge University Press.

Rushdie, Salman. 1992. *Imaginary Homelands: Essays and Criticism 1981–1991*. New York: Penguin.

Russell, Bill. 1993. "The White Man's Paper Burden: Aspects of Record Keeping in the Department of Indian Affairs, 1860–1914." In *Canadian Archival Studies and the Rediscovery of Provenance*, edited by Tom Nesmith, 50–72. Metuchen, NJ: Association of Canadian Archivists and SAA.

Ryan, Lyndall. 1981. *The Aboriginal Tasmanians*. St. Lucia: University of Queensland Press.

Sandbothe, Mike. 2007. *The Temporalization of Time: Basic Tendencies in Modern Debate on Time in Philosophy and Science*. Translated by Andrew Inkpin. www.Sandbothe.net (accessed February 15, 2012).

Saussure, Ferdinand de. 1983. *Course in General Linguistics*. Translated by R. Harris. London: Duckworth.

Schleiermacher, Friedrich. 1977. *Hermeneutics: The Handwritten Manuscripts*. Edited by Heinz Kimmerle. Translated by James Duke and Jack Forstman. Missoula, MT: Scholars Press.

———. 1998. *Hermeneutics and Criticism*. Edited and translated by Andrew Bowie. Cambridge, UK: Cambridge University Press.

Schmitt, Carl. 1922. *Politische Theologie: Vier Kapitel zur Lehre von der Souveränität*. München: Duncker & Humbolt.

———. 1933. "Führertum als Grundbegriff des nationalsozialistischen Rechts." *Europäische Revue* 9: 676–79.

———. 1974. *Der Nomos von der Erde*. Berlin: Duncker & Humbolt.

———. 1985. *Political Theology: Four Chapters on the Concept of Sovereignty*. Translated by George Schwab. Cambridge, MA: MIT Press.

Schneider, Rosa B. 2003. *"Um Scholle und Leben" Zur Konstruktion von "Rasse" und Geschlecht in der deutschen kolonialen Afrikaliteratur um 1900*. Frankfurt am Main: Brandes & Appel.

Schönberg, Arnold. 1957. *Die formbildenden Tendenzen der Harmonie*. Mainz: Schott.

Scott, David. 2006. "The 'Concept of Time' and the 'Being of the Clock': Bergson, Einstein, Heidegger, and the Interrogation of the Temporality of Modernism." *Continental Philosophy Review* 39: 183–213.

Scott, Joanna Vecchiarelli. 2002. "Hannah Arendt Twenty Years Later: A German Jewess in the Age of Totalitarianism." *New German Critique* 86 (2): 19–42.

Scott, Walter. (1818). 1982. *The Heart of Midlothian*. Edited by Claire Lamont. Oxford: Oxford University Press.

Shakespeare, William. 1968. *Hamlet*. Edited by Bernard Lott. London: Longman.

Sherry, Mark. 2004. "Overlaps and Contradictions between Queer Theory and Disability Studies." *Disability & Society* 19 (7): 769–83.

Shipway, Jesse. 2003. "Wishing for Modernity: Temporality and Desire in *Gould's Book of Fish*." *Australian Literary Studies* 21 (1): 43–55.

Showalter, Elaine. 1977. *A Literature of Their Own: British Women Novelists from Brontë to Lessing*. Princeton, NJ: Princeton University Press.

Sicher, Efraim. 2000. "The Future of the Past: Countermemory and Postmemory in Contemporary American Post-Holocaust Narratives." *History & Memory* 2 (12): 56–91.

Simpkins, Scott. 1988. "Magical Strategies: The Supplement of Realism." *Twentieth Century Literature* 34 (2): 140–54.

Silverman, Kaja. 1983. *The Subject of Semiotics*. New York: Oxford University Press.

———. 1996. *The Threshold of the Visible World*. London: Routledge.

Smith, Babette. 2008. *Australia's Birthstain: The Startling Legacy of the Convict Era*. Sydney: Allen and Unwin.

Smith, Dominic. 2007. "Deleuze's Ethics of Reading: Deleuze, Badiou, and Primo Levi." *Angelaki: Journal of the Theoretical Humanities* 12 (3): 35–55.

Smith-Pryor, Elizabeth M. 2009. *Property Rites: The Rhinelander Trial, Passing, and the Protection of Whiteness*. Chapel Hill: University of North Carolina Press.

Southern, Eileen J. 1971. *The Music of Black Americans: A History*. New York: Norton.

Span, Christopher M. 2002. "'I Must Learn Now or Not At All': Social and Cultural Capital in the Earliest Educational Initiatives of Mississippi Ex-slaves, 1862–1869." *Journal of African American History* 87 (3): 196–205.

Spinks, Lee. 2001. "Thinking the Post-political: Literature, Affect and the Politics of Style." *Textual Practice* 15 (1): 23–46.

Spinoza, Baruch van. 1985. *The Collected Works of Spinoza*. Vol. 1. Translated by Edwin Curley. Princeton, NJ: Princeton University Press.

———. 2000. *Ethics*. Edited and translated by G. H. R. Parkinson. Oxford: Oxford University Press.

Spivak, Gayatri Chakravorty. 1983. "Displacement and the Discourse of Woman." In *Displacement: Derrida and After*, edited by Mark Krupnick, 169–95. Bloomington: Indiana University Press.

———. 1985. "The Rani of Sirmur: An Essay in Reading the Archives." *History and Theory* 24 (3): 247–72.

———. 1987. *In Other Worlds: Essay in Cultural Politics*. New York: Methuen.

———. 1988. "Can the Subaltern Speak." In *Marxism and the Interpretation of Culture*, edited by Cary Nelson and Lawrence Grossberg, 271–311. Urbana: University of Illinois Press.

———. 1992. "The Politics of Translation." In *Destabilizing Theory: Contemporary Feminist Debates*, edited by Michele Barrett and Ann Phillips, 177–200. Cambridge, UK: Polity.

———. 1993. *Outside the Teaching Machine*. London: Routledge.

———. 2003. *Death of a Discipline*. New York: Columbia University Press.

———. 2005. "Feminismus und Dekonstruktion, noch einmal: Mit uneingestandenem Maskulinismus in Verhandlung treten." Translated by Doro Wiese. In *Forschungsfeld Politik: Geschlechtskategoriale Einführung in die Sozialwissenschaften*, edited by Cilja Harders, Heike Kahlert, and Delia Schindler, 239–57. Wiesbaden: VS Verlag.

Stein, Howard. 1991. "On Relativity Theory and the Openness of the Future." *Philosophy of Science* 58 (2): 147–67.

Stevens, Christa. 2004. "De la société répétée à une mondialisation imprévisible: Les discours insulaires de Gilles Deleuze et d'Edouard Glissant." In *Discernements: Deleuzian Aesthetics / Esthetiques deleuziennes*, edited by Joost de Bloois, Sjef Houppermans, and Willem Korsten, 223–33. Amsterdam: Editions Rodopi.

Stevenson, Daniel C., and Web Atomics, eds. 1994–2009. The Internet Classics Archive. http://classics.mit.edu/index.html (accessed February 15, 2012).

Stoler, Ann Laura. 1992. "'In Cold Blood': Hierarchies of Credibility and the Politics of Colonial Narratives." Imperial Fantasies and Postcolonial Histories. Special issue of *Representations* 37: 151–89.

———. 1995. *Race and the Education of Desire: Foucault's History of Sexuality and the Colonial Order of Things*. Durham, NC: Duke University Press.

———. 2002a. *Carnal Knowledge and Imperial Power: Race and the Intimate in Colonial Rule*. Berkeley: University of California Press.

———. 2002b. "Colonial Archives and the Arts of Governance." *Archival Science* 2 (1–2): 87–109.

———. 2009. *Along the Archival Grain: Epistemic Anxieties and Colonial Common Sense*. Princeton, NJ: Princeton University Press.

Stölzl, Christoph. 1979. "Prag." In *Kafka Handbuch in zwei Bänden*. Bd. 1, edited by Hartmut Binder, 40–100. Stuttgart: Metzler.

Suleiman, Susan. 2000. "Problems of Memory and Factuality in Recent Holocaust Memoirs." *Poetics Today* 21 (3): 543–59.

Szafraniec, Asja. 2007. "Knowing the Leech's Mind." Paper presented at Inside Knowledge: (Un)doing Methodologies, Imagining Alternatives, ASCA, University of Amsterdam, March 28–30. Available in reader "Producing/Resisting Knowledge," accessible to conference participants. 119–26.

Tasker, Elizabeth, and Frances B. Holt-Underwood. 2008. "Feminist Research Methodologies in Historic Rhetoric and Composition: An Overview of Scholarship from the 1970s to the Present." *Rhetoric Review* 27 (1): 54–71.

Taylor, Talbot J. 1982. "Communication and Literary Style: The Principle of Inter-subjectivity." *Poetics Today* 3 (4): 39–51.

Thompkins, Jane. 1985. *The Cultural Work of American Fiction, 1790–1860*. New York: Oxford University Press.

———. 1986. "'Indians': Textualism, Morality, and the Problem of History." *Critical Inquiry* 13: 101–19.

Trouillot, Michel-Rolph. 1995. *Silencing the Past: Power and the Production of History*. Boston: Beacon Press.

Truchot, Pierre. 2006. "Une approche bergsonienne de la spatialité en musique." *Astérion* 4: 217–36.

Twine, France Winddance. 1998. *Racism in a Racial Democracy: The Maintenance of White Supremacy in Brazil*. New Brunswick, NJ: Rutgers University Press.

Vaessens, Thomas. 2009. *De revanche van de roman: Literatuur, autoriteit en engagement*. Nijmegen, Netherlands: Vantilt.

Villarejo, Amy. 2005. "Tarrying with the Normative: Queer Theory and Black History." *Social Text* 23 (3–4): 69–84.

Vinken, Barbara, ed. 1992. *Dekonstruktiver Feminismus: Literaturwissenschaft in Amerika*. Frankfurt am Main: Suhrkamp Verlag.

Wagenbach, Klaus. 1958. *Franz Kafka: Eine Biographie seiner Jugend (1883–1912)*. Bern: Franckel.

Walker, Alice. 1983. *In Search of Our Mother's Gardens*. New York: Harcourt, Brace, Jovanovich.

Walker, Cheryl. 2002. "Feminist Literary Criticism and the Author." In *The Death and Resurrection of the Author?*, edited by William Irwin, 141–61. Westport, CT: Greenwood.

Wandhoff, Haiko. 2003. *Ekphrasis: Kunstbeschreibungen und virtuelle Räume in der Literatur des Mittelalters*. Berlin: de Gruyter.

Webb, Ruth. 1999. "Ekphrasis Ancient and Modern: The Invention of a Genre." *Word and Image* 15: 7–18.

Webster, Yehudi O. 1992. *The Racialization of America*. New York: St. Martin's Press.

Wellek, Rene, and Austin Warren. 1956. *Theory of Literature*. New York: Harcourt Brace.

White, Hayden. 1973. *Metahistory: The Historical Imagination in Nineteenth-Century Europe*. Baltimore: Johns Hopkins University Press.

———. 1980. "The Value of Narrativity in the Representation of Reality." *Critical Inquiry* 7 (1): 5–27.

———. 1982a. "The Politics of Historical Interpretation: Discipline and Desublimation." *Critical Inquiry* 9 (1): 113–38.

———. 1982b. *Tropics of Discourse: Essays in Cultural Criticism*. Baltimore: Johns Hopkins University Press.

———. 1987. *The Content of the Form: Narrative Discourse and Historical Representation*. Baltimore: Johns Hopkins University Press.

———. 1999. *Figural Realism: Studies in the Mimesis Effect*. Baltimore: Johns Hopkins University Press.

Whyte, Jessica. 2009. "Particular Rights and Absolute Wrongs: Giorgio Agamben on Life and Politics." *Law Critique* 20: 147–61.

Wiese, Doro. 2000. "Textgewebe und Körpertexte: Körper und Sprache bei Judith Butler und Elspeth Probyn." In *Wieviel Körper braucht der Mensch: Dokumentation der FachNacht der Geschlechter*, edited by Hessischer Jugendring, 13–19. Wiesbaden: Hessischer Jugendring.

———. 2008. "HalluciNation: The Entanglement of Race, Gender, and Sexuality in the Varuh Meje—Guardian of the Frontier." Идентитети: Списание за политика, род и култура (*Identities: Journal for Politics, Gender, and Culture*) 13: 269–94.

———. 2009. "Crimes of Historiography, Powers of the False and Forces of Fabulation in *Gould's Book of Fish* by Richard Flanagan." In *Deleuzian Events—Writing|History*, edited by Hanjo Berressem und Leyla Haferkamp, 356–70. Berlin: Lit Verlag.

———. 2011. "My Dissertation Photo Album: Snapshots from a Writing Tour." In *Theories and Methodologies in Postgraduate Feminist Research: Researching Differently*, edited by Rosemarie Buikema, Gabriele Griffin, and Nina Lykke, 118–36. London: Routledge.

———. 2012a. "Evoking a Memory of a Future: Jonathan Safran Foer's *Everything is Illuminated*." *CLC Web: Comparative Literature and Culture* 14 (4). http://docs.lib.purdue.edu/cgi/viewcontent.cgi?article=1865&context=clcweb.

———. 2012b. "Die Posthumane." In *What Can a Body Do? Praktiken und Figurationen des Körpers in den Kulturwissenschaften*, edited by Netzwerk Körper, 185–90. Frankfurt am Main: Campus.

Wiesel, Elie. 1990. *From the Kingdom of Memory*. New York: Summit Books.

Wieviorka, Annette. 1998. *L'ère du témoin*. Paris: Plon.

Wilde, Oscar. 1969. "The Soul of Man under Socialism." In *The Soul of Man under Socialism and Selected Critical Prose*, 125–63. London: Penguin.

Wilkomirski, Binjamin. 1996. *Fragments: Memories of a Wartime Childhood*. Translated by Carol Brown Janeway. New York: Schocken.

Winant, Howard. 1999. *Racial Democracy and Racial Identity: Comparing the United States and Brazil*. Racial Politics in Contemporary Brazil, edited by Michael Hanchard, 98–115. London: Duke University Press.

Windschuttle, Keith. 2002. *The Fabrication of Aboriginal History*. Vol. 1: *Van Diemen's Land, 1803–1947*. Sydney: Mecleay Press.

Wolpoff, Milford, and Rachel Caspari. 1997. *Race and Human Evolution: A Fatal Attraction*. Boulder, CO: Westview Press.

Woolf, Virginia. 2005a. "A Room of One's Own." In *Selected Works of Virginia Woolf*, 561–635. London: Wordsworth Edition.

———. 2005b. "The Waves." In *Selected Works of Virginia Woolf*, 635–781. London: Wordsworth Edition.

Yacobi, Tamar. 1997. "Verbal Frames and Ekphrastic Figuration." In *Interart Poetics: Essays on the Interrelations of the Arts and Media*, edited by Ulla Britta Lagerroth, Hans Lund, and Erik Hedling, 35–46. Amsterdam: Rodopi.

Yahil, Leni. 1998. *Die Shoah: Überlebenskampf und Vernichtung der europäischen Juden*. Translated by H. Jochen Bußmann. München: Luchterhand.

Young, Robert J. C. 1995. *Colonial Desire: Hybridity in Theory, Culture and Race*. London: Routledge.

———. 2008. *The Idea of English Ethnicity*. Oxford: Blackwell.

Young-Bruehl, Elisabeth. 1982. *Hannah Arendt: For Love of the World*. New Haven, CT: Yale University Press.

Zeitlin, Froma. 2003. "New Soundings in Holocaust Literature: A Surplus of Memory." In *Catastrophe and Meaning: The Holocaust and the Twentieth Century*, edited by Moise Postone and Eric Santner, 173–209. Chicago: University of Chicago Press.

Ziarek, Ewa Płonowska. 2008. "Bare Life on Strike: Notes on the Biopolitics of Race and Gender." *South Atlantic Quarterly* 107 (1): 89–105.

Zimmermann, Michael. 1996. *Rassenutopie und Genozid: Die nationalsozialistische "Lösung der Zigeunerfrage."* Hamburg: Wallstein.

Žižek, Slavoj. 2004. "Against Human Rights." http://libcom.org/library/against-humanrights-zizek (accessed November 1, 2011).

Index

 FLASHPOINTS